Dec 85.

90 Meetings 90 Days

90 Meetings 90 Days

Ernie K.

A Journal of Experience, Strength, and Hope

Johnson Institute

Library of Congress Catalog Card Number: 84-82082

ISBN: 0-935908-26-9

Printed in the United States of America

ACKNOWLEDGMENTS

Angyal, Andras. *Foundations for a Science of Personality.* Published for the Commonwealth Fund by Harvard University Press, 1967.

Anonym, Kenneth, *Understanding the Recovering Alcoholic.* Alba House Communications, 1974.

Barrett, William. *Irrational Man.* Doubleday, 1958.

______. *The Illusion of Technique.* Anchor Press, 1978.

Bateson, Gregory. *Steps to an Ecology of Mind.* Ballantine Books, 1972.

Bettelheim, Bruno. *The Uses of Enchantment.* Knopf, 1976.

Clark, Walter Houston. *The Chemical Ecstasy.* Sheed and Ward, 1979.

Eliot, George. *Middlemarch.* Harcourt, Brace, and World, 1962.

Emerson, Ralph Waldo. *The Essays of Ralph Waldo Emerson.* The Heritage Press, 1934.

Essays of Michel de Montaigne. Translated by G.B. Ives. Heritage Press, 1947.

Farber, Leslie. *Lying, Despair, Jealousy, Envy, Sex, Suicide, Drugs, and the Good Life.* Basic Books, 1976.

Fontenelle, Bernard le Bovier de. *A Plurality of Worlds.* The Nonesuch Press, 1929.

Gaylin, Willard. *Caring.* Knopf, 1976.

Gelvin, Michael. A *Commentary on Heidegger's Being and Time.* Harper and Row, 1970.

Hammarskjold, Dag. *Markings.* Foreword by W.H. Auden. Knopf, 1964.

James, William. *Talks to Teachers on Psychology, and to Students on Some of Life's Ideals.* Dover Publications, 1962.

______. The Principles of Psychology. Dover Publications, 1950.

______. *The Varieties of Religious Experience: A Study in Human Nature.* Penguin Books, 1982.

Jung, Carl Gustav. *Answer to Job*, Princeton University Press, 1973.

______. *The Development of Personality.* Princeton University Press, 1981.

Kaufman, Gershen. *Shame: The Power of Caring.* Shenkman Publishing Company, 1980.

Keller, Mark. "The Oddities of Alcoholics." *Quarterly Journal of Studies on Alcohol* 33:1147-1148, 1972.

Kierkegaard's Concluding Unscientific Postscript. Published for the American Scandinavian Foundation by Princeton University Press, 1941.

Kierkegaard, Soren. *Purity of Heart.* Harper Torch Books, 1956.

Kolakowski, Leszek. *Religion, If There Is No God.* Oxford University Press, 1982.

Lewis, C.S. *Perelandra*. Macmillan, 1968.

Lynd, Helen Merrell. *On Shame and the Search for Identity*. Harcourt, Brace, and World, 1958.

MacIntyre, Alasdair. *After Virtue.* University of Notre Dame Press, 1981.

McNeill, Donald P., Morrison, Douglas A., Nouwen, Henri J.N. *Compassion: A Reflection on the Christian Life.* Doubleday, 1982.

Mullen, John Douglas. *Kierkegaard's Philosophy: Self-Deception and Cowardice in the Present Age.* New American Library, 1981.

Nietzsche, Friedrich. *Beyond Good and Evil.* Vintage Books, 1966.

O'Connor, Flannery. *Mystery and Manners.* Farrar, Straus, and Giroux, 1969.

Peabody, Richard R. *The Common Sense of Drinking.* Little, Brown, and Company, 1931.

Peter, Laurence J. *Peter's Quotations: Ideas for Our Time.* Morrow, 1977.

Ricoeur, Paul. *Time and Narrative.* University of Chicago Press, 1984.

Rieff, Phillip. *The Triumph of the Therapeutic: Uses of Faith After Freud.* Harper and Row, 1968.

Szasz, Thomas. *The Second Sin.* Anchor Press, 1973.

Thomson, Robert. *Bill W.* Harper & Row, 1975.

Tillich, Paul. *The Courage To Be.* Yale University Press, 1952.

Unamuno, Miguel de. *Tragic Sense of Life.* Dover Publications, 1954.

Unger, Roberto Mangabeira. *Knowledge and Politics.* Free Press, 1975.

Webb, Mary. *Precious Bane.* The Modern Library, 1938.

Wordsworth, William. *Poetry and Prose.* Harvard University Press, 1967.

Zimmerman, Michael E. *Eclipse of the Self.* Ohio University Press, 1981.

CONTENTS

THE 12 STEPS OF A.A.

1. We admitted we were powerless over alcohol — that our lives had become unmanageable.
2. Came to believe that a Power greater than ourselves could restore us to sanity.
3. Made a decision to turn our will and our lives over to the care of God *as we understood Him*.
4. Made a searching and fearless moral inventory of ourselves.
5. Admitted to God, to ourselves, and to another human being the exact nature of our wrongs.
6. Were entirely ready to have God remove all these defects of character.
7. Humbly asked Him to remove our shortcomings.
8. Made a list of all persons we had harmed, and became willing to make amends to them all.
9. Made direct amends to such people wherever possible, except when to do so would injure them or others.
10. Continued to take personal inventory and when we were wrong promptly admitted it.
11. Sought through prayer and meditation to improve our conscious contact with God *as we understood Him*, praying only for knowledge of His will for us and the power to carry that out.
12. Having had a spiritual awakening as the result of these steps, we tried to carry this message to alcoholics, and to practice these principles in all our affairs.

 Throughout this book, the opinions expressed in interpreting the Steps are those of the author. The interpretation accepted by A.A. appears in the books published by A.A. World Services, Inc., Box 459, Grand Central Station, New York, New York 10163. 212/686-1100.

THE 12 TRADITIONS OF A.A

1. Our common welfare should come first; personal recovery depends upon A.A. unity.
2. For our group purpose there is but one ultimate authority — a loving God as He may express Himself in our group conscience. Our leaders are but trusted servants; they do not govern.
3. The only requirement for A.A. membership is a desire to stop drinking.
4. Each group should be autonomous except in matters affecting other groups or A.A. as a whole.
5. Each group has but one primary purpose — to carry its message to the alcoholic who still suffers.
6. An A.A. group ought never endorse, finance, or lend the A.A. name to any related facility or outside enterprise, lest problems of money, outside property, and prestige divert us from our primary purpose.
7. Every A.A. group ought to be fully self-supporting, declining outside contributions.
8. Alcoholics Anonymous should remain forever nonprofessional, but our service centers may employ special workers.
9. A.A., as such, ought never be organized; but we may create service boards or committees directly responsible to those they serve.
10. Alcoholics Anonymous has no opinion on outside issues; hence the A.A. name ought never be drawn into public controversy.
11. Our public relations policy is based on attraction rather than promotion; we need always maintain personal anonymity at the level of press, radio, and films.
12. Anonymity is the spiritual foundation of all our traditions, ever reminding us to place principles before personalities.

 Throughout this book, the opinions expressed in interpreting the Traditions are those of the author. The interpretation accepted by A.A. appears in the books published by A.A. World Services, Inc., Box 459, Grand Central Station, New York, New York 10163. 212/686-1100.

90 Meetings 90 Days

INTRODUCTION

ALTHOUGH MY FIRST EXPOSURE WAS WITH another "Twelve-Step" program, there is no way that this journal can conceal that its author is a member of Alcoholics Anonymous (A.A.).

Long before they chose the name "Alcoholics Anonymous," the first members of that fellowship — which is both the ultimate source and the proximate parent of all Twelve-Step programs — referred to their way of life as "The Day At A Time Program."

The words *journal* and *journey* both derive from the French word *jour*, which means *day*. A journal records the events of a day. A journey originally implied the distance traveled in a day.

This is a journal that tells the story of a journey. Because that journey is more an interior one involving a way of life rather than a literal one through spaces and places, it is — like the journal recording it — highly personal. What brings such a personal journey/journal to publication?

Two of A.A.'s Traditions, in fact, ultimately underlie the decision to publish these thoughts in this form. The Eleventh Tradition, beyond enjoining "personal anonymity at the level of press," reminds that Alcoholics Anonymous flourishes by "attraction rather than promotion." These pages, offered anonymously, seek to promote nothing: whatever attraction they might have is founded only in the attractiveness — to one alcoholic — of growth in the A.A. way of life.

But A.A.'s Twelfth Tradition even more so, I hope, infuses these pages. Most obviously, the author presents himself anonymously because any who might choose to follow this journey — whether as spectators or as participants — will certainly wish to "place principles before personalities." In this journal, the journey is far more important than the journeyer.

More deeply, however, echoes the final Tradition's reminder: "Anonymity is the spiritual foundation. . . ." Within Alcoholics Anonymous, "the spiritual" is — at the very least — the "foundation." Within the boundaries of anonymity, then, it seems appropriate to share the story of how this journeyer's understanding of the spiritual, which led to this journal, evolved along that journey.

Some months ago, for the first time in several years of sobriety, I was asked to sponsor less a "newcomer" than our group's periodic "slippee." Pete, my "pigeon," readily acknowledged that he chose me for a sponsor because he did not find my sobriety overwhelming. "You seem a lot like me," he commented, "only you don't drink. Maybe you are the one to help me get at least that far."

It was a backhanded compliment, but I appreciated its honesty: it is on a foundation of honesty that all sobriety is built. Almost by accident, however, my own honesty soon came to be tested. In one conversation with Pete, while urging him to attend ninety meetings in ninety days, I was asked if I had ever done so. Back where and when I first found Alcoholics Anonymous, the suggestion had been thirty meetings in thirty days. I had done that and it had apparently worked: I have not taken a drink of alcohol nor sampled another mood-altering drug since.

But there is more to sobriety than not drinking. Indeed, one reason I welcomed the opportunity for sponsorship was that my own sobriety — if I may call it that — had somehow gone dry. It was not so much that the "pink cloud" had disappeared — that had occurred during my second year — as that I increasingly seemed to be feeling the haunting emptiness that had dominated my actively alcoholic experience. A.A. meetings — I attended at least once, usually twice, and fairly often three times weekly — were more and more leaving me feeling hollow, somehow passed by in the journey of growth that is sobriety. I often offered insight, I felt, but I rarely found any into or for myself.

Those who noticed, those to whom I turned for guidance and suggestions, advised many things, but one consistent theme was "the spiritual." That somewhat frightened me, for I am — at best — an unconventional believer. Indeed, I found — and still find — a great deal of consolation and hope in the realization that A.A.'s co-founder Bill W. was the same, and remained so for the whole of his sober life. I recalled that my own sponsor, Sam, when I told him of my "ninety days" suggestion to Pete, suggested that I spend less time exploring A.A.'s history and expend more effort working A.A.'s Steps.

Sam's pointed suggestion stung, but it was warranted. And the bite in his truthful remark reminded me that we are most vulnerable at precisely those points where we are most in need of being — and able to be — healed. In my line of work, I read and think much about Alcoholics Anonymous. Sam's comment led me to reread — *for myself*, for the sake of my own sobriety — the Twelve Steps, and then *The Big Book*, and then the *Twelve and Twelve*. In that context, then, I undertook to attend ninety meetings in ninety days — with or without Pete, because I was going to do it for myself, for my own sobriety.

For some reason, which I am not sure that I understand but which some of the pieces that follow explore, from the beginning I viewed that endeavor as a journey. Many people, when they travel, carry cameras. I do so also, but beyond taking pictures, when I travel, I keep a journal. Perhaps because I am a person who likes to read, I find that the discipline involved in trying to write down my observations and thoughts helps to formulate my experience into strength and hope. And so at the end of each day of traveling or, more often, in the morning before beginning a new day, I write — reviewing for myself where I have been that I may better understand where I am and thus move more awarely toward where I am going. Recalling what I saw yesterday helps me to see more clearly what I might come across today.

The practice of journaling, begun in college, had of course fallen prey to my alcoholism when I was drinking. During those too-long years, I did not want to know where I was because I loathed where I had been and feared where I was all too clearly headed — alcoholic bottom.

After my hitting bottom in treatment, one of the great first gifts of dawning sobriety was the resurrection of my habit of keeping a journal.

Now, a journal — or at least my journal — is a kind of conversation. When I was in school, that conversation had been with a mentor or an author. In treatment, I had communed imaginatively with my counselor or at times with figures in A.A.'s history or with those whose stories I had heard. For whatever reason, such people now seemed remote. With whom, then, was this conversation to be carried on? For a time, in my imagination, I tried to choose as my interlocutor Pete or Sam, my pigeon or my sponsor. But, quite simply, this did not work.

Turning again to *The Big Book*, I discovered why: "We have entered the world of the Spirit." Despite all my doubts and hesitancy, it seemed, the program of Alcoholics Anonymous was suggesting — perhaps insisting — that I somehow get to know my Higher Power better. Checking that guess out in *Twelve Steps and Twelve Traditions* left no room for doubt.

To me, at least, to claim to speak *to* God has always smacked of the same arrogance as to claim to speak *for* God. Perhaps I feel that way because, when I was drinking, I claimed to do both. Perhaps because I am not exactly a silent type, my Higher Power has always seemed to be so. Wrestling with those fears, trying to let go of them, I found myself repeatedly drawn back to the Steps — not to the Third and Eleventh, which name "God *as we understood Him,*" but to Steps Six and Seven. I could, it seemed, at least converse with my Higher Power about my defects of character and their removal. In fact, the awareness began to dawn that perhaps this was the only way in which I could become "entirely ready" and "humbly ask" for their removal.

These pages began, then, as a journal recording my ninety-day journey to ninety meetings that led me to review the Sixth and Seventh Steps of my A.A. program in light of my understanding of that program's Tenth and Eleventh Steps. They are, nevertheless, only most vaguely "inventory"; nor would I dare suggest that they represent "prayer and meditation." They rather offer, quite simply, the daily record of one part of the journey of one overeducated and undersober recovering alcoholic (as I have been called) toward what he hopes is "spiritual progress rather than spiritual perfection." That journey was generally joyous, but at times it proved painful; it was always deeply moving.

How came these pieces, then, to be published? Not easily, at least for me. Any journal is preciously private; but the fact that I journal is not. Sharing my thoughts with friends is a necessary part of my ongoing growth. One friend, who works in publishing, suggested the obvious: after the Tenth and Eleventh Steps, we must confront — and live — the Twelfth.

Although I am wary of claiming a spiritual awakening — and in fact would be inclined to deny any such occurrence were it not for A.A.'s Twelfth Step — a part of my sobriety must also be, as Alcoholics Anonymous tells me, "carrying the message." I do that, of course, at meetings — and even on occasional Twelfth Step calls. But my friend pointed out that sharing my journal, or at least the not strictly personal parts of it, with him and with others could do the same.

These pages are offered simply as they were written: as conversations with myself — or perhaps at times with a Higher Power — about my day-to-day journey into the too-often-to-me foreign but always wonderful terrain that is the sobriety of the A.A. way of life. As is true of all journeys, then, these pieces record some doublings-back and missed connections as well as the familiar sights and new discoveries that make all journeys both a challenge to grow and a joy to live. Now that they come to publication, I can say only this: if the journal of my journey can on any day aid any reader on his or her journey, I am happy; for, as the experience, strength, and hope of Alcoholics Anonymous make clear, no one of us can ever make that journey — or even one step of it — alone.

1

Unfortunately, nothing in life is nothing but; it is always something more.

— William Barrett

TONIGHT'S SPEAKER SEEMED TO KNOW NOT only that I was present but also why I had undertaken this journey of ninety days. His story captured both what had been one fatal treachery in my own drinking and what seemed to be one dangerous flaw in my thinking.

How did he put it? —

> I was so smart, back when I was drinking, that I thought I could explain anything. I surely used to come up with some dandy explanations of my drinking — like that I really hadn't been drinking, but my cough medicine sure tasted funny! Then one day someone pointed out to me that I could never explain anything. All that I was really good at was explaining things away. And I have learned in sobriety that if there is any trap more dangerous than saying "Yeah, but," it is the treacherous self-deception of thinking "nothing but."

That insight hit home. In my active alcoholism, I thought only in terms of "nothing but"; today, I too often still do the same. I recall feeling skewered on first reading William Barrett's indictment of all tendencies to reductionism: "Unfortunately, nothing in life is nothing but; it is always something more." That is a truth that I as an alcoholic need to learn: as the way of thinking that characterized my drinking, "nothing but" is an attitude of mind that surely jeopardizes my sobriety.

Back when I was drinking, after I knew I was in trouble but before I found A.A., that trap of thought often took the form of "nothing but a couple of drinks." A.A. teaches the inevitability of what happened next — if not at the party, soon after I got home. The alcoholic who thinks "nothing but" about any form of alcohol is doomed by the "something more" of alcoholism.

That kind of thinking, of course, trips us up in other ways too. When someone first suggested A.A. to me, long before my life fell completely apart, I rejected the idea because A.A. was "nothing but a lot of talking." I needed, I thought, real help.

I probably would have changed my plan to begin this ninety/ninety tonight had I not promised beforehand to accompany Pete to the meeting. A movie I have wanted to see came back to town for a brief showing, and I remember thinking, momentarily: "Why bother with this ninety day project? After all, I won't drink at the movie, and being sober is nothing but not drinking." Maybe — probably — I would not have had a drink of alcohol at or after the movie, but being sober is not "nothing but not drinking."

What not-funny games I play, with myself and with my sobriety, when I fall into that kind of thinking. How easily I forget how, in the form of just one little ol' drink, "nothing-but" thinking led to so much grief. How often, for example, do I still tell myself that it is okay to hang onto "nothing but a little upset" when actually I am harboring the seed of a real resentment.

As I think on it now, I also suspect there is "something more" even about "nothing but." Part of being an alcoholic, it seems, is that what we do not deflate or minimize, we tend to inflate or exaggerate. And the trap of "something more" can be as treacherous as the snare of "nothing but."

For instance: lots of people can fix a car, but when I do, I like to think it makes me a mechanical genius. When someone tells me, for another example, that I have given a good lecture, I often put on the mask of "Aw, shucks" humility; but I also make very sure they realize how hard and how diligently I worked on it. And when I do some little job around the house, I can get really upset if my wife does not acknowledge my heroic goodness. Last year, it pains me to recall, she bought a box of those little stars used in kindergartens, and she stuck one on my forehead every time I did the dishes. Somehow, it is difficult to interpret that as a tribute to real sobriety.

There seems to be, for us alcoholics, a very fine line between thinking we can take nothing but one drink and thinking we are something more than sober just because we do not take that first drink. Sobriety, in a way, involves finding that line and settling on it with some degree of comfort — even of joy.

Sobriety also involves remembering that comfort is not complacency. We can be comfortable because that line — that middle space between minimizing and exaggerating, between putting down and puffing up — that line is not that thin. There is room there for the comfort of serenity.

I suspect that if I could live in the middle area of balance, I might discover something very important not only for me as alcoholic, but for me as human being. And, the thought comes, out of gratitude for that insight, perhaps I should try it . . . so I will.

2

Implicit in the combination of [A.A.'s first] two steps is an extraordinary — and I believe correct — idea: the experience of defeat not only serves to convince the alcoholic that change is necessary; it is the first step in that change. To be defeated by the bottle and to know it is the first "spiritual experience." The myth of self-power is thereby broken by the demonstration of a greater power.

—Gregory Bateson

THE CHAIRMAN LAST NIGHT TOSSED OUT QUITE a challenge: "Okay — this is an A.A. meeting, and so we're supposed to share our experience, strength, and hope with each other, and to do it by telling 'what we were like, what happened, and what we are like now.' We've all heard each other's stories, and so we pretty well know 'what happened.' What I would like to do tonight is to go around this table and have each of us tell the main difference between 'what we were like' and 'what we are like now.' "

His words touched off a rollicking good discussion. I think there must be well over a hundred years of sobriety in the dozen alcoholics who were present, but they poured out that "what we were like" as if for each one it had been only yesterday. It was good sobriety, too, because each speaker at once got down to talking about the inside changes. A few indicated in their asides that they thought it important that we used to miss work and now we don't; that we used to kneel down only to vomit in the toilet and now some of us kneel down to say thanks for no longer having to do that. But as we went around the table, most people seemed to talk mostly about the changes in their thinking. The group painted a detailed picture of the sober A.A. way of life, and I think I learned from every brush-stroke each speaker added.

One contribution stood out, however, as I think on it. Perhaps it struck me with such impact because of its source; Good Old Ed, as just about everybody refers to him, almost as if that were his full name. Ed has the gentlest smile in three counties. He is without doubt the softest-spoken, most serene man I have ever met. But those who knew Ed when he was drinking say he had the hottest temper in six counties, and his own story is replete with tales of fights and jail because of fights and even some pretty ugly violence toward his own loved ones. Ed doesn't usually say much at meetings — he just exudes serenity. So when he opens up, like tonight, I listen very carefully.

Born dramatist that he is, Ed got our attention by announcing that his main difference concerned a kind of fighting that he had learned about only in A.A. "I never could understand people who had resentments," he observed. "That just means to me keeping things bottled up. Well, as a good alcoholic, I never believed in that. I didn't believe in keeping anything bottled up when I was drinking." Ed went on to detail, very briefly, how he had always found relief by "punching out." "But I knew all along," he concluded, "that the punching out wasn't my real problem. It was the hassling within that finally got to me, that finally brought me to this program."

That strikes a chord in my own experience. I have never been one to engage in much punching out. Perhaps, when I was drinking, that was due to cowardice. But hassling within? That is the whole story of how I approached life when I was drinking, and much of that old habit still clings even as I strive to grow in sobriety. The question, it seems to me, is basic, for it concerns how I confront reality: by fighting it, trying to change everything that does not suit my taste; or by acknowledging that there are some things that it is useless to fight, because I cannot change them. That latter, as the echo of the Serenity Prayer reminds, I need to accept and fit into rather than change.

Especially in the late stages of denial, it seems to me, the alcoholic's problem is that he is a fighter. That is the only way he knows how to relate to unpleasant reality. And so when alcohol, the former friend, turns into the enemy, the alcoholic tries to fight the bottle. So long as the alcoholic fights the bottle, he is destined to lose; for it is a sure truth of being human that as long as we try to fight against any ultimate reality, we are sure to be the losers.

Gregory Bateson called the active, suffering alcoholic's

relationship with the bottle "symmetrical." It is a one-against-one struggle; and the odds are infinitely uneven, for the bottle cannot change its mind, but the alcoholic can — and therefore inevitably does so just at the point when he thinks he has won. As soon as the alcoholic thinks, "I have won: I can control it," he drinks again to prove his victory. Because winning must be proven, the active alcoholic fighting alcohol provides a classic example of losing by winning.

Surrender, of course, as understood within Alcoholics Anonymous, is winning by losing. We are able to get sober only by acknowledging that we are no match for the bottle — that, in a sense, alcohol has won. Superficially, that is not a pleasant admission — that we are powerless over alcohol. Yet one does not have to hang around A.A. very long before insight dawns: these "losers" are the ultimate winners.

Winning, of course, means to us in A.A. something very different from our juvenile and adolescent concept of it, which saw victory as the only favorable outcome of conflict, of fighting. The philosopher, Alasdair MacIntyre, who represents a very different tradition of thought than does Gregory Bateson, recently posed two questions about winning and losing that may help to locate the place of the A.A. way of life in the history of thought. Studying what he terms "the heroic society" of ancient peoples, MacIntyre proposed, might teach us to think more deeply about the meaning of human life itself. We would attain that depth by learning to ask these two questions whenever we catch ourselves thinking in terms of winning and losing: (1) "Can a human life *as a whole* be envisaged as a victory or a defeat?" and (2) "What do winning and losing really consist of and amount to, anyway?"

It seems to me that within A.A. we learn to ask those questions, to think habitually in those heroic terms. The very format of our story-telling reminds us that our human life has meaning only as a whole. And having triumphed, in a sense, over the destructiveness inherent in our alcoholic drinking — having achieved that victory in our humanity only by admitting and accepting that both alcohol and a Higher Power are more powerful than we — we reevaluate the meaning of power as well as the true nature of victory or defeat.

For a considerable time, as I slid down the long, slippery slope of alcoholism, I seemed to be an apparent winner destined to become an ultimate loser. Then I found A.A. The fellowship of Alcoholics Anonymous, it seems to me, is a fellowship of apparent losers who are the ultimate winners.

Gregory Bateson, when he wrote, was directly treating of A.A. Alasdair MacIntyre, so far as I know, is ignorant of our fellowship and its program. Both, however, help me to understand the nature of my sobriety. As Ed put it at the conclusion of the meeting last night: "It seems to me that our main choice is between fighting and not fighting. We fear that if we do not fight, we shall lose. But in A.A. we learn that it is only by losing that we win. I do not know how widely that principle applies, but — in my own case — it has proved valid not only for my relationship with alcohol, but in my relationships with others."

I do not know how widely that principle applies either; but it is good to be reminded of it, as I am each time I walk into a meeting of Alcoholics Anonymous.

3

We ourselves want to be needed. We do not only have needs, we are also strongly motivated by neededness. . . . We are motivated to search not only for what we lack and need but also for that for which we are needed, what is wanted from us.

— Andras Angyal

THERE IS ALWAYS SOMETHING SPECIAL ABOUT a meeting at which an absolute newcomer arrives. By "absolute newcomer" I mean someone who is coming to his or her very first A.A. meeting. Even though I slipped around in A.A. for my first few months and therefore sort of have two first meetings under my belt, I identify with such newcomers in a way that vividly recalls my own very first A.A. meeting.

When a newcomer arrives, like last night, I try very hard to identify precisely with his identification. That first glimmer of identification seems to me always a mixed experience. On the one hand, the newcomer almost invariably arrives dazed and confused. Further, we necessarily carry into our first meeting some not-so-accurate ideas about what A.A. is, about just what to expect. Rarely if ever does someone come for the first time without some remnant of alcohol or other drugs still in his or her system. The admonition of the A.A. program is to identify, but despite all our pretense of being all right, our misery and our confusion and our pain make that very difficult. The others we meet seem so happy, so healthy, so sober; how can we ever identify with them?

On the other hand, however, there does seem to be something in the air that invites at least the beginnings of identification. For want of a better term, I think of it as hope. The newcomer hopes to find sobriety; the veterans hope to grow in it, to progress in the A.A. way of life. That, I think, is the first bridge to identification — the sense that everyone in the room is united by hope. For those of us who came in fear, half expecting to find fear dominating this anonymous group, that is a powerful revelation.

But on its heels, mingled with it, comes another even more potent source of identification. Everyone in the room hopes because everyone in the room is aware of needing. At first, the reception accorded the newcomer puzzles him. He came because he needed, and wanted, what these others so obviously have — sobriety. Slowly it dawns on the newcomer, however, that those others — the sober alcoholics — also seem to need what he has. He is welcomed precisely because of his alcoholism.

The recently drinking alcoholic is not accustomed to feeling needed. No one needs anyone's alcoholism — except Alcoholics Anonymous. It is a strange feeling to realize, slowly or suddenly, that these happily sober people, the members of Alcoholics Anonymous, want not our talents nor our skills nor anything else on which we pride ourselves — that they want and need rather the very reality that is making us miserable, our alcoholism, our shamefully felt inability to drink alcohol normally.

It is fortunate for most newcomers — it was very fortunate for me — that that is so, that our alcoholism is needed. For, on the one hand, we need to be needed; but, on the other hand, all that most of us as newcomers have to offer is our alcoholism. The psychologist Andras Angyal well captured the deep sense of homecoming that so startles the newcomer to Alcoholics Anonymous who has hit bottom:

> We ourselves want to be needed. We do not only have needs, we are also strongly motivated by neededness. . . . We are motivated to search not only for what we lack and need but also for that for which we are needed, for what is wanted from us.

We can feel at home only where we are needed. That powerful insight seems to me to capture one of the great gifts of Alcoholics Anonymous to any newcomer. Usually, by the time most of us get to A.A., we have become so dysfunctional that it is difficult even to imagine being needed. That is probably why I found it so difficult to believe the welcome that A.A.s offered me at my first meeting. That is surely why I find it so helpful to identify with every newcomer's dawning identification as an alcoholic.

For the truth endures: what is needed in Alcoholics Anonymous is ourselves — ourselves as alcoholics. That means that what

A.A.s need from any alcoholic is precisely his or her alcoholism. We are needed not for some strength or talent or ability, but precisely because of our weakness, our inability, that about us which causes us to feel worst about ourselves.

Some of us stumble on that insight. At least I did, at first. Delighted in the discovery that I had finally found a place where I seemed needed, I somehow failed to realize that those recovering alcoholics needed me not for my ideas and articulateness, but for my alcoholism. I thus missed one of the main points in A.A.: we come in order to get, but we stay in order to give, and the main thing we have to give is our continuing need to get. We are needed because we need; and thus the moment we forget that we are in A.A. for our own sobriety, the moment we no longer need, we are no longer needed.

In a way, that is scary; or at least it will become so if I ever forget that the root of my early failure in A.A. was forgetting my failure in life. Too readily, when I first came around, did I forget the true nature of my "bottom." Each newcomer is a precious gift, reminding me of that truth. At first, I for a time thought that my hitting bottom was having to go to A.A. meetings. Somehow, I did not learn that if bottom means saying "I need," then there is no way to grow beyond bottom and still remain in A.A.

That may sound stark, but one of the speakers last night, a recently returned twice-around newcomer, vividly drove the point home. Jane told how, during her earlier visit over a year ago, she had come to feel that she graced A.A. meetings with her cool intelligence. She had become, in six short months, a sort of "pigeon-hunter" especially watchful for new women approaching the program. With mordant humor, Jane described how she had tried to glow with her best intellectualized "sobriety" by having all the answers for any newcomer's questions. She would wait impatiently until they got sober enough to realize how much she had to give them from her profound understanding of A.A. Needless to say ("of course and fortunately," Jane concluded), most newcomers, as they got sober, steered a pretty wide path around her and her way of thinking.

I identify deeply with Jane, for my own early days in A.A. were not much different. Newcomers, as soon as they gained a smidgen of sobriety, avoided me; for my attitude signaled that while I thought they might need me, I surely did not need them.

Today, then, I rejoice that at last night's meeting I was happy to see the newcomer not primarily because I thought I had something to give him, but because I have so much to get from him. Or, maybe another way of putting it: I was happy when he walked in because I know that we as A.A.s have so much to give him — the new way of life that is sobriety — while he had so much to give me from his experience, strength, and hope for my own growth in sobriety.

Reading over what I have written in today's entry, thinking about what struck me both about the presence of the absolute newcomer and about Jane's story last night, I notice something that makes me feel good about myself as a sober person. Without using the exact words, I have been describing humility and gratitude — or at least the faint beginnings of them — in my own sobriety. Somehow, what those qualities signify seems to come through more clearly when we momentarily forget to label those spontaneous feelings of sobriety. For far too long, I have not known them well enough to call them by name. Perhaps, then, they are the greatest gift brought to me by last night's newcomer.

4

Marx said that religion was the opiate of the people. In the United States today, opiates are the religion of the people.

— Thomas Szasz

I SUPPOSE I SHOULD HAVE LEARNED BY NOW that alcoholics come in all ideologies as well as all shapes and sizes, but the itinerant visitor who descended upon our usually staid discussion meeting last night came as a surprise. After assuring us that he had no sectarian bone to pick because he himself inclined to be "a religious Marxist," our unexpected guest challenged us to discuss A.A.'s claim that its program is spiritual rather than religious.

That can be a touchy topic within A.A. Although we do not exactly engage in a conspiracy of silence on the subject, most A.A. speakers approach it with a degree of timidity and often apologetically. Most of us, even those willing to address the topic directly rather than gingerly, at least seem to reserve this as the only area where we never offer comment on any other A.A.'s experience, strength, and hope.

The valid reasons for that sensitivity are clear from A.A.'s history. Alcoholics Anonymous grew out of a culture explicitly secular yet superficially respectful of religious diversity. In such a context, A.A. found pragmatic reasons for caution. Alcoholics, especially when they hit bottom, can be very touchy people. Denial dies hard, so A.A. has been vigilant to avoid any artificial barriers to its program and fellowship.

Our visitor seemed to realize that. Yet, as he pointed out in suggesting the topic, even A.A.'s "only requirement for membership" implies reaching out to something greater than oneself. "The desire to stop drinking" implies inability to implement that desire by oneself. The very concept of Alcoholics Anonymous involves a reaching out for help. "But is not that admission religious rather than spiritual?" our guest challenged.

The first acceptance of all religion, he pointed out, is precisely this: that one is in some sense a dependent being. All religions, of course, also go further. Does "spiritual rather than religious" then mean that Alcoholics Anonymous simply stops there, allowing individual members to go further if they so choose?

Some around the table thought so. In general, however, the more sober members of the group, those generally ackowledged as winners in the program, expresed dissatisfaction with such an understanding. Although it is enough to begin with, a few pointed out, most sober alcoholics, after a relatively short time, want more.

In our group, the words *enough* and *more* always spark spirited discussion. Some insist that sobriety means accepting "enough," that wanting "more" is the danger signal hallmarking alcoholic thinking. Others point to the need for growth and progress, and last night this second group vociferously made much of the fact that the chapter, "How It Works," from *The Big Book*, speaks precisely of spiritual progress. For what it was worth, I observed that, in my own experience, virtually all A.A. members who seemed to have good sobriety seemed to place much emphasis on the spiritual, rarely suggesting that anyone had enough of it.

Fred, whom I would include in that group, pointed out that, nevertheless, "virtually all" is not "all." He went on to suggest that, too often, we seem to get hung up on words; that perhaps therefore we ourselves create some sort of false distinction between those overly familiar terms, *spiritual* and *religious*.

Our visitor, who had been listening with undisguised glee, his eyes darting around the table as he followed our words, pounced into the discussion, pulling dog-eared scraps of paper from one of his pockets. "Exactly!" he exclaimed. "I have been interested in that for a long time in my sobriety, so let me share with you some quotations that on occasion help to jog my thinking. In this area, I think, just because it is so 'familiar,' we really need the jostling of outside ideas, of differing insights. Anyway, here are some ideas I've heard; try them on for size:

> 'Religion is where therapy leads when it takes on hope.'
> 'Religion is the lived admission of failure.'
> 'Formerly, when religion was strong and science weak,

> men mistook magic for medicine; now, when science is strong and religion weak, men mistake medicine for magic.'
>
> '. . . Kierkegaard's statement of the religious position is so severe that it has turned many people who thought themselves religious to atheism. Analogously, Sartre's view of atheism is so stark and bleak that it seems to turn many people toward religion. This is exactly as it should be. The choice must be hard either way; for man, a problematic being to his depths, cannot lay hold of his ultimate commitment with a smug and easy security.' "

The group stirred silently under the barrage. Although we are not used to being read at from non-A.A. sources, we were obviously all thinking, wrestling with our own understanding of "spiritual" and "religious." I remembered reading an incident from Bill W.'s own story.

In 1940, when A.A.'s co-founder was living in the old Twenty-fourth Street clubhouse and on the verge of a real depression, he too had had a visitor — the Jesuit priest, Edward Dowling. At that moment, as often later, Bill himself was wrestling with "spiritual rather than religious"; the change described in *The Big Book's* appendix on "Spiritual Experience" was being agitated. Dowling, the Catholic priest, almost impatiently brushed aside Bill's anxiety over the appropriateness of that change with an epigram that then and later helped to free the co-founder's own mind from troubling over the non-topic of "spiritual or religious": "If you can name it, it's not God!"

"Is it not precisely our need to label that gets us into trouble?" someone asked. "We try to find the right name for something, instead of really thinking about its meaning." Perhaps because it was getting late, most around the table agreed.

The chairman suggested that A.A. accomplished precisely that — to get us thinking — by its insistence that its program is spiritual rather than religious. Our visiting gadfly seemed to agree: "Yes, it is too easy for a smart-assed alcoholic like me to think I know all there is to know about religion, but the word *spiritual* makes us pause and think. That is why I suggested the topic: We are aware, first of all, that we do not know exactly what it means."

I warmed to the visitor after that comment. I tend to agree that "spiritual rather than religious" is, among other things, yet another way in which Alcoholics Anonymous reminds its members of their essential limitation. That is why A.A.s speak on the topic as diversely — and as warily — as they discuss the meaning of "alcoholism."

Within A.A., we share our experience, strength, and hope with each other. Because this sharing takes place by identification, labels and names that we might try to apply to our experience, strength, and hope tend to get in the way of the understanding that heals. The important thing is our experience, not what we call it. That is why, it seems to me, in A.A. we tell our stories rather than analyze our condition.

I never found out who our strange and intense visitor was. I know, of course, that he was an alcoholic, trying to stay sober and to grow in sobriety. Most often, visitors at our meetings remain relatively silent. I rejoice today that last night's visitor did not.

5

It is better to encounter one's existence in disgust than never to encounter it at all.

— William Barrett

LAST NIGHT'S MEETING REALLY JOLTED PETE — and me, too, if I am honest about it. I usually disdain and therefore tend to avoid speaker meetings. "They do not give me enough to think about," I tell myself with a touch of arrogance. I am hearing the suggestion, I think, that I should try to be a tad more open-minded.

Pete chose the meeting because it was to be a special birthday party. It was special all right, and not because of the cake: the speaker turned out to be perhaps the ultimate "low-bottom drunk" of all I have ever heard. Lots of laughter punctuated the telling of his story, but I doubt that anyone in the hall found it pleasant to hear many of the escapades he told. Sometimes I think we laugh in order not to cry.

If Pete or I needed any reminder that if you keep drinking it gets worse, the story told last night hit us both right between the eyes. As Pete commented during the ride home: "I have often been told not to worry if I can't identify because some things haven't happened to me — that if I keep drinking, they will. But that message never touched me as deeply as it did tonight, when the speaker said it so calmly and quietly in conclusion, after telling the story of his drunken abuse of his own children."

For each of us in A.A. or any other Twelve-Step program, I suspect, "hitting bottom" is a uniquely and incommunicably painful experience. We rarely talk about it in detail, because even thinking about it scrapes a sore nerve, rendering us able only to scream . . . or to collapse . . . or both. Hitting bottom happens inside. What goes on outside may trigger our hitting it, but bottom involves at the very least seeing oneself and being sickened to death by disgust at the sight.

Last night's meeting, and Pete's reaction to it, reminded me of the time, years ago, when I came across a quotation that became a part of my own bottom. I read the words for the first time while still trying to avoid A.A., while yet striving to deny that I was an alcoholic. In fact, after initial exposure to Alcoholics Anonymous and genteel disdain for the low-bottom drunks I met there, I was at the time trying to solve what I acknowledged was my "slight drinking problem" by reading philosophy. Then one day a phrase hit me from one of those books — hit me in a way that suddenly helped me understand why I needed A.A., despite all my reservations about those low-bottom drunks with whom I could not yet identify. The words were plain, simple, and painfully clear: "It is better to encounter one's existence in disgust than never to encounter it at all."

The comic strips of my youth used to portray a scene in which, suddenly, a light bulb went on inside somebody's head. That's what happened to me when I read those words. I realized that the disgust I felt at A.A. meetings was actually disgust at myself, because deep down I knew that I belonged where those "disgusting" drunks told their "disgusting" stories. I was resisting disgust because I was refusing to face myself, because I was trying to avoid confrontation with the all-too-obvious nature of my own situation.

Even the recollection of that moment cuts through me like a jagged knife. Yet, during subsequent weeks and months, as my sense of being different fell away, I recall also feeling for the first time some glimmer of hope — even, I think, some tiny shred of healing. At least for a moment, I had confronted my existence; or, better, the true nature of my actual alcoholic existence had confronted me. Stories like tonight's, though on one level they make me uncomfortable, seem to do something special for my sobriety: they recall me to the moment of my own "Remember when . . .": that instant when I first received A.A.'s perhaps most precious gift — honesty with myself, about myself.

I saw then, and I remember now, that when I first came to A.A., despite my air of superiority, I was not pretty. That observation concerns not my physique nor complexion nor bearing, nor the clothes I wore nor whether I had bathed and shaved: I was favored in those things, I had performed the social amenities. But what counted — and what at the time I was trying to deny — was that I was not very pretty on the inside, especially in how I was thinking. I suspect, in fact, that if anyone could look inside the head of anybody who has been boozing for years, boozing badly enough that he or she finally stumbles into an A.A. meeting, even a few days or a few weeks after they stop drinking, even if they have been through treatment for alcoholism, if you could look inside that head you would find a tangle of confusions and fears, of very sick thinking.

The alcoholic, as I now well know, is sick — physically, mentally, and spiritually sick. Researchers talk quite a bit about the physical side of it, and maybe some people get so physically sick that that is why they come to A.A. But in my case, my thinking was a lot sicker than my body when I first came around; and it is very good for me to remember this, even if the memory is neither a proud nor happy one.

Because of that conviction mingled with painful memory, tonight's birthday meeting suddenly takes on a whole new meaning for me. I am sure it is not exactly a new idea, for we do celebrate birthdays in A.A. just as we do in life. But have you ever seen a baby being born? On just about every level, it is not a pretty sight. In a way, the baby surely doesn't want to be born. We come into this world yowling and screaming in protest, covered with stuff that hardly makes us pretty, literally forced and spanked into life. I guess being born to sobriety is not too different. At least my own birth into the A.A. way of life was not.

Birth and rebirth, of course, are metaphors today too glibly abused. Yet how else am I to understand what happened when I finally confronted my existence in disgust? I was not only not pretty when I first came to A.A. — my thinking was not only ugly — the sheer reality is that what I then thought was my best thinking was actually my sickest thinking. In fact, I now realize that I had — that I was capable of having — only one even marginally healthy idea in my head at the first meeting I attended: that I wanted to get well and that I was where that might happen. It is good to remember this, even if it is not exactly a pleasant, pretty memory. It *is* better to encounter one's existence in disgust than never to encounter it at all.

Although the words have flowed easily, this morning's journaling has not been an easy experience, any more than was last night's meeting. Remembering the bottom — being invited by another's story to relive one's own — is not pleasant. Yet it does please me to be here, now, thinking these thoughts. Perhaps, as the old after-shave commercial put it, "I needed that." Which leads me to remember the first word of that advertisement: "Thanks." I do not know exactly what is happening, and I am not sure I like it. But something is occurring as I begin these ninety days that I know is good for me — and for that, I am grateful, and that gratitude feels good.

6

Man is, in his actions and practice . . . , essentially a story-telling animal. . . . I can only answer the question "What am I to do?" if I can answer the prior question. "Of what story or stories do I find myself a part?"

— Alasdair MacIntyre

Everything that needs to be said has already been said. But since no one was listening, everything must be said again.

— Andre Gide

WHEN I FIRST CAME AROUND A.A., FOR THE first several months I did not stop drinking. The main reason for that, I now realize, was that I did not really want to stop. Eventualy, I heard enough, and things got worse enough, that I did finally attain A.A.'s only requirement for membership, a desire to stop drinking. Even during that time, too, I learned many other useful truths — about alcoholism and alcoholics, about sobriety and being human.

But I also picked up one bad habit, a mannerism that persisted long into my sobriety. Until beginning this ninety/ninety, I did not really like speaker meetings. Whenever possible, I chose to attend discussion meetings. That was true not so much because I liked to be able to say something, if I chose, nor even mainly because I naturally prefer the generally smaller and more intimately friendly atmosphere of the discussion setting: I felt that I learned more from discussions. The topics and themes of sobriety seem to be explored more deeply and more thoroughly when sober alcoholics directly examine them, each different expression contributing a sort of overall panoramic view of possible growth and progress in the A.A. way of life.

The experience of this ninety/ninety has led me to reevaluate that preference. In the first place, I recalled that the purpose of A.A. meetings really did not have very much to do with whether or not I liked them. I did not come to Alcoholics Anonymous because I liked it, but because I had to. "Liking," it strikes me, may be a luxury that my sobriety can afford as little as could my drinking, albeit for different reasons.

But a second purpose of this ninety/ninety, it seemed clear, was that I explore the variety of different riches that A.A. makes available for my sobriety. I should become familiar with them, I felt, because some day I may need to draw on them. I already knew the merits and value of discussion. It helps me to hear a single topic treated from the differing points of view of those gathered around the table at a meeting. No one individual says everything I need to hear, but everyone's contribution helps me to think differently, even about some very familiar topic. And usually, I find, I do need that.

Also, at meetings of discussion groups, it seems to me, we get to know each other and each other's sobriety more deeply. The identification is ongoing, and so we plumb levels of honesty rarely attained otherwise. Self-deception is always a trap for us alcoholics, and my own experience indicates that those who get to know us in discussions can spot signs of stinking thinking and warn us about it much more easily than can others — even A.A.s with whom we do not have such an ongoing relationship.

Those are, of course, very powerful considerations. But they do not mean that all the benefits of A.A. can be found only at the discussion meetings. The more I attend speaker meetings, the more convinced I become that my sobriety needs both speaker and discussion meetings. Both promote growth — each in its own way.

Perhaps because there were only two speakers at last night's meeting, this morning I seem to see more clearly the benefits of hearing their stories at such length, in such detail. Last night I heard in depth something only rarely glimpsed in discussions — whole stories of "what we were like, what happened, and what we are like now." And for some reason, that strikes me as more fundamental A.A.

What do I mean by "more fundamental"? I have noticed, over time, that when I am "sort of" hurting, or when something very specific seems to be blocking my growth in sobriety, I definitely prefer to attend a discussion meeting. That chance to talk about whatever is bothering me, that opportunity to draw on the experience, strength, and hope of other A.A.s on that specific topic, makes the discussion format especially useful.

But there are two circumstances in which, even before this ninety/ninety, I seem to be drawn instead to a speaker meeting. One occurs when I am "really" hurting; the other is when I feel just plain "blah." What those two cases have in common is that I seem unable to put into words — even for myself — whatever it is that is bothering me.

When I first came around A.A., I learned that it was good for me, at times like that, just to listen. It is not that I just passively sit at a speaker meeting. Listening — really listening — can be hard work, perhaps especially when I myself feel speechless. It seems, in fact, to be the kind of work I need just then. What goes on, I suspect, is that hearing whole stories best reminds me and puts me in touch with who I am — an alcoholic who has not taken a drink of booze that day. That is perhaps the most important sense in which listening to stories brings one back to fundamentals.

Even if the speaker's story is very different from mine in the externals, even if the feelings described are not ones with which I can identify at just the moment, still . . . the reminder that it is a "story" that I am living seems somehow to help. Why and how does it help? I am not sure that I know, but I find hints here and there in reading:

> "Man is, in his actions and practice. . . , essentially a storytelling animal. . . . I can only answer the question "What am I to do?" if I can answer the prior question "Of what story or stories do I find myself a part?"
>
> "Everything that needs to be said has already been said. But since no one was listening, everything must be said again."

The first quotation struck me, when I first read it, as both capturing and shedding light on the genius of A.A. in using the practice of telling stories. It also helps me to understand why I need that format most at precisely those moments when I am hurting, in one way or another. It is only by telling our story that we discover who we are. And it is mainly by listening to others tell their stories that we are reminded of that truth.

The second observation, Gide's, strikes a similar response. In a way, we tell the same story: what we were like, what happened, and what we are like now. It is not the variations of that story that are important: it is the sameness of its substance. And yet . . . however well we think we listen, we never fully hear. And so that story must be told again and again that we may come to hear.

If there is a world of wisdom hidden in the first words of A.A.'s Second Step — "we came, we came to, we came to believe" — that wisdom finds reflection in the twofold way in which it is possible to understand the claim that, from going to meetings of A.A., we "come to hear."

For we come to hear stories. Bill W.'s favorite phrase and image for growth in sobriety was borrowed from Bunyan's *Pilgrim's Progress.* The concept of pilgrimage is ancient and rich: it combines movement, uncertainty, and joyful hope. And any pilgrimage captures the best, as Chaucer knew, when it is made up of people telling stories. That is why, it seems to me, "telling stories" fits A.A. so well: We are on a pilgrimage of recovery, a journey toward sobriety.

The classic understanding of "pilgrimage" bears this out. It saw the pilgrim as knowing the general direction in which to head but having no clear and distinct idea of his goal. On the way, the pilgrim learns more about both his exact goal and himself as the seeker of that goal. Stories are the perfect motif for describing a pilgrimage, because they convey that very style of understanding.

Ancient people wove their whole literature around that idea. In the works of the earliest Greek dramatists, we find their characters answering the question, "Who are you?" by telling first what they were seeking and then how they came to be in this place in their search. And each time one of them told the story, some listener would suggest some detail or some connection or some perspective that allowed the journeyer to move forward in both ways: toward better understanding of the goal he sought and toward better understanding of himself as its seeker. And that, it seems to me, is exactly what happens in Alcoholics Anonymous.

This entry has run away from me; in a way it is on a pilgrimage of its own. The idea of telling stories is so rich — perhaps my own pilgrimage on this ninety/ninety will bring me back to it.

7

His Majesty, the Baby

— Dr. Harry Tiebout's 1944 diagnosis of A.A. co-founder Bill W.

If we cannot or will not achieve sobriety, then we become truly lost, right in the here and now. We are of no value to anyone, including ourselves, until we find salvation from alcohol. Therefore, our own recovery and spiritual growth have to come first — a right and necessary kind of self-concern.

— Bill W.

THERE SEEMS TO BE ONE KEY THEME THAT unites all understandings of the alcoholic, whether psychiatric or lay or derived from A.A.'s own experience, strength, and hope. The psychologists and psychiatrists portray us as proud, defiant, and grandiose; Alcoholics Anonymous insists that "self-centeredness . . . is the root of our troubles."

If that is true, and from my own experience I surely have no reason to think it untrue, then humility has an important place in my recovery. But what is humility? When I ask the question, a voice seems to warn me. "Can the asking of the question itself be an act of pride?" Is that because it is impossible to know humility?

Somewhere recently, I recall reading that "Seeking to 'know' humility is like trying to pick up the ocean with a pair of scissors." I think I understand the meaning of that image: the mind seems incapable of grasping whatever it is that the word *humility* signifies. Recognizing that need not trouble me; the mind also finds difficulty distinguishing between dryness and sobriety.

To say that it is impossible to know humility, then, is not to deprecate mind: it is rather to understand the proper place and function of mind. In some areas of human experience, it seems, mind must follow rather than lead. Having experienced some realities, we are able to understand them. But those experiences can never be attained merely by knowing them. Understanding involves more than merely knowing. Or, in the words of William James, "knowing" is different from "knowing about."

Humility is an ancient term for even more ancient experience. The experience that it describes has to do with place, with being at home at one's place. The word *humility*, my dictionary tells me, derives from the same root as the words *human* and *humor*. In all that, I think I find a message — at least for me.

Because to be human is to be middle — to be both beast and angel — humility seems to require, first, accepting that middleness of my human being. "You must remember that we alcoholics tend to be 'all or nothing' people," ran one of Bill W.'s favorite reminders. But *to be human* means precisely to be *both* all and nothing. As humans, we are essentially "both-and" beings. In that reality lies both our sorrow and our joy, both our tragedy and our comedy, as humans.

Does that seem a puzzle, a paradox, a mystery? Of course it does: we are, as our own experience testifies, puzzling and mysterious and paradoxical beings. That is why we so often feel not only that no one else can really understand us, but also that we do not even really understand ourselves. Both our active alcoholism and our growth in sobriety reflect that paradox, that mystery. How can one crave for what he knows is destroying everything true and good and beautiful in his life? Yet we did. How is it that one can succeed by failing, can triumph by surrendering, can gain by giving? Yet we do.

Humility involves, first, acceptance of that reality — the reality of our mixed, middle, paradoxical nature. Humility means, then, acceptance of the place in which the reality of our nature locates us. As neither beast nor angel, but somehow sharing in both; as neither all nor nothing, but somehow partaking of both. Our place is in the middle.

To be in such a middle place involves a kind of tension. Both extremes pull against the center. But if humility means accepting and embracing that middle place — our own middleness — then humility equally excludes grandiosity, the claim to be more than middle, and self-abasement, the pretense of being less than middle.

All the classic virtues involve precisely the living out of the experience of human middleness. The prudent person is neither foolhardy nor cowardly. The just person neither gives too much nor takes too little. The humble person, then, esteems himself rather than either flaunting and inflating or debasing and degrading that self. The virtue of humility, like the A.A. program, recognizes the distinction between self-centeredness and self-respect — in Bill W.'s term, *self-concern.* That is why we say, "This is a selfish program." It is the selfishness of self-centeredness that gets us in trouble, and self-hatred can be as self-centered as self-flaunting.

I am beginning to glimpse, I think, the depths available in the topic of humility. Humility, I intuit, has a profound connection with a term we hear often within Alcoholics Anonymous: *appropriate.* The appropriate fits; it fits us into reality, into the reality of our alcoholic humanity.

Because it fits, the appropriate bestows comfort — comfort with ourselves. Comfort, of course, is neither complacency nor stagnation: we need to grow, but we can grow fittingly. I recall a gibe of the nineteenth-century theologian, Horace Bushnell: "Abiding in Christ is to abide: it is not to bask." The same could be said of our sobriety.

8

Good theology ought to answer every man's question: "Do I live in a rational universe under a just and loving God, or do I not?" . . . Theology doesn't seem to answer this any more.

— Bill W.

. . . We discovered that we did not need to consider another's conception of God.

— *Alcoholics Anonymous*

LAST NIGHT I SAW SAM, MY SPONSOR, ANNOY some people and amuse a few others during our discussion meeting. I learned something from his contribution, and so I want to record his thoughts and what I remember of our conversation about them. In a way, this entry will be Sam's, but I can well identify with his concern and effort to grasp the spiritual.

"Oh, hell, I don't know what got into me at that meeting tonight," Sam began, as we stopped for coffee and ice cream on the way home. "What bothers me most, right now, is that what I did say was probably not completely honest, even if I got people to listen."

"Perfect honesty might be impossible, especially for us alcoholics," I said, a mite uncomfortable at hearing my sponsor admit to less than perfect anything. "But tell me, just what was your point?"

Sam was silent for a time. I outwaited him, and finally he spoke up: "Okay. What I said was this, a mere phrase: 'My Higher Power, whom I choose to call Gertrude.' And then I added that I did find it useful and helpful to read the Third and Eleventh Steps as saying, 'God as we understand Her.'

"In hindsight, that comment was probably more smart than wise, but I doubt anyone in that group is going to take a drink over it. I mean I don't think I hurt anybody, and I am sorry if I did.

"Still, although how I said what I said was probably even dumb, I think my point was valid. What I said was for me: I go to meetings for my own sobriety, and my sobriety needed that point at that moment, even if the alcoholic in me got in the way of it coming out very well. I needed the reminder, so I offered it to myself."

"Huh?" I said. "What point? What reminder? What does Higher Power have to do with male or female?"

"That's exactly my point," Sam said. "What I said had nothing to do with gender or sex. It did have to do with Higher Power — God, if you wish."

He went on: "Like many within the fellowship, I wrestle with spirituality, with A.A. as a spiritual program. Like most of A.A.'s earliest members, I had a fairly religious upbringing. And also like them, I had trouble with religion and fell away from it during the drinking years. Now, in sobriety, I am still not sure that I want to get back to it — in fact, I am pretty sure that I do not want to go back to what, when I was a child, they told me was religion.

"But I have found something in A.A., and just calling it spiritual sometimes doesn't seem to be enough. If we have 'made a decision to turn our wills and our lives over to the care of God as we understand Him,' and if, in order to maintain and to grow in sobriety we must seek 'through prayer and meditation to improve our conscious contact with God as we understand Him,' then I have to work on my understanding of God.

"At A.A. meetings, and especially around the tables at discussion meetings, I am often helped to do that. In fact, in trying to understand, there is nothing like hearing a large number of individual, sober alcoholics share their understanding of their Higher Power — about the place of God, or spirituality, or whatever you want to call it in their progress in sobriety, in their continuing exploration of the art of living sober.

"But sometimes, like tonight, it seems to me that someone just might be trying to lay his or her 'God-trip' (if you'll pardon the jargon) on me. I always bristle inside at that, but I usually keep quiet and listen. Listening, after all, is one reason I am there. On a very few occasions, however, like tonight, I begin to feel that things are getting out of hand — out of hand, that is, for my sobriety. Somebody says something, admittedly for his or her own sobriety, that seems to threaten my serenity because it raises the specter of a religious understanding that my own experience has taught me will not work for me.

"I grew up with a God who was more interested in spying on me than in caring for me, and I reciprocated by just trying to keep out of trouble. That God to whom I was introduced as a child was not very interested in either my understanding or love — it was all fear and obedience.

"Today, of course, largely thanks to A.A., I am pretty sure that God is not like that. Also, despite my flippancy about 'Gertrude,' I do not really think that there are many higher powers. But being idiosyncratic helps me to avoid controversy, and therefore, I think, to grow in the spiritual side of my sobriety. For I sometimes need to remind myself that some other people's ideas about their higher powers are not the same as mine.

"Saying 'my Higher Power' recalls that. I do not mean 'my' possessively, as if I owned my own Higher Power. But I do mean it seriously. I am sure that, if I had to accept some other people's ideas of their Higher Power, I would go out and get drunk. Their Higher Power cannot keep me sober. My Higher Power can and does, one day at a time — and that is why I can keep turning my will and my life over to His, or Her, care.

"Does anyone, I wonder, really think that a Higher Power minds whether we think 'Him' or 'Her'? Mine, I suspect, is so happy to be thought of at all by this former drunk that I doubt the gender of my imagination makes much difference. All I know is that as long as I keep trying to turn my will and my life over, I seem to be beginning to find in the Eleventh Step's 'prayer and meditation' a glorious adventure as I seek, a day at a time, to improve my conscious contact with Him, or Her, or whatever helps me to remember and to be grateful for my sobriety today."

"But what about people like me," I asked. "Those who do not labor under the handicap of your kind of upbringing? I guess what I am trying to say is that I feel myself identifying with you on this topic, but I am not sure exactly why or how."

"Let me play sponsor again, then," Sam replied. "As I think of the stories in the back of *The Big Book* and remember also a lot of stories that we hear at meetings, I begin to understand something that maybe, because of our differing backgrounds, we will never be able to experience in exactly the same way: the freedom to be spiritual that seems for so many of us to be the most important gift of A.A. to our sobriety.

"Maybe that is why serenity seems to correlate with spirituality in Alcoholics Anonymous. We come to A.A. in chains, it seems to me — in many different kinds of shackles. The chains of our alcoholic drug dependency are only the most obvious. But those shackles of alcoholism are also a model for what happens in the A.A. way of life on every level, to every fettering bond: accepting the A.A. way of thinking means that our chains are dissolved and that we become free. And to feel free and to be free is, of course, the meaning as well as the gift of true sobriety.

"And it is also, I think, the ultimate meaning of all spirituality. That is why, tonight, I insisted on my freedom to call my Higher Power 'Gertrude'. It's that simple: A.A. frees us to be spiritual, it doesn't tell us how."

Although I doubt I could ever bring myself to call my Higher Power "Gertrude," Sam's final point fits me well. This day, I shall try to live by its insight.

9

Being human is a terminal disease.

— A.A. Speaker

BECAUSE I AM SOBER TODAY, BECAUSE I HAVE not had a drink of alcohol in the last twenty-four hours, I can and do feel good about myself. Because I am still an alcoholic and therefore powerless over alcohol in a society in which most people can drink it normally, because I know that whatever sobriety I have I owe to the grace of my Higher Power and the fellowship and program of Alcoholics Anonymous, I am preserved from feeling too good about myself. Those are both great gifts: I rejoice daily in their reality, for, of course, it was not always thus. But that dual sense of feeling good, but not too good, about myself has been a constant thread in my life since I first glimpsed the beginnings of true sobriety. Last night's lead speaker, John, spoke to that sense in a profound way.

Two phrases used last night stick in my mind — in fact, I almost feel they are lodging in my gut. "Terminal self-centeredness" was the phrase he used to describe "the lingering disease that still hinders my efforts at living sober." And, he pointed out in a sentence that is memorable: "Being human is a terminal disease." Striking as those phrases are, each somewhat discomfits me. Like the speaker last night, I assumed, when I first came around, that even if "putting the cork in the bottle" was not the whole story of sobriety, it would solve at least 90 percent of my problems. And it did. Or at least that simple step made solvable, one day at a time, most of the problems I consciously brought to A.A.

But putting the cork in the bottle not only eliminated drunkenness: it also started me on the road to sobriety. And on that road, I find new problems, even if I now recognize them as opportunities. I learned first — as did John and as I suspect do we all — that not alcohol but self-centeredness lay at the root of my troubles. And although I can, with help, avoid taking the first drink, one day at a time, the tendency to view myself as the center of the universe — or if not to view, to act and to feel as if I were — is a much more tricky and treacherous trap.

John's phrase — terminal self-centeredness — offers consolation even as it rouses wariness. The wariness, in fact, can approach terror, for the connotation of "fatal" hangs onto the term *terminal.* Happy and sober as I am, the idea that Ernie has to live with Ernie for the rest of his life can also at times be pretty disconcerting. "Terminal self-centeredness": when the speaker said that last night, I felt both scared and freed. It scared me because I would like to deny it. I would like to think that someday, at least, I might be free from the bondage of self of which my active alcoholism was only the most blatant manifestation. But if I ever did succeed in denying it, I suspect, I would also be denying that I am an alcoholic. I have gone that route before — it doesn't work. Denial never works.

But it is scary, given the nature of my disease, to realize that my self-centeredness will always cling to me — and that at least some part of me will always cling to it. It says in A.A.'s *Big Book* that self-centeredness is "the root of our troubles." Yet it is the kind of scare that keeps me coming to meetings and working the Steps and just plain not taking the first drink, one day at a time. Those who "graduate" from A.A., it seems to me, do so because they are no longer scared. Seeing what happens to them, I think I will try to stay scared — and recalling my terminal self-centeredness may help me to do that.

The term *scared*, like the word *fear*, does not frighten me. Realistic fears are healthy. They can be good for my sobriety, for my health. It seems to me that my fear of drinking alcohol is not very different from my fear of eating tainted food. I certainly do not fear eating, but I am afraid to eat spoiled food. I am not afraid of drinking water, coffee, or whatever nonalcoholic beverage may be at hand; but for me, as an alcoholic, alcohol is spoiled drink. It is not, of course, the alcohol that is spoiled — it is me. But the results of consuming it, as I have often proved, are therefore for me just as fearsome.

Yet fear is only half the story — and was only half my feeling on hearing the phrase, *terminal self-centeredness.*

Accepting the part of me that tends ever to be self-centered means that I do not have to feel bad about myself when it pops up. I have to keep watch over self-centeredness; I certainly have to try to work against it. But because I am not only human but also an alcoholic, I will never be completely without it.

Just as my self-centeredness, although terminal, is not fatal (so long, at least, as it does not lead me to drink alcohol), so also the bondage of self, although real, is not total. I can, therefore, attain limited freedom, from and within both. John's phrase reminded me of my human condition: because to be human is to be both/and rather than either/or, any freedom we attain can only be limited. That realization is why I find freedom in being reminded of my terminal self-centeredness. It is the demand for all or nothing that destroys freedom. The acceptance that we cannot be all or nothing bestows freedom — or so, at least, as I am coming to understand from my own experience.

That acceptance signals why, as in John's second phrase, being human is a terminal disease. Because we are urged to and promised spiritual progress rather than spiritual perfection, our lives as humans are ongoing efforts at growth and progress that free us from inflicting upon ourselves the requirement that we be perfect — free us from the alcoholic way of thinking that demands perfection. Being freed of that alcoholic way of thinking is a part of being freed from the bondage of alcohol. The bondage of self is slavery to some inflated, impossible image of self. That is partially why grandiosity is an all too familiar characteristic of the active alcoholic.

"Being human is a terminal disease" reminds me that I will die imperfect. It offers the same message as terminal self-centeredness: our task, as humans and also as alcoholics, is spiritual progress rather than spiritual perfection.

To try to be more — to attempt to deny terminal self-centeredness and that being human is a terminal disease — as I did in and through most of my drinking — is inevitably to become less than human. But to pretend to be less, as I did near the end of my drinking, also as inevitably fails. I can neither be perfect nor be nothing. It is the attempt to do either that is fatal. I will never stand still on the road. To accept that my task is progress along a road, the terminus of which I shall never reach — that, it seems to me, is sobriety.

10

. . . While it is true that every self as such is angular, the logical consequence of this merely is that it has to be polished, not that it has to be ground smooth."

— Soren Kierkegaard

THERE IS A DIFFERENCE BETWEEN "HUMILITY" and "humiliation." It is not unlike the difference between hitting bottom and staying there. At least for alcoholics, it is difficult — perhaps impossible — to attain humility without humiliation: we don't gain sobriety without hitting bottom. But that does not make them the same. Hitting bottom, to build on Kierkegaard's image, softens out angles so that they can be polished.

But those angles are then to be polished; the attempt to grind them smooth is not humility. All alcoholics know humiliation. Those who gain true sobriety build on that experience, developing humility. Sometimes, however, the tendency arises to cling to humiliation, rather than seeing it as the necessary starting point on the journey toward humility.

For me, that tendency shows itself, I suspect, in my perhaps excessive relishing of First–Step discussion meetings. To "remember when" is a salutary practice; to wallow in "bottom" cannot be true sobriety. My story describes what I was like, what happened, and what I am like now. Too often, when I tell it, the gap between the first two seems inappropriately wider than the difference between the last two. Understanding our own stories provides an attitude that distinguishes humility from humiliation, that differentiates between remembering bottom and centering one's life in that memory.

The speaker at tonight's meeting clearly knew and lived that difference. Our backgrounds and drinking histories were similar; but more important, the feelings that he described in approaching bottom had also been mine. Although not many external things had been lost, the sense of wrenched out emptiness, of a world collapsed hollowly in on itself, of a despairing going through the motions of living even when dry —

those had been my feelings, too, and in his description, I recognized feelings to which I still clung.

When the speaker turned to "what it is like now," much of my identification fell away. He described a serenity, a peace, a fullness that is surely not currently mine. I have known glimpses of that sobriety; I recall even, for a time, feeling that I had attained it. Lately, however, something has happened.

"What we really have is a daily reprieve contingent on the maintenance of our spiritual condition," *The Big Book* tells us. Our "daily reprieve," I am learning, is not only from alcoholic drinking: it is also from alcoholic thinking. It helps me to remember that Bill W. himself long suffered a kind of depression. Especially in A.A.'s earliest years, such bouts were almost frighteningly common among the newly sober. But the line of thought suggested by tonight's speaker perhaps helps me to see the bottom line of that daily reprieve, at least in my own case, by focusing my attention less on my experience of bottom and more on its meaning.

We always carry our memory of hitting bottom with us. It is the turning point, the denouement, of our story. But denouement is not climax. It is not enough to see the light: we must live in and by the light we find. Let me, at the risk of apparent silliness, extend the metaphor. We always carry our bottom with us, but it is behind us.

At times I tend to live as if my having hit bottom were an incandescent culmination of my life, and that from this point on its light is shed on all my choices. Seeing everything in its light, however, does not mean finding its reflection in everything that happens to me. Having been humiliated, I am free to grow in humility. But I abdicate that freedom, I refuse that humility, if I insist on clinging to my humiliation. Bottom, to use a more modern metaphor, is a launching pad. It exists not to be cherished for itself, but as a point to be flown from and grown from. In our present technology, launching pads are not airports. Those launched into space land elsewhere, if the mission is successful.

What does all this mean to me, right now? Practically, that I stop finding in every setback, in every disappointment, in every hurt, a renewed invitation to hit bottom. I am an alcoholic, but not every untoward event that occurs in my life happens because

I am an alcoholic. The line between modesty and self-pity, between accepting that I need to be polished and feeling that I am being ground smooth, may be narrow — but it is real.

Those closest to me, even if themselves nonalcoholic, know and accept me as an alcoholic. There are times, in every relationship, when hurt occurs and weapons are reached for. Those who love us can wound us most deeply: they know our vulnerabilities, the places where we can be hurt. On occasion, those who love me attribute that about me which they do not like to my alcoholism. On one level, that is dirty pool. More profoundly, it is part of the game of being human, part of the challenge inherent in loving and in allowing oneself to be loved.

The Serenity Prayer teaches me that I can change what others say no more than I can change the reality that is my alcoholism. When I hurt in this way, then, sobriety suggests that I need to examine whether such an accusation, though painful, may not be true. If, then, part of my pain comes because the dagger strikes truth, it would be well for me to review A.A.'s Seventh Step.

That Step begins, however, with the word *humbly*. It does not suggest wallowing in humiliation. Humility is the ability to rise above humiliation. And that involves sobriety's second reaction, whether the wounding accusation be true or false.

Unlike a stone under a mason's pumice, I have some choice over whether I will be polished or ground smooth. And the first element in that choice, it seems to me, involves deciding whether to view even false accusations as occasions of humiliation or as invitations to humility. When the wound, the abrasion comes from a loved one, that choice can test my sobriety. It helps, on such occasions, to remember another loved one, another lover. Count Leo Tolstoi once published a series of folk-wisdom stories under the title of one such tale: "Though the mills of God grind slowly, yet they grind exceeding small."

The image of my Higher Power as a miller does not attract me. But if I stretch my mind in an attempt to embrace this bit of quasi-Pietist wisdom, I can discern a fit with Kierkegaard's image that heads this piece. Those who love me, and perhaps especially my Higher Power, abrade to polish, not to grind smooth. Remembering that might help me more often find humility where now I too frequently see only humiliation.

11

. . . "Of all the world's wonders, which is the most wonderful?" the Bhagavad Gita asks, and answers, "that each man, though he sees others dying all around him, never believes that he himself will die."

— Willard Gaylin, M.D.

DEATH IS NOT A COMMON TOPIC OF CONversation, even within A.A. That is strange, in a way, for I suspect that every member of A.A., at his or her bottom, in some way stared death in the face. We know, in a way, what it is to die, or we would not be alive, much less sober.

Yet thinking of death makes us uncomfortable. I did not relish, last evening as I set off for my meeting, the realization that on the way I would be stopping by the wake of one of our oldtimers.

Perhaps because my background is part Irish, I always wonder on such evenings how the custom got started in A.A.: a bunch of sober alcoholics descend on the wake of a deceased fellow alcoholic. Perhaps I am uncomfortable less with the phenomenon of death than over my associations with wakes. I recall a ditty that, I am ashamed to say, I sometimes drunkenly sang at them: "The Night That Paddy Murphy Died." Most of its verses detail rampant alcoholic behavior, the memory of which perhaps frightens me more than death itself.

I choose this topic today because something strange seemed to happen at Tom's wake last night, to happen to me and to my attitudes, and perhaps to my sobriety. The wake itself was practically an A.A. meeting. Tom had no family, and just about everyone gathered there seemed to be in the program. The first thing that struck me was the large size of the gathering. Most of us, if we had died when we were drinking . . . . Well, the kind of friends I had then would not have been coming to my wake — unless, of course, booze was being served as in the Paddy Murphy song. In fact, there would not have been any real mourners of any kind, I suspect, if I had died when I was drinking. Unless a remark like "that poor bastard" can be taken as an expression of mourning.

Yet "mourning" did not last night and does not now seem to be the right word. I doubt that I have ever seen so many joyous people gathered together, exchanging stories about how old Tom had helped them. Some of those people Tom had twelfth-stepped; others had been his pigeons at some point in their sobriety; still others were recalling times when a quiet word from Tom, or even just his own example of living sober, had helped them over some rough times.

I find it difficult to put into words what I am just now feeling as much as thinking, and I hope this attempt does not sound morbid. But when I die, I want it to be like that — like Tom's wake last night. Back when I was drinking, sometimes I used to imagine what it would be like to die. I would imagine all those people who had hurt me, standing around the coffin and feeling sad that they had hurt me. In other words, the best I could do was to wallow in self-pity and resentment. Now that I am sober, I realize how sick that was, and I can even laugh at it — at my drunken imaginings of my own wake.

Since I have gotten sober, I have not thought much about dying: it is too much fun finally being able to think about living. But the wakes of A.A.s, like Tom's tonight — I don't know exactly how to describe what I feel, but the beauty of it makes me shiver. When I was growing up, or was supposed to be growing up, people used to talk sometimes about "a happy death." Well, I am still not sure I know what that means, but if it means anything, then good old Tom is having a happy death.

A story comes to mind about when the philosopher Plato was dying. His followers gathered around, hoping to hear his last words of wisdom. One of them asked the old man — Socrates' pupil, Aristotle's teacher — what was the secret of living a good life. Plato, according to the story, slowly opened his eyes and with smooth effort spoke two last words: "Practice dying."

That irritated me when I first read it not too many months ago. I felt that as a recovering alcoholic I had my hands full practicing living. But in light of my experience last night, the outpouring of joyfully serene remembrance that was Tom's wake, I think I might be beginning to understand the deeper import of Plato's injunction, "Practice dying."

Living is in some sense dying. What does "a day at a time" mean, if not that each day we are to live as if that were all we had? Truly, as we learn in this program, that is all we ever really do have: this day, this twenty-four hours of sobriety, to continue our growth and our recovery. "Alcoholics live in the past or in the future," Bill W. once wrote: "they have no present tense." We learn in A.A. that all we actually do have is a present tense — a "daily reprieve," as *The Big Book* says. I suspect that Plato meant something similar when he said, "Practice dying."

Although I dislike the term — probably because I still have some growing to do in the area of tolerance — we are, in a way, *born again* in Alcoholics Anonymous. Any alcoholic who walks through those doors has stared death in the face, or he or she wouldn't be there. Life, for most of us, had become utterly meaningless. I recall what one woman said, telling the story of how she felt just before coming to A.A.:

> For more than thirty years I lived with the sneaking suspicion that I had not found the answer to the most basic meaning of my existence. This suspicion grew into a terrible desperation. Nothing made sense, nothing mattered. I was not afraid of death; I was afraid of having lived for no reason at all.

That woman told her story in prison — she is a convicted murderer.

But it doesn't have to be that dramatic. In A.A., most of us, it seems, discover a reason for living. And that reason, summarized in the words of the Twelfth Step, involves, in a way, practicing dying, for that is precisely what it means to live a day at a time, trying to practice these principles in all our affairs.

Some pretty good philosophers and psychologists insist that we cannot imagine our own death. "The limit of our experience cannot be the object of our experience," as one of them has put it. Perhaps that is why we so cling to intimations of immortality: we are incapable of imagining the cessation of our own being.

That is interesting speculative philosophy, perhaps; but all those A.A.s at Tom's wake tonight, and what I have just been thinking about Alcoholics Anonymous: that concretizes it, puts flesh on it, in a way that might enable me to use that idea to progress in sobriety. At least to the kind of sobriety that was Tom's.

Someone once asked the great medical researcher, Sir William Osler, the secret of a long and full life. His answer pretty well sums up what we do in A.A.: "Contract a chronic, terminal disease and take care of it." I do not know the nature of Osler's own disease, but his insight is profound. Only when we know that we are sick do we fully know — and care for — our wellness.

These thoughts, inspired by Tom's wake, are concerned less — it seems to me now — with death than life. We cannot think of death without thinking of life. Perhaps we usually shun thinking about death because we fear thinking about life. Yet, being human *is* a terminal disease. Perhaps it is my greatest privilege, as an alcoholic, that on some level I glimpse this truth of the human condition from the perspective of my own alcoholic malady.

12

Humans are those beings who understand what it means for things to be. . . , a change in one's understanding of Being presupposes a change in one's existence.

— Michael E. Zimmerman

MANY PEOPLE REFER TO ALCOHOLISM AS A medical entity, but I doubt that anyone sees it as a condition helped by surgery. Nevertheless, a recent experience of recovering from surgery seems to be teaching me something about the process of recovery from alcoholism.

Before surgery (not for alcoholism, but for a problem disc), the surgeon told me all that he would do, and it did not sound like the "minor procedure" he called it. This minor surgery required a team, and especially a skilled surgeon to do the work. During the operation, I just lay there, unfeeling, devoid of all responsibility for outcome.

But after leaving the recovery-room — inappropriately named, it seems to me — the story changed. The surgeon's work was done, but I was in more pain than when I first consulted him. And now it was up to me to recover. Upon discharge from the hospital the next morning, I was given a list of "Don'ts" — warnings that, although the surgeon had successfully performed the operation on my back, I could render all his labor valueless by one incautious step. I had been repaired, but I was not healed.

In any case, becoming healed suddenly became *my* responsibility. And so I asked, "What can I do to foster postsurgical healing?" "Nothing." came the response. My body, I was told, would ultimately heal itself — so long as I did not interfere with its natural healing processes.

I found that bit of information both consoling and disturbing. Consoling because I like to trust my body — at least now that I am free from chemicals. It is good to hear affirmation that my body is on my side — that it is a good body, capable of healing. But I also found that news disturbing. Even though I do not believe that I am my body, I am not accustomed to think of "having" a body, like having a pair of shoes that I can change at will. Although it is not all of me, my body is me. So how is it that I can do nothing while my body heals?

Because I respected my surgical team and therefore the sagacity of their counsel, I tried to follow their advice, accepting that they having done their part, it was now up to me to do mine. The problem was that there was, in a sense, both everything and nothing to do. I lay motionless while my body healed. In other words, because of one's peculiar relationship with his body, I found myself in the contradiction of doing nothing while doing everything.

As I lay meditating on that, it struck me that there was an analogy between that aspect of healing from surgery and how I attain healing from alcoholism within the program and fellowship of Alcoholics Anonymous. Stated most simply, our most important task as human beings, if we would be healed, if we would become whole as truly human beings, is simply to be — but to be in a sense of that word rarely recognized in its common usage.

Last night I began to think about this again.

Is it possible to recapture the most basic meaning of the word and idea: *to be?* Understanding be-ing is not an effort in philosophical gamesmanship. It is a matter of life and death for those of us who suffer from chronic disabilities such as alcoholism. Because we are human beings, living a truly human life involves the activity of be-ing. Our primary task, as human beings, is to be humanly. We may do good; we may even do well; but be-ing well is our most essential action.

But how are we to understand that and to live it, if our usual use of language blinds us to simplicity? The very vocabulary available to us for understanding ourselves seems to inhibit the thought as well as the talk that might aid our understanding of be-ing. The conversation after a recent meeting brings to mind an example. Some of the group's members were carelessly hassling a relative newcomer, who seemed to be incautiously sharing the beginning of his Fourth Step inventory, about "practicing these principles in all our affairs." They seemed, against one of Bill W.'s favorite cautions, to be pushing him "to try to get too good by Thursday."

Finally the neophyte blurted out, "Look! I don't come here to learn how to get good — I come here to learn how to get well!"

Our resident sage in sobriety heard him and put the matter into even better perspective. "A noble purpose and indeed the best reason for being here," Tom proclaimed in his best imitation of pomposity — the clue to the rest of us to heed what would follow. "But let me share somthing with you: after quite a few twenty-four hours working this program, I am not sure that I am 'well,' but I sure do seem to be getting weller."

In a setting other than an A.A. meeting, the phrase *getting weller* would have jarred ears. Yet Tom had expressed a simple idea that the rest of us intuitively understood. Later, I began thinking about it, albeit in uncommon terms and unconventional use of language. There is a great difference between claiming "I *am* well" and stating "I *be* well." The former implies static well-being — a condition of ease. One who is well feels the soft contentment of unagitated wholeness. "I *am* well" signals the kind of rest experienced by one stretched out in relaxation.

To *be* well is different. It involves the activity of dynamic wholeness. And what is dynamic wholeness? An acceptance of the reality of dis-ease that fosters becoming whole, of healing, because that acceptance *is* that process. If someone should ask, concerning my recent surgery, "How are you?" I could not truthfully answer, "I am well." Nor, probably, would I reply, "I be well" — but the temptation to do so would be present. How else transmit what I understand to be going on? I am recovering from my surgery. But I am not merely "getting well" because I am actively and even passionately involved in that recovery. Nor am I being healed: rather, I heal. Insofar as I and my body are one, that verb must be used intransitively. I am, in a sense, working on my recovery from back surgery precisely by not working at all.

Be-ing, in this sense, signifies more than the existence of some status or condition. It is an action. My body — and therefore also I — are involved less in *an* activity than in *the* activity that undergirds everything else that I now or ever hope to do. Healing, understood in this light, is an act of be-ing.

Yet how rarely do we think to examine how we *be*, how we

heal — unless, that is, we are trying to live a Twelve-Step program. The Twelve-Step program guides us, most simply, in how to be. Chapter Five of *The Big Book* presents not "the things we did" but "the Steps we took" that are suggested as a program of recovery. One takes rather than does a Step. And, as all of the Twelve Steps imply and some make very explicit, even much of that taking involves open readiness rather than frantic activity. As I try to live the program, the Steps take me at least as much as I take them.

In other words, I not only work the program: the A.A. program also in some way works me. That is why *"Willingness, honesty and open-mindedness are the essentials of recovery,"* as the famed *Big Book* "Appendix" reminds in italics. And that is also why, if one is serious about recovery, sobriety, and serenity, one must attend to be-ing if one's doing is ever to produce benefits. I must be well, for — as an alcoholic — I can never say in perfect truthfulness that "I am well." Because I am an alcoholic, I am always in some way dis-eased.

We introduce ourselves, we qualify, at A.A. meetings, not by telling what we did but by acknowledging who we are. The words, "I am an alcoholic," spoken at an A.A. meeting, denote not a static condition but a profound activity of our being. That is why we are there: to be a certain kind of alcoholic — one engaged in the spiritual progress that is our recovery. I attend A.A. as a way of be-ing well, and I need to do that because in some way I am not well. And that will be as true, though I hope differently true, at the last A.A. meeting I attend as it was at the first.

Someday I will be able to say, concerning my back, "I am well." But my alcoholism — and my recovery from it — is different. Because Alcoholics Anonymous promises progress rather than perfection, be-ing sober is an unending process. Our task, in the phrasing of the title of one piece of A.A. literature, is *Living Sober.* And that is not the same as living soberly. Yet living sober is not a chore — nor even so passive an activity as lying in bed. Being sober is rather the only possible expression of my truly human being. As an alcoholic human being, I have no other choice than to be truly human, for only thus do I heal, only thus can I even approach becoming whole.

13

I would rather have [a virtue] than know how to define it.

— Thomas à Kempis

ONE PARTICULAR PHRASE THAT I WROTE yesterday has stayed on my mind, inviting deeper exploration. "As I try to live the program, the Steps take me at least as much as I take them." My postsurgical disability is teaching me something that I thought I already knew. There exist two kinds of knowledge — or, perhaps better — two ways of knowing.

The surgeon, I am sure, knows more about my surgery than I either know or care to know. And his knowledge is not merely theoretical: he performed the operation, bringing to bear all his experience as surgeon. I know my surgery differently — in a way that no one who has not undergone the same experience can know it. My surgeon knows a great deal *about* my operation: I know it from *within* the experience itself.

Surgery, and the wider field of medicine, afford one example. Two other models come readily to mind: first, the ineffable experiences of spirituality and love; second, the most obvious example, the experience of sobriety within the program and fellowship of Alcoholics Anonymous.

Thinking on my A.A. experience, it seems to me that perhaps a more profound truth underlies the oft-repeated axioms, "Identify, don't compare" and "Utilize, don't analyze." Do those suggestions not urge knowing from within rather than merely knowing about? The phrase will never catch on in A.A., I am sure, but let me at least try to formulate this idea in terms of what I am just now undergoing. "Experience, don't just examine." There are some realities like wisdom, love, healing, spirituality, and sobriety of which it is true that to know them from within, deeply, by the participation of immersion, is quite different from knowledge about them, however extensive.

Different — neither better, nor worse. Perhaps extending the metaphor implicit in contrasting depth of knowledge with extensiveness of knowledge can help me to remember and clarify that understanding. This line of thought involves more than metaphor: our world is, after all, in reality three-dimensional.

The diver knows the sea in a way different from the mariner. The knowledge of each person is good and useful. But a sailor is not an oceanographer, not every philosopher is wise, nor is every theologian a saint, every professor of economics a good manager of household finances, every psychologist a well-adjusted human being. To know any reality from *within*, to be a reality by participation in the reality, differs from knowing *about* that reality, however useful and valuable such knowledge about it may also prove.

Just about everyone knows this, and knows it from within, by experience. Those who do not know it from their experience of healing likely understand it from their experience with spirituality or with love. Perhaps spirituality is the easier example. Many individuals are certain that they know much about their Higher Power — God as they understand Him. Few of them, in my experience, seem very spiritual in the sense of that word that I have learned to cherish within A.A. Others, who rarely speak the word *spiritual* and almost never claim much knowledge about the details of their Higher Power, exude not only spirituality but what the ancients termed *sanctity*. They may speak of their Higher Power hesitantly, but anyone touched by their lives feels contact with a Power greater than themselves. Such seem to know their God from within.

And then, what of love? Fools speak of it; lovers seem content quietly to practice it. Would anyone who has loved, who has known the experience of love from within, doubt that to have much knowledge about love differs vastly from knowing love itself? Some — poor, tortured souls — have asked, "How can I come to know love?" Who would respond by suggesting a course of study or reading a book? The answer, most of us know, lies not in knowledge about love but in the practice of loving itself. I cannot imagine a greater difference than that between knowing about love and knowing love itself.

The one who knows from within participates in the be-ing of the reality that is known. Ironically, such depth may lead to a certain blindness: the diver on the sea-floor remains heedless of storm clouds on the horizon unless someone on the surface informs him of them. But the sailor who scans the horizon, whose skill lies in recognizing storm clouds even at great distance, also remains partially blind, ignorant of the deep, rich reality of the sea on which he floats. Each knowledge, that is to say, is purchased at a price. And it is good to know what price we have paid. Here, then, the example of Alcoholics Anonymous may be most useful. And here also seems where these ideas on knowing connect with yesterday's thoughts on be-ing.

To understand be-ing as an action distinct from being as a condition or a status is to be prepared to understand the difference between the knowing that derives from objective observations, however extensive, and the knowing that flows from participation, from the depths of actually living. Many nonalcoholic (and some nonrecovering) scholars know much about the program and fellowship of Alcoholics Anonymous. Some of them, indeed, know much more about A.A.'s history and psychological dynamics, for example, than do most members. But even the simplest, newest member of Alcoholics Anonymous, who yet struggles with the second half of the First Step, knows the nature and the be-ing of the recovery that is Alcoholics Anonymous in a way that no nonmember ever can.

Because we tend to confuse being as a passive condition with the active behavior of be-ing, we seem also prone to confuse one kind of knowledge or one way of knowing with the other. Yet, if there is a difference between dryness and sobriety, if putting the cork in the bottle is not the whole of the A.A. way of life, then there is also a vast difference between the knowledge that comes from studying the A.A. program and the kind of knowledge that flows from living and loving that program from within.

I need the reminder that this journal represents an effort at the latter. Although learning about Alcoholics Anonymous does not (and I hope never will) bore me, learning A.A. itself is clearly the task at hand on this ninety/ninety. Because of the kindness of many A.A. friends, my sudden surgery has not imposed an interruption of that project. "If you can't bring your body to the meetings, well, we'll just bring the meetings to your poor old body," one of them declared. And the one hospital and one sick-room meetings have been great therapy for my back as well as for my spirit, as I suspect my doctors would agree, for they lead me to think and therefore to lie still.

But these last two days of largely silent thinking, as I prepare again to venture cautiously out to "a real meeting," have been of inestimable value in calling me back to the purpose of this whole endeavor — this ninety/ninety and its journal. If I would grow and truly progress in spirituality, whatever it is, I need remember that my goal is not to know more about A.A., even as a way of life. In order to live, I must *be* an Alcoholics Anonymous. And though that term may sound strange, I am now clearer about what it means: knowing the fellowship and its program in my being, not just in my head nor in these jottings.

14

Thales was asked what was most difficult to man; he answered: To know one's self.

— Diogenes Laertius

It is as easy to deceive oneself without perceiving it as it is difficult to deceive others without their perceiving it.

— La Rochefoucauld

"WHAT IS THE MOST IMPORTANT PART OF ANY A.A. meeting?" I remember my first sponsor, Phil, asking me that question one night as we drove home. Although my head was still groggy from my most recent binge, I tried hard to think of the answer he seemed to be looking for. The Serenity Prayer? The stories? The friendly greeting that welcomed each speaker who introduced himself? Phil listened quietly until I ran out of suggestions, then he even more quietly made the point that I needed that night: "The most important part of any A.A. meeting, for you, is the moment you walk through the door into it."

Phil's wisdom lingers in my mind, reawakened by something I observed last night — an identification with a less than happy "Remember when." A newcomer is making many of the meetings I attend. In conversation, he told me that he is not trying to make a ninety/ninety, nor even thirty meetings in thirty days: he is shopping around.

There can be wisdom in shopping, but the way this newcomer is going about it troubles me, for he is doing what I did when I first came around, and for me that style of attendance was a mistake. He arrives at any meeting one minute before it starts and rockets out less than one minute after it ends. He is missing much, and he doesn't even know it.

I realize I should not be taking his inventory — maybe he works late or has to get to work, or maybe he has a sick wife or child at home. But I didn't have any excuses like that back when I was doing the same thing. The truth is, I just did not understand the nature of an A.A. meeting.

It was Phil who took me aside and explained this to me, some weeks after he had made his walking-through-the-door point. "You seem to know," Phil observed, "all about the two kinds of A.A. meetings, speaker and discussion. But all A.A. meetings also have two parts — what goes on within them and what happens before and especially after them. Just as, for good sobriety, most of us need both kinds of meetings, so — perhaps for sobriety itself — especially newcomers need both parts of what an A.A. meeting really is."

Phil had — wittingly, I am sure — touched a sore point. During my last detoxification, I had noticed something: the A.A.'s who came and twelfth-stepped me in the hospital, those who had time and love for a guy who had just flunked out of A.A., were those who had always been at meetings when I got there and who had always still been there when I left. Of course, it wasn't too difficult to be in that category, given how narrowly I used to budget my A.A. time.

And so I began to learn something — by thinking about that experience that had seemed so devoid of strength and hope, by listening to Phil's comments. Within meetings, during the time between the Serenity Prayer and the Lord's Prayer, we share with each other primarily in order to identify with each other — to learn from each other. That is not only good, it is necessary: identification is the only way — or at least the best way — that people who suffer from a chronic disability such as alcoholism can truly communicate what is meaningful to them, the only way in which we are able actually to share — to give and to receive — experience, strength, and hope about our disability.

Also within meetings, we see another manifestation of mutuality — of our need both to give and to receive — that builds upon that one of experience, strength, and hope. Inevitably, for example, after a speaker has finished telling his or her story, one person will come up and say: "Thanks for what you said — it really helped me." And as inevitably someone else comes up and says: "About what you said — I think maybe that I can help you." That experience furnishes an effective reminder of the mutuality of our giving and our getting.

But there is another kind of mutuality — of giving by getting, of getting by giving — that runs deeper. It seems most evident in what happens before and especially after the meeting itself. I once asked an oldtimer about his meeting attendance — why he attended so frequently and so regularly — when according to any realistic appraisal, he was in very little danger of drinking alcohol on any given day.

Ben first informed me that an alcoholic is an alcoholic; and that therefore the day any alcoholic forgets that he might all too easily take a drink on any given day — the day any alcoholic becomes sure he won't take a drink and therefore neglects to ask for help — is usually the day when he or she does drink, because an alcoholic is an alcoholic. But having cleared up that point, Ben went on readily to admit that that was not the only reason he attended so many meetings.

Honesty, Ben reminded me, is the foundation of all sobriety. And getting honest with ourselves, while important, is never easy. Getting honest with ourselves is, in fact, an ongoing and neverending process, as the story of the Delphic oracle's advice, "Know thyself," was intended to convey. As the ancient Greeks understood it, good people are those who spend their lives trying to heed that counsel; evil people seem to devote their lives to trying to avoid it — usually by pretending or deceiving themselves that they have fulfilled it once and for all, that they have attained perfect honesty with themselves.

As A.A.'s explanation of "How It Works" reminds us, we cannot attain "perfect" anything. But we must try to progress in — to use the ancient terms — those virtues that are spiritual. Yet how can we do that, for example, with *honesty?* Well, experience teaches — and A.A. certainly verifies — that we get honest with ourselves by being honest with others; and, of course, we are able to be honest with others only by becoming honest with ourselves.

That is a healing rather than a vicious cycle. It all begins with the word *alcoholic* — with saying out loud, to someone else, "I am an alcoholic." On the one hand, we do not say that until we believe it; on the other hand, we really do not believe it until we say it. But that honesty is only our first honesty, if we would grow in sobriety. We must progress in that saving honesty by continuing its practice — by telling what we come to know of ourselves as the only way of coming to know what we tell of ourselves.

A.A.'s Tenth Step, it seems to me, captures this insight. Step Ten has two parts, and together they reflect the mutuality between honesty with self and honesty with others, in sobriety. "Continued to take personal inventory and when we were wrong promptly admitted it." We take inventory in order to know ourselves better; but when we obtain that self-knowledge, we need to share it with someone else. Likewise, sharing whatever self-knowledge we attain leads to deeper self-knowledge and therefore to more profound honesty with self.

There are, of course, many reasons for the wording of that Step: no one is ever going to encapsulate the depths of wisdom in each Step of the A.A. way of life in some single narrow idea, even that of honesty. But it seems to me that this — the mutuality of honesty — is one bit of the wisdom of that Tenth Step in which I am being invited to grow. And I plug into that wisdom not only by taking inventory, but at meetings — and especially during the conversations that take place before and after those meetings, because they are a part of the complete A.A. meeting experience. Unfortunately, they are a part of the meeting of which many newcomers, and perhaps even many not-so-newcomers, unwittingly deprive themselves.

Because, as a newcomer, I deprived myself of it for too long, I pray that the newcomer with whom I identified last night does not follow too closely in my footsteps. That the program of A.A. requires honesty is only half the story: the fellowship of A.A. enables that honesty, if we but give it the chance. Coming early and staying late opens us to that: may every newcomer learn it less painfully than did I.

15

Meanwhile, back at the ranch . . .

— Owen Wister

GETTING TO MEETINGS EARLY AND STAYING late has another advantage: one discovers the nature of what one of my early sponsors liked to refer to as "A.A. conversations."

"A.A. conversations" is not a technical term. To the best of my knowledge, the phrase does not appear in any of the fellowship's literature. It is rather a shorthand expression for any exchange that is infused with the A.A. way of thinking, that supports and promotes the A.A. way of life. Such conversations gain that quality less from their content, from what is talked about, than from their style, from how any topic is approached.

Humor, for example, is a frequent characteristic of A.A. conversations. A.A. humor rarely directly concerns drinking or sobriety: rather, it highlights the incongruity of life. In A.A. conversations, as I understand them, participants talk not *about* the A.A. way of life but *within* it — thus applying to "all our affairs" the principles of the Twelve Steps.

When my own sponsor first introduced me to the concept of A.A. conversations, after I had about six or eight months of budding sobriety, I recall that he explained the idea less with his words than with his hands. Sam had impressive hands: to see them even at rest was to be reminded of Durer's famous woodcut of hands at prayer. His words, as best as I can recall, concerned "finding wholeness by seeing wholes," but I remember more vividly his gestures as he spoke. For it was those beautifully gnarled hands cupping and balancing the empty air that finally led me to see his point — and to learn a reality that has helped me to learn much more, over the years, about the riches of healing provided by the program and fellowship of Alcoholics Anonymous. Without those hands, mere words seem deprived. But the point is too important not to recall in this journal, too sobriety-enhancing not to attempt to set down, even if only in words.

As alcoholics, and perhaps also as human beings, we are healed — we become whole and complete — only by finding and seeing wholes, by looking at the full picture, by viewing things in context. Within A.A. we gain that difficult but necessary skill primarily because, in telling our stories and listening to those of others, we learn to think in terms of stories. Any story is always, in some way, whole; or at least it reflects as much wholeness as we who are human can comprehend.

Stories, then, in a way impart "chronic" wholeness. But at times, our dis-ease — our fractured alienation — becomes "acute." On such occasions, when current happenings rather than the larger vicissitudes of life threaten to pull us off balance, we need an intensively abridged reminder of the larger truth taught by "whole stories." And that is what A.A. conversations provide.

The evening when Sam first tried to explain that idea to me, I recall how strangely came the realization that the movements of his workman's hands were reminding me of the delicately precise gestures of the professor who had long ago instructed me in the rudiments of the Greek language. Suddenly I realized that both were trying to teach me the same truth. My academic mentor had suggested, decades before, that the greatest contribution of the ancient Greeks to civilization consisted in two untranslatable particles, *men* and *de.* The closest we can come to translating them, maybe, is "on the one hand" and "on the other hand." But the classical Greeks used those particles in a much classier way. That ancient civilization, although it possessed a written language, was composed of people who were primarily storytellers. Not only does their great literature tell stories, but often those stories are about people who spend a great deal of their time telling *their* stories.

A Greek storyteller would, as I recalled, habitually begin his narration of some occurrence with the particle *men.* Then he would go on — for hours or for pages and pages — telling about that event, but all the while his readers or hearers knew that sooner or later would come the *de,* the description of what else was going on at the same time that was also significant. *Men* and *de,* my Greek prof insisted, taught Western humanity to suspend judgment, to look for and to see the "other side" that any reality always has. The practice of its use thus promoted tolerance as well as truly sophisticated thinking about the complexity inherent in human affairs.

It helped me then, and it helps me now, to ponder how the implicit *men* and *de* of A.A. conversations infinitely improves on the hack writer's "Meanwhile." That modern technique sort of sneaks up on the reader, often with a kind of jolt: it betrays that the reader needs reminding that something else is going on. The Greek usage, like the A.A. style, subtly makes certain that that "something else" is never forgotten, is kept always in mind.

A.A. conversations work like this. Imagine an A.A. member who arrives at a meeting at the end of a particularly rough day. He or she had car trouble and was late for work; maybe there was a spat at home, the news that one child is ill and another seems to be in some kind of trouble, and maybe there's more. Other A.A.s stand around and listen attentively as his day's tale of woe is recounted over coffee, and then — invariably — one speaks up: "Yes, you sure did have a rough day, but at least you didn't take a drink." His or her day becomes at least a partial success.

Another member, perhaps at the very same meeting, enjoyed just the opposite kind of day. He or she tells, over coffee, what a great twenty-four hours it has been: there was an unexpected raise in pay; a daughter has just won a scholarship to a prestigious college; and the marriage seems to be recapturing the joy and wonder of its first weeks. As invariably, a fellow coffee-sipper also speaks up: "Yes, that sure is great — but don't forget that you are still an alcoholic and therefore just one drink away from a drunk that would blow it all."

The ancient Greeks and sober members of Alcoholics Anonymous, it seems to me in other words, share and participate in the same wisdom. According to that vision, to be human is in some way to be in the middle: we are necessarily always "both/and" rather than ever "either/or." Or, in a frequently expressed insight of A.A. co-founder Bill W., because "we alcoholics tend to be all-or-nothing people," we need all the help we can get to smooth out our highs and our lows. A.A. conversations achieve that. By so consistently inviting us to look at the other side of any reality, they impress upon us the insight that all reality — and especially our own reality — always is two-sided. It is not only that every cloud has its silver lining: every silver lining also has its cloud. That's life, and A.A. conversations recall us to the reality of life.

A final thought intrudes — one that concerns this practice of keeping a journal of my experience, strength, and hope during these ninety days. Most often, I jot down thoughts late at night, on returning home from my meeting, and polish them for clarity only the next morning, in light of the previous night's day-end inventory and that day's sense of fresh gratitude for a new day in which I do not have to drink.

Because of that framework, I would like to think, this journal may at times record a kind of A.A. conversation with my Higher Power. Seeing that possibility, I hope I can remember better to listen as I ponder each day's events, each meeting's meaning to my sobriety. It is good to recall that, because my Higher Power speaks to me in such richly diverse ways, especially through A.A., an attitude of attentive listening is always important — and perhaps especially for one who seeks to capture those insights in writing.

16

Knowledge about God, whether gained in contemplation or through speculative effort, lies beyond the power of language and appears paradoxical.

— Leszek Kolakowski

As a computer scientist, I agree with Ionesco, who wrote, "Not everything is unsayable in words, only the living truth.

— Joseph Weizenbaum

IF ANY SUBJECT IS LIKELY TO PROVOKE SILENCE when suggested as a topic for a discussion meeting, it is the Eleventh Step's reference to prayer and meditation. Last night proved no exception. But a good chairman, one who knows the group and their sobriety well, knows how to wait. For the waiting, the silence, is not empty. Each person around the table is working hard, albeit silently, trying to formulate into words a rich but also profoundly unarticulated aspect of his or her own experience, strength, and hope.

When he is chairing, Len waits well. Relaxed, but perched expectantly, not quite on the edge of his chair, he glances with encouragement but with no hint of obligation at each face as its expression signals the possibility of dawning insight to be shared. The group last night began gingerly. Several observed, in various ways, that A.A. literature is more helpful — more specific — in explaining prayer. Meditation is treated more briefly, especially in *The Big Book*, but also in the *Twelve and Twelve*. Those passages seem written primarily for people who gagged at the very term *meditation*.

But that, we agreed, was not our problem. At least in this group, no one found either the term or the concept objectionable. Several of us in fact, although our educational and religious backgrounds greatly differ, have some familiarity with the rich history of meditation. That knowledge, however, seemed pointless to the discussion at hand. Our interest concerned what, precisely, meditation means within A.A. — how it relates to living the A.A. way of life.

Even framed thus, the topic proved difficult to discuss. For most of us, prayer and meditation have to do with something very precious and very personal in our lives. Talking about them too easily seems to cheapen them, to violate their meaning in our experience. Important realities cannot be put easily or well into words. That is why we have so many artists, and such varied arts. To ask me to tell about my meditation is like asking a painter to explain what his picture means. The artist replies, "If I could put it into words, I would not have had to paint the picture." When asked about prayer and meditation, then, I am inclined to answer: "If you cannot understand it from my life, you will never come to understand it by my words."

But the group was not asking that. An A.A. discussion meeting involves not "show and tell" but "live and let live": we are there to identify, not to compare. And so a few members tried. Len summed up our efforts well, pointing out that to him, at least, what we were then doing involved a kind of meditation. We were engaged in a thoughtful exchange of ideas about something deeply important to us. That, he suggested, caught at least one aspect of meditation: it involves a kind of A.A. conversation with one's Higher Power.

Although most did not agree with our chairman's implication that the A.A. group served as his Higher Power, Len's point was well taken. Everyone accepted that it seemed to capture two things essential to any meditation: it involves one's Higher Power, and it is a two-way process in which listening is more important than speaking.

Yet during last night's inventory, and again this morning as I inevitably meditated on meditation, I began to suspect that that initial understanding, for all of its usefulness, also contains a glaring weakness. Meditation, after all, can and perhaps should go beyond mere words. Any conversation is composed of words, but it seems to me that meditation worthy of the name ought at least occasionally to transcend our usual ways of speaking and thinking.

The *Twelve and Twelve* helps a lot, just here, in its treatment of the Eleventh Step. A.A.'s co-founder writes therein of "*constructive* imagination" — the italics are his. In *The Big Book's* passage on meditation, Bill's treatment had been very cognitive, very idea-oriented. Its brief description presents meditation mainly as an extension of the Tenth Step inventory. That aspect of it, of course, does come first. It is also probably the best way for a beginner in the program to get started on meditation.

But it seems to me that the *Twelve and Twelve*'s treatment of the Eleventh Step takes a large leap forward. That reflects, I am sure, Bill's and the other early A.A.'s growth in sobriety over the years. It is good for me to remember that they, as we, had to *grow* in sobriety. In the *Twelve and Twelve*, although Bill again links prayer and meditation with self-examination and follows the classic spiritual writers in suggesting that we begin with words — his example is the St. Francis Prayer — he immediately goes further. He encourages, to put it most briefly, visualizing an atmosphere — seeing and feeling our relationship with reality in the very same act of our being.

The words, *visualizing an atmosphere*, are my own rather than Bill's. Yet I find the very paradox implicit in that phrase, which it seems to me does accurately reflect what Bill suggests, to be helpful. Verbal paradox can open the mind to those realities that transcend the possibility of precise verbal expression. As playwright Eugene Ionesco once put it: "Not everything is unsayable in words, only the living truth."

Meditation is a kind of living of truth that somehow puts us in touch with ultimate reality. The practice of meditation, that is to say, is a kind of presence to reality. And because it deals with or is at least open to ultimate reality, that presence is a kind of "*be*-ing there" (as in Heidegger's famed formulation) that locates *us* rather than us locating reality. Meditation involves then, it seems to me, the kind of "understanding" in which we literally *stand under* ultimate reality. We thus become open to that reality in a way that enables us better to be, and so to live, who and what we truly are.

Difficult as that is to put into words, I believe the *Twelve and Twelve* ratifies that sense. Bill goes on in those pages to call the "first fruits" of meditation "emotional balance." And, at the conclusion of the treatment of Step Eleven, he names as "perhaps one of the greatest rewards of meditation and prayer . . . the sense of *belonging* that comes to us." Again, the italicized emphasis is his.

Although it is as difficult to meditate about thinking as it is to think about meditation, I find it helpful to recall that a way of thinking does underlie the A.A. way of life. In treating of prayer and meditation, Bill W. emphasized that both involve a learning process.

Within A.A., we learn first what we are — the meaning of being alcoholics. But then, as we progress in the A.A. program and grow in the A.A. way of life, we find ourselves invited to discover who we are, as sober alcoholics. And that involves learning more about and understanding more deeply our relationships with all those realities other than alcohol and alcoholics.

The main such reality, of course, is the ultimate reality of our Higher Power. Because that relationship is ultimate, not too much can be said about it, nor can we even think very well about it. Thinking about our Higher Power is as useless as was thinking about our alcoholism when we were drinking. As William James knew and taught, there are some things that thinking about necessarily distorts. We know them, then, not by thinking *about*, but by thinking *within* them.

The difference between "thinking about" and "thinking within" is anything but a mere play on prepositions. As James pointed out, it is the difference between even expert theoretical knowledge of how a violin produces sound and possessing the skill of a concert violinist. In a more recent metaphor, it is the difference between the ways in which a pediatrician and a mother care for an infant's health.

Meditation thus seems to involve a letting go of "thinking about" in the hope of becoming able "to think within." The difference between "thinking about" a spiritual topic and the "thinking within" that is meditation thus resembles the difference between, on the one hand, reading and thinking about and even studying the Twelve Steps and, on the other hand, actually practicing and taking those Steps. In both cases, thinking occurs; but one can see the vast difference betwen those two kinds of thinking at just about any meeting at which both newcomers and oldtimers are present.

In a sense, "thinking about" is to "thinking within" as dryness is to sobriety. In both instances, from the outside, they look similar. But as anyone who has moved from the one to the other in his or her own life knows, it is difficult to imagine a greater difference — unless it be that between drinking and not drinking.

Meditation, in other words, eludes such efforts as this one at thinking about it, precisely because it is meditation. I need, then, not so much a conversation about it as the practice of doing it. I did not come to accept "powerless" and "unmanageable" by thinking about the meaning of those words: I came to know their meaning only by identifying with their experience.

The same, I suspect, is true of "prayer and meditation" as those words appear in the Eleventh Step. My task, then, in that Step as in the First, is to identify rather than to compare; and meetings such as the one I attended last night, or journal entries such as this one this morning, can at best only point out the way.

17

To be able to recognize a freak, you have to have some conception of the whole man. . . . [Some people seem] very much afraid that [they] may have been formed in the image and likeness of God.

— Flannery O'Connor

As I BEGIN MORE AND MORE TO LIKE SPEAKER meetings and to appreciate the special healing that flows from hearing whole stories, I am also discovering in such meetings another benefit that I used to resent as a liability. Many speaker meetings are open meetings: nonalcoholics are welcome to attend them.

For too many years I unthinkingly felt that visitors — especially when they presented themselves as observers rather than as problem-drinkers who wondered whether or not they might themselves be alcoholics — turned A.A. meetings into a zoo. As a member of A.A., such meetings left me feeling like some kind of freak. I did not relish being stared at by "earthpeople." Why should my disability — alcoholism — be treated less politely than any other handicap?

Perhaps I reacted so strongly, emotionally, because when I first came around, I often pretended to be one of the observers. I feared being thought — and in fact I was terrified of being — one of the observees, an alcoholic. Perhaps because I now accept that I am an alcoholic, I can feel differently about observers.

At times, when they attend our meetings, I almost feel flattered by their attention — not for myself, of course; no one likes to be regarded as a freak. But for A.A. It strikes me as literally wonderful that some of the great and wise of the world — or at least those who sometimes see themselves as great or wise — come to learn from A.A., from us alcoholics, who are perhaps the most "foolish" beings in the world.

All the great philosophers and religious thinkers, I believe, commented on and encouraged that — not about alcoholics, but that the wise should learn from the foolish. Among modern writers, it was almost an obsession with Flannery O'Connor. She once wrote an essay explaining some of her stories and why she set them in the American South.

> Whenever I'm asked why Southern writers particularly have a penchant for writing about freaks, I say it is because we are still able to recognize one. To be able to recognize a freak, you have to have some conception of the whole man, and in the South the general conception of man is still, in the main, theological. . . . While the South is hardly Christ-centered, it is most certainly Christ-haunted. The Southerner . . . is very much afraid that he may have been formed in the image and likeness of God.

Quoting O'Connor seems singularly appropriate: there are a lot of colleges around here, and so we get a lot of college people at meetings. Actually, I dislike the term *collegepeople* as much as I despise the term *earthpeople*. Someone once suggested that the most obscene four-letter word is *they*, if that syllable be used to push off from other people, to make them more "other" and less "people." Nonalcoholics are human beings, just as we are human beings. We might be in different and perhaps closer touch with our humanity because we are also alcoholics; but the joys and the pains, the pleasures and the sorrows of being human are as real for them as those experiences are for us.

In that context, it strikes me that although being an alcoholic is never funny, there is often an almost humorous side to our anonymity. Sometimes, for example, I think at least some of the outsiders who visit our meetings envy us. Some of them seem to sense that we possess something, have plugged into something that they want but cannot have because they are not alcoholics. I remember a colleague once, complaining only half-jokingly that he seemed "cursed to a life of being a social drinker."

And so some of them observe or visit, I think, because they hunger — they want what we have, in a strange way, in a world where there seem to be too few vehicles of the spiritual for the needs that some people have. At least some of our visitors, I think, call themselves "observers" humbly rather than proudly. They acknowledge that they are different from us — they are not alcoholics — but it is almost as if they wanted to be alcoholics, because to learn from is to become like. And so I often feel that A.A. is being honored, not that its members are being spied upon or degraded, when such visitors come to our meetings.

That may, of course, sound excessive. As any alcoholic well knows, nobody stands in line to become an alcoholic. I have heard people honestly say, "I am grateful that I am an alcoholic"; and I pretty much feel that gratitude myself, in context. But that comes, if it comes at all, only slowly, as the A.A. way of life seeps into all of our thinking. No A.A. member I have ever met is grateful to be an alcoholic in his or her first month, or even first year, in the program. Nobody wants to be an alcoholic. And anybody who truly knows us, who listens to our stories, can only rejoice that he or she did not have to pay the dues that we did to get into A.A.

Still, it is also true that we alcoholics have something very precious and very attractive that, at times, other people can honestly and validly wish that they had. I guess the question is almost philosophical: Is it possible to be a sober alcoholic without ever having been an active alcoholic?

Defining terms strictly, the answer must be "No." But there is another, deeper question: Can the way of life that the sober alcoholic learns in A.A. be learned by others who are not alcoholic? And the answer to that question, I think A.A. history and practice proves, is "Yes."

I never cease to be impressed by how generous our fellowship is with its program. The different groups of variously disabled people who use the Twelve Steps, all with A.A.'s permission and blessing, are virtually uncountable. That tells much about the attractiveness — and the significance — of A.A. and the way of life that its simple program enables.

Thus I like to think — and I know from experience that I am not just making this up — that at least some outsiders who come to our meetings come not to laugh or to inspect but to learn. They may ask seemingly stupid questions sometimes. They can sometimes make us uncomfortable because they feel uncomfortable, sensing that they are outsiders. Some of them, of course, may even be early-stage alcoholics who get defensive when they hear something that threatens the denial they are just beginning to develop. Others, of course, maybe especially the social workers, do come to study us. But even most of them are doing that not to mock us or stare at us, but rather in the hope that they can learn from us so they can help others.

Alcoholics Anonymous really practices what it preaches. Its primary purpose remains, as always, "to help the alcoholic who still suffers." If others can learn from us, that is just great; but we do not push that aspect of A.A.'s potential. Alcoholics Anonymous, it seems to me, has a great faith in its Higher Power: it believes that if it does its job, one day at a time, its Higher Power will take care of anything more.

Of course, it is also true that Alcoholics Anonymous is not "it": G.S.O. is not A.A. — we are, I am. And thus I do not think it grandiose that feeling good about A.A. makes me feel good about me. My task is to live as best I can the blend of humility and generosity that characterizes the fellowship of which, today, I am honestly and soberly proud to be part. And, to me, that does include welcoming outsiders and visitors and even observers to our open meetings. Some of them, I suspect, might be used by A.A.'s Higher Power to carry the message in ways in which we ourselves cannot. For there are, out there, not only alcoholics who still suffer: there are also other human beings who suffer, who, even though they are not alcoholic, might in some way be healed by our way of life.

18

The problems of the pill taker are the same as those of the alcoholic and the pill-taking alcoholic is just as incapable of safely using pills as he is of drinking — he simply doubles his risks.

— *The Grapevine*

Probably a third of the women and many of the men, on their arrival in A.A., are already pill addicts. And pill addiction, for us drunks, often proves more damaging, physically and emotionally, than alcohol.

— Bill W.

LAST NIGHT'S MEETING REMINDED ME OF THE tiny discrepancy between A.A.'s Tenth Tradition and the "Preamble" that is read at the beginning of our meetings. The Tenth Tradition of Alcoholics Anonymous reads:

> Alcoholics Anonymous has no opinion on outside issues; hence the A.A. name ought never be drawn into public controversy.

The relevant portion of the Preamble states:

> The only requirement for membership is a desire to stop drinking. . . . A.A. . . . does not wish to engage in any controversy, neither endorses nor opposes any causes.

There is a difference, it seems, between *public* controversy and *any* controversy. Or — more accurately, perhaps — there exists a narrow range for one type of controversy within A.A. itself.

Last night's controversy — if that word does not too misrepresent the spirited and respectful discussion that actually took place — concerned the problem of "other problems." It began when a new member introduced himself by saying: "My name is Glen, and I am a chemically dependent alcoholic."

The group whose meeting I attended last night has a reputation for "fundamentalist" A.A. I am not sure that I like the adjective, but its meaning is clear, and I am sure I like — and occasionally need — that meaning. These are people who stick to A.A.'s fundamentals. Some who feel less need for those fundamentals than do I, at times refer to them as "The Don't-Drink-and-Go-To-Meetings Group." And so several of them rose to what I am sure was not intended as bait.

"A.A. means *Alcoholics* Anonymous," the chairman immediately greeted Glen's quiet introduction of himself. "Our purpose is 'to stay sober and to help the alcoholic who still suffers.' Talking about pills and other chemicals just confuses me. 'Booze' is booze. The oldtimers, the early A.A.s, had it down right when they concentrated their effort on that. It seems to me dangerous to expand on it. Like they say: 'If it works, don't fix it.' Well, for me, A.A. works just fine if we stick to talking about alcohol."

Fortunately for all present, that gauntlet was immediately picked up by another regular member of the group who also seemed to have about three centuries of sobriety. "Which oldtimers have you been talking to recently?" Russ asked. "I seem to recall that as early as 1945, in one of the very first issues of the *A.A. Grapevine*, Bill W. wrote an article on 'Chewing Your Booze: The Sleeping Pill Menace.'

"Pills and other chemicals are not a new problem for alcoholics and therefore for A.A. The problem has gotten bigger, what with modern medicine and chemistry and all, but it is not a new concern in A.A. Bill wrote another article specifically about pills, about some of the then-new mood-changing drugs that some physicians were prescribing for alcoholics. He titled that article, 'Those Goof Balls.' So far as I can tell, the title referred to the pills, not to those who took them nor to the physicians who prescribed them."

That set the boundaries and defined the terms of the debate. The oldtime members set off: Glen, I, and a few others following their thrusts as if watching a tennis match.

"Russ," George suggested to the most recent comment, "It's good you are reading about A.A., but what about A.A. literature itself? I mean, besides the *Grapevine*, which is, after all, unofficial. Do you find anything in *The Big Book* or the *Twelve and Twelve* about chewing booze or goof balls?

"I don't mean to be harsh: this twenty-four hours, nobody in this room has taken a drink, and you love A.A., and it seems to me that you have at least a little bit of pretty good sobriety. Most A.A. groups, largely because of the nature of the world we live in, seem made up of alcoholics at least half of whom also had problems with other chemicals. And I can identify with them when they talk about alcohol. But when they talk about 'doctoring prescriptions' or going to three physicians at one time . . . well, I just can't identify. And I come to these meetings for myself, so that I can stay sober, so identifying is pretty important to me."

"Now wait a minute, George," another member chimed in. "You mean you never protected your supply of booze? Or found a way of getting it illegally after hours or on off days? Or never lied about how much you were drinking? Did you always go to the same package store to buy your booze — to the same clerk? Or even to the same bootlegger? Don't forget what we say around here so often: our basic problem was not our drinking, it was our thinking. It was the way in which alcohol dominated our lives to the point of destroying everything else in our lives, and especially our honesty."

Al went on. "You just talked about identifying. I agree: that is the key. It has always been the key in and to A.A. But we identify not on the basis of externals like car accidents, or jailings, or lost jobs, or broken marriages, or even on the basis of how much or what we drank. In A.A., alcoholics identify, it seems to me, on the basis of the inside — the feelings, the fears, and especially the thinking that, when described, allow us to recognize ourselves in each other and each other in ourselves.

"Look: if some of that thinking — some of those same feelings and fears — led some alcoholics to use other drugs as well as alcohol, does that make us any less alcoholic? I have never lost a job because of my drinking — well, hardly ever. Anyway, does that make it right for me to complain, 'This is becoming Unemployment Anonymous,' when some poor fellow alkie who is an A.A. member describes losing jobs while drinking and how he is feeling now in sobriety when he fears losing his job even though he is not drinking? It seems to me rather that I can learn from him about the ways we handle our fears and feelings when we are not drinking."

For a brief moment, the room grew quiet. Al's logic seemed incontrovertible, although I doubt anyone there would have used that word. Even the evening's chairman and George had nodded as Al spoke and now sat in obvious silent agreement. Glen seemed about to continue to "qualify," when from the back of the room rumbled the rarely heard voice of Jake. Jake, it was generally agreed, has six centuries of sobriety: he had been present at the second A.A. meeting ever held in this state.

"I am glad this topic came up," he began, "because it reminds me of my first A.A. meeting." Needless to report, that revelation got attention. "At my first meeting," Jack went on, "I felt just like some of you drunken bums are making Glen feel right now. When I first came around I was sucking cheap wine: it was all I could afford. Well, at that first meeting, when I told them that — as if they couldn't have smelled it — one of the guys said: ' "Booze" means liquor. If you didn't get drunk on liquor, you are not really a drunk . . . at least not like I was.'

"There was a loud silence in the room after that. I guess everybody was wondering what to say to the newcomers like me, whom they had rounded up, trying to get us interested in this new thing, 'A.A.' A lot of us had had most of our real bad trouble with cheap wine. And we were sitting there quietly, sort of wondering whether we were really alcoholics, I guess. I remember the thought crossed my mind that even if A.A. didn't seem to know much about wine, maybe if I would just keep my drinking to a couple of beers, I would be able to stay out of trouble.

"Well, there was another fellow in that room sort of like I'm here tonight. That was still A.A.'s early days — *The Big Book* was just out a few months, I guess — but he seemed to have been around always, from the very beginning. After a few minutes of silence, this guy — I never did get his name, but I think he was from New York — he spoke up. 'Well,' he said, 'then I guess I'm not an alcoholic either. I used to get drunk on Scotch, mainly. And from what I hear around here, most of you lousy alkie-holics had your trouble with bourbon, and maybe, especially — around the time you hit bottom — with bootleg corn likker and gin. I guess that means I didn't drink like you did, and I guess that means I am not an alcoholic. I mean, hell: if you can see through it, it's not really booze.' "

Laughter broke whatever tension lingered in our meeting. Disagreement, the specter of controversy, seemed to melt. The group got down to what everyone agreed was "brass tacks" fundamentals. It wasn't what we drank or even so much how we drank, it was what our drinking did to us, and especially to our thinking, our honesty.

On that basis, everyone agreed, it did not matter what kind of alcoholic one was. "An alcoholic is an alcoholic is an alcoholic," was the consensus. The bottom line in A.A. is trouble with booze. If you have trouble with booze, and if you want what A.A. has, then it doesn't matter if you are also male or female, or Black or Chinese, also Baptist or Catholic or Jewish, or rich or poor, or a convicted criminal or a high government official. Why should it make any difference if you are also addicted to other chemicals or not? An alcoholic is an alcoholic.

But a few, apparently inspired by the evening's earlier discussion of identification, pushed further. In this view, squelching the "what kind of alcoholic" pseudoproblem did not solve the deeper opportunity presented by "chemical dependence." As one of them put it: "I think there is more here. Remember 'Those Goof Balls' and 'Chewing Your Booze.' For some alcoholics, being 'also addicted to other chemicals' is different than those other things you mentioned. Because using other chemicals can be chewing your booze, talking about it seems to belong at A.A. meetings more than those other things, which — let's face it — we do not usually talk about.

"The ultimate bottom line in Alcoholics Anonymous," Ted continued, "is identification. We go to meetings to save our lives by learning a new way of life. We learn that way of life by identifying with others who are making the same effort. I travel quite a bit. Most A.A. groups, I find, are like most A.A.s: very tolerant of lots of, at times, weird experiences — so long as the members can identify with them. If I say something at an A.A. meeting that alcoholics cannot identify with, then I am helping neither them nor me. And if those members seem intolerant, it is not because I have violated some rule, but because I am not giving what they came for — the identification that keeps them sober — and because they know that if I cannot identify with them, they have nothing to give me."

By that time it was getting late, and the chairman moved to tidy up the topic.

I recalled my own story: how, before coming to A.A., I had tried to use tranquilizers to get off booze, only to find that I soon became addicted to the pills too. Changing my chemical did not help: it just made things worse until I finally learned that what I had to change was not my chemical but my way of life. What I have found in A.A. is a new way of life in which I can do without any chemical.

For me, identification is all-important, for that is the only way in which to learn that way of life. I thus deem it a great gift of my growth in sobriety that, although "an alcoholic is an alcoholic is an alcoholic," we come in so many different sizes and shapes, with so many varieties of experience, strength, and hope. Because of that variety, we can not only identify with each other — we can learn from each other. And learning this way of life, learning it by practicing its way of thinking, is, to me, the best way to progress in sobriety.

19

We have to go back to James to meet ourselves in our actual quandaries and uncertainties. . . . William James had an instinct for "going to the guts" of any issue.

— William Barrett

TWICE IN THE LAST TWO WEEKS OF MEETINGS I have attended, the name of William James has been mentioned. Members of Alcoholics Anonymous are not, in general, name-droppers, and most with whom I share meetings are far from being avid readers.

William James and Herbert Spencer are the only authors cited by name in *The Big Book.* I have never heard Spencer's name mentioned at an A.A. meeting. Why, then, the frequent — or even occasional — attention to James?

Thinking about that, it seems to me that although James' study of *The Varieties of Religious Experience* marks the most direct contribution of his thought to Alcoholics Anonymous, William James the man lived a life that could almost be an A.A. story — without the booze. As near as I can figure out, James died at just about the time that A.A. co-founder Bill W. was taking his first adolescent drink of booze in 1910. In some ways, it seems almost providential how James, more than any other American thinker, left the impress of his thoughts on the program and fellowship of Alcoholics Anonymous. His book not only helped Bill W. understand his own spiritual experience: it became almost a guide for the early A.A.s who had trouble with the spiritual.

Trained in medicine, both a philosopher and a psychologist, William James lived at a pivotal time in the history of ideas in America. Favored first son in an intellectually prominent family, he also knew much suffering and even despair in his early life. Largely because of those experiences, and perhaps especially because of the nature of his triumph over them, James developed almost into an art form a quality rare among American academic intellectuals: an open-mindedness that led him to take seriously spiritualistic seances as well as Sigmund Freud, the random jottings of his Harvard students as well as the mad ravings of chained asylum inmates.

Far more than for any other reason, it seems to me, William James stands out in American intellectual history for his open-mindedness in an age when humanistic intellectual horizons seemed to be contracting in direct proportion to the expansion of the outlook that characterizes the physical sciences. William James was a unique phenomenon — a social scientist who was convinced that his wisdom could benefit all of mankind. He never lost the vigor of his excitement with the whole of human life, with all human experience.

It is not always easy to read James today. The style in which he wrote can seem a bit florid to our modern tastes. The free flow of his ideas at times seems to follow a logic that is all its own. Often his references are not to technical monographs that one can look up, but to popular books that are today all but forgotten. And he loved controversy — especially arguments about how we think — in which he relished challenging those who seemed to him to deny human uniqueness.

> In the average man . . . the power to trust, to risk a little beyond the literal evidence, is an essential function. Any mode of conceiving the universe which makes an appeal to this generous power, and makes the man seem as if he were individually helping to create the actuality of the truth whose metaphysical reality he is willing to assume, will be sure to be responded to by large numbers.

That, it seems to me, is exactly what we do in A.A. Alcoholics Anonymous invites us to "conceive the universe" in such a way that we know that we can "create" sobriety just by not taking the first drink, one day at a time, and by going to meetings. No wonder it has been "responded to by large numbers."

I also like that quotation because it seems to capture the twinkle in James's eye as well as his vision itself. William James had a passion for being human. Perhaps that is why his thought so aptly fits for the alcoholic. He reveled in both human ability and human disability — in the capacity of every human being to transcend limitation and in the very limitations that he understood as inevitable and even necessary to the human condition.

The only thing of which James was intolerant was intolerance. In a way, it was that passion that led him to his study of religious experience. As he wrote to a physician friend at the time of the book's publication: "I regard *The Varieties of Religious Experience* as in a sense a study of morbid psychology mediating and interpreting to the philistine much that he would otherwise despise and reject utterly."

That explanation may seem two-edged, unless one realizes how much James himself identified with the "morbid psychology" of the "twice-born." That identification was always one facet of his abomination and playful twitting of "the philistines."

Recently, inspired in the rediscovery of William James to which my embarking on this ninety/ninety has led me, I again picked up and began to reread *The Varieties of Religious Experience.* And as I read it in light of what I hear at each day's meeting, it more and more strikes me that the three words of the book's title sum up not only James himself but also his precise contribution to Alcoholics Anonymous. "Varieties," "Religious," "Experience": open-minded honesty and enthusiastic willingness to grow seem to underlie each of these concepts. William James may not have been an alcoholic, but I feel sure he would have read *The Big Book* and praised it and learned from it.

James's title seems embodied in the very fiber of the program and fellowship of Alcoholics Anonymous. *Varieties* is a word that offers clues to A.A.'s tolerance and diversity. Even on the important topic of spiritual awakening, as *The Big Book*'s Appendix II makes clear: ". . . the personality change sufficient to bring about recovery from alcoholism has manifested itself among us in many different forms." Far from being a straitjacket, A.A. welcomes variety and diversity as best witnessing to the deep truth of its fundamental insights — the insight that there *is* "religious experience."

Religious is the second term. Wariness of it has increased since James's own time, which is why A.A. presents itself as spiritual rather than religious. Yet the thrust of William James's title and of A.A.'s claim is the same: there remain realities uncaptured by the scientific method — realities important to human be-ing. *Experience* is the third word. What can be said of experience more clearly than both William James and Alcoholics Anonymous say by their careful presentations of actual case material? Theory comes all too easily; only experience can validate understanding. Few phenomena have better lived out that Jamesian appreciation than the experience, strength, and hope of members of Alcoholics Anonymous.

It seems to me, in sum, that A.A. affirms much in both the philosophy and the psychology of William James. Unfortunately, today, neither James nor A.A. is regarded as a reputable scholarly topic. But fashions change, and not least in scholarship. When the present fashion does change, A.A. will be there to illuminate the thought of William James as much as the ideas of William James will be there to facilitate understanding of A.A.

20

To thine own self be true and thou canst be false to no man.

— Polonius

SOMETIMES I DISAGREE WITH WHAT I HEAR AT an A.A. meeting. That experience, I have learned, usually becomes strength and hope if, after the meeting, I find opportunity to explore the disagreement. This ninety/ninety has afforded many examples of that process already.

The disagreement we explored last night had been latent in the differing angles from which two of the participants had framed the meeting's discussion. Walter chose the topic of "people-pleasing," proclaiming that one great freedom he found in A.A. was liberation from that callow need. "Today, I don't have to care what anybody thinks of me," Walter concluded.

I readily identify when A.A.s talk about the tendency to be people-pleasers, when they discuss how the deep self-loathing of the active alcoholic leads us to become fawning doormats in our sick hopes of winning approval. And I especially like being reminded that I don't have to do that any more, in A.A., because my task each day is to put "First things first" and to not take the first drink no matter what generally hidden priorities others have in their expectations of me.

But Walter's point, or perhaps the passion with which he made it, also disturbed me. It seems to me that no matter how much we try to deny it or how mature we are, what other people think of us always does make a difference to us. I do, for example, care what sober A.A.s — the "winners" whom I meet — think of my sobriety and my efforts to grow in it. If that is so, and it is, am I still unfree? I do not think so: but how, in this area, does "living sober" differ from "alcoholic thinking"?

Even as I wrestled with the question, Peggy broke into the discussion with a suggestion that helped. "My problem," she stated quietly but emphatically, "was not so much that I was a people-pleaser — it was the kind of people I tried to please."

I liked that, and I savored it, although the group went off in a different direction. After the meeting, however, over coffee, Peggy and Walter and a few others and I returned to the topic. In that setting, Walter readily agreed with the obvious fact that, when we were drinking, we used to try to please other drinkers and our suppliers, whereas now in A.A. we are more interested in pleasing other A.A.s.

"But you see!" he exclaimed: "There's the problem! Somehow the idea of pleasing A.A.s doesn't quite fit. I really do not think that is what I am trying to do, or that it is very important, or even that many A.A.s with good sobriety would respond very well to someone who came around trying to please them. That sounds to me, at best, like a very tenuous way to get dry, and surely not at all like a good way to get sober."

Mike spoke up, agreeing that it is difficult to think of any kind of people-pleasing as having any place in sobriety. We in A.A. find it a useful term to describe life before A.A., because it well captures how the self-loathing active alcoholic seeks support for his or her denial. The drinking alcoholic seeks external affirmation of being okay precisely because deep down inside, he or she knows that everything and especially self is not okay. The term *people-pleasing*, then, always implies a wishy-washy attempt at denial — if not of our drinking, at least of the nature of what we need for true sobriety.

Peggy rejoined the discussion in a way that pleased me deeply. She admitted she had been reading William James (my suggestion). "James's great topic was 'making a difference.' He was interested in how 'what other people think' makes a difference in our lives. If something makes a difference, it is important. James would have loved A.A., I am certain, simply because so many people testify that A.A. makes a very important difference in their lives." As she continued, my thoughts wandered to my own reading of James.

As a psychologist, James was a realist as well as a pragmatist. He was fascinated by a topic that has not found much favor since his time — the human will, our capacity to choose. In his understanding, people chose wondrously and variously. In fact,

James virtually says that to be human is to choose: we define our humanity by the choices we make. Again, I am certain James would have taken very seriously and applauded the A.A. member's choice not to take the first drink, one day at a time.

I tuned into Peggy again. She was saying, "On this topic, then — the topic of how what people think of us makes a difference to how we think and feel about ourselves — James's point is that while that is inevitably true, we can at least choose the people whose thought will make a difference to us. A lot of very different people live in this old world. There are even an awful lot of very different people who might, at least momentarily, 'think something' about me. But of those people, I can choose whose thinking will make a difference to me — whose thinking, that is, will make some difference to my understanding of myself."

Then Walter, despite his earlier head-shaking at the mention of William James and his muttering about "Keep it simple" as Peggy and I held forth, suddenly brightened: "You haven't said anything new," he said.

"In A.A. we are able to choose to not drink so long as we restrict that choice to not taking the first drink, one day at a time; then we become free to make other choices — such as whose thinking about us will make a difference to us. What other A.A. members think, at least about living sober, makes a difference to me because I want to choose what they have — sobriety. That is not people-pleasing, it is just intelligent sanity."

Walter's contribution pretty well summed up the evening's conversation for the rest of us. And today, I less ponder people-pleasing than the nature of occasional disagreements within Alcoholics Anonymous.

Perhaps disagreement is too rare within A.A.; perhaps we are at time too politely respectful. I, at least, am grateful for the opportunities afforded by this ninety/ninety to explore, with people like Peggy and Walter and Mike, the riches of our diversity of understanding.

21

The thing of which I have most fear is fear.
— Montaigne

LAST NIGHT'S DISCUSSION RECALLED AN OLD hobby: playing anagrams. The topic was HALT — an exploration of the painfully learned truth that, as recovering alcoholics, we are especially vulnerable when we are Hungry, Angry, Lonely, or Tired.

The group quickly agreed on three things. First, it is wise to take precautions against becoming hungry, angry, lonely, or tired. Second, despite precautions, no one can completely avoid those experiences. Third, just as when we were drinking we seemed almost instinctively to turn to alcohol in such situations, today — in sobriety — we need to turn to A.A. As one participant pointed out: that is not substitution or sublimination — it is sanity.

We covered those points rather quickly. For a bare moment I wondered whether this would be one of those very rare A.A. meetings that ended early. But then good old Ed spoke up, and we ended up running quite late.

His question concerned fear. "Perhaps I am just lucky," Ed began by suggesting ever so innocently, "but it seems to me that I am in danger of taking a drink, or at least of falling into a kind of alcoholic thinking, less when I feel hungry, angry, lonely, or tired than when fear invades and begins to dominate my life. Fear of economic insecurity, fear of being unloved or unloving, fear of what others might think, fear of you-name-it. Fear, it seems to me, underlies just about all the problems I have with living sober."

Ed's comment struck a deep chord in several of us. Perhaps defensively, my mind began to play with the acronym HALT: "Yes, fear surely fits in," I thought. "Now let's see — can I make any sense of THALF or FLATH?"

Others, fortunately, responded more constructively. "I can

identify," Paul piped up. "In fact, now that you mention it, it seems to me that the main difference between what I used to be like and what I am like now has to do precisely with fears and being fearful. When drinking, I was fear-ridden: afraid that I would run out of booze; afraid that someone would think that I was a drunk; afraid that I was a drunk; afraid of what I might have done in a blackout. . . . Hell, I was afraid to wake up in the morning, but also afraid at times that I might not.

"Today I do not know those fears . . . or, in a way, any fears, so long as, one day at a time, I do not take the first drink and do go to meetings and try to work A.A.'s Twelve Steps. I am, I think I can claim with gratitude, free of fears, or at least of being fearful. And that freedom is one of sobriety's greatest gifts to me. It is great to be free of those fears, to be free of fear itself . . . or at least of being fearful. Before I found A.A., I was full of fears."

Several attentive listeners picked up Paul's careful qualifications. "I hear your point," Jane injected, "and I identify with both Ed and you, Paul. But I think I identified most with your saying 'in a way' and 'at least,' because it seems to me that I now do have one very healthy fear — the fear of taking a drink. In fact, maybe that is one way of putting the main difference A.A. has meant in my life: it keeps it simple. I too used to be fearful — full of fears, most of them ridiculous. Now I have just one fear, and it is healthy. I am afraid to drink alcohol."

Others quickly joined that theme, exchanging ideas about good fears and bad fears, about appropriate fears and inappropriate fears. Steve offered the most significant contribution. He distinguished between two styles of fears: those that push us and those that pull us. "Both kinds move us around," he pointed out, "but push fears are concerned with trying to maintain things as they are — they push us to avoid what we sense as dangers. Push fears can be important. It is good for us to avoid danger, like the danger of taking a drink. But when that is all that fear is, a push away from something, and when that fear dominates our lives, as it does the life of the drinking alcoholic, then it seems to be that such push fears dehumanize us. They get in the way of our being fully and truly human.

"Pull fears, on the other hand, move us toward something. They lead us to seek — to attain more than to avoid. We go to A.A. meetings, it seems to me, at least partially out of fear. The push fear is that if I do not go, I may take a drink. But for most members of A.A., that is only a very small part of why they go to meetings. It is only rarely and exceptionally the main reason for going to meetings, because if that were the main fear, why, you could just get yourself locked up in jail or get in a small boat, without booze, and float out to the middle of the lake and stay there.

"We go to A.A. far more to get something than to get away from anything. There is an element of fear, if you wish, but it is mainly a pull fear. In fact, it seems to me that it is less a fear than the fare we pay for sobriety. Knowing that booze is a danger to us, we seek to strengthen ourselves and to progress in our sobriety rather than merely running away. I guess the point is that some things, like booze, we cannot just run away from: to try just to run away from them is inevitably to be running back to them."

Steve's words hit home. At the end of my drinking, I learned all too well the frustration inherent in the impossibility of the effort to just run away from my alcoholism. The more and the harder I tried to run away from it, the sooner and the deeper I sank back down into it. Only when I finally discovered A.A. did I begin to glimpse the answer. Some realities, some dangers, we get away from only by going toward something else. There may be and probably is an element of fear in that; but there is a universe of difference between the fear that moves us to run away and the fear that leads us to run toward. In fact, only the former seems correctly termed *fear:* the latter is hope, one of the great virtues and therefore one of the courageous strengths of being human.

That rediscovery, by itself, made last night's discussion significant for my sobriety. I need to be reminded that, for the alcoholic, drinking booze is running away from reality, while going to A.A. is running toward the reality of life as well as of sobriety. The question, when I feel fear as well as when I get hungry, angry, lonely, or tired, is the same: What do I do? Try to run away from something that cannot be run away from, which is a dangerous endeavor? Or try to move toward something else that can protect me from the danger, which signals sober thinking and sane living?

It is time, also, to stop playing anagrams. The question is not how to fit fear's *F* in the HALT of hungry, angry, lonely, tired: my task is rather to live the freedom that A.A. sobriety gives me. I do fear booze; but so long as running signifies progress in the A.A. way of life, I am not running away from anything. To run toward rather than away: that is freedom, and I am grateful for it.

22

It is not enough to be busy . . . the questions is: what are we busy about?

— Henry David Thoreau

TONIGHT'S MEETING MUST BE WRITTEN OF tonight, for the memories awakened beg to be captured in their freshness. Ben was there — Old Ben, as he seems always referred to these days. And, as he used to years ago, Ben was "working the meeting" — walking around between the speakers, chatting briefly but intensely with everyone he recognized.

Ben isn't too healthy any more, by wordly standards. He jokes about having five terminal diseases, but I guess it's his arthritis that keeps him from getting to many meetings. Of course, lots of A.A.s stop by to visit him at home — to chat over coffee about anything that seems to be bothering their sobriety. And Ben always finds something to say that helps.

One relative newcomer, who did not know Ben, seemed puzzled and perhaps even annoyed at how he worked the meeting tonight. "What is he doing," the neophyte asked me, "selling insurance?"

I had never thought of it like that before, but in a way Ben was selling insurance. I suggested the questioner listen in, try to hear the query Ben was addressing just about everyone with whom he spoke: "What Step are you working on?" That question has been Ben's trademark for the many years he's haunted these halls. And it remains his mark despite his sickness and the fact that he pretty much has to stay at home.

Whenever anyone comes by with some problem or to express some question about or difficulty with living sober, Ben sits very still and listens carefully, looking at you with that serious, pain-tinged yet also serene and joyful face, giving your every word all his attention. He never interrupts; but finally, when you are through pouring out whatever it is that is troubling you, Ben always begins whatever he has to say by asking the same question:

"What Step are you working on?"

Sometimes, merely hearing that reminder is enough to solve the problem. Not surprisingly, I recall, after a time, as Ben's penchant for asking the question became well known, people who were deciding to go see him started asking themselves the question first, so they would have some answer when Ben asked it. Often, of course, the inevitable happens: after someone does that, he or she very likely no longer has to see Ben, except to say "Thanks." Just asking oneself the question very often provides a good start down the road to solving whatever problem one faces.

There is, of course, no magic in A.A. At best, we receive gifts earned by others' often painfully acquired experience, strength, and hope; and we work our own program. But Ben's question reminds that we do have to work the program. And that means, of course, working on the Twelve Steps that are the A.A. program. And because we are finite and limited human beings, because we are alcoholics who need to be reminded about "First Things First" and "Easy Does It," we can work the program only one Step at a time. That is why we have Twelve Steps, with numbers in front of them, instead of some flowery paragraph or philosophical essay.

Though I accept that I cannot do it justice, let me try to recall, from and for my own memory, the vivid recollection I have of the first time, years ago, that I heard a far healthier Ben tell his whole story.

"Lots of people think A.A. is too simple," Ben began, eyes twinkling from a face that he was trying to keep somber. "But I knew as soon as I saw the Steps that they would stretch my mental capacity, such as it was after decades of drinking. You know the first thing I noticed? There were twelve of the blasted things! 'Hell,' I thought, 'I'll never make it! Moses only got ten commandments, and God knows I have enough troubles with them.' Why, I can't even count to twelve, unless I take my shoes off."

Ben went on to tell how, after learning how to count to twelve without taking his shoes off, it dawned on him that maybe he should try to keep on learning. "One day," he continued, "I had this momentous revelation: it was time to stop counting the Steps and to start reading them." Ben allowed as how that pretty well kept him busy for the next six months, until he had another even more momentous revelation.

"A little bird, or maybe it was my Higher Power, one day suggested that, while I was reading those Steps right well, maybe the time had come to start working them. Well, you could have knocked me over with a feather. I guess I had come to A.A. for the same reason — one of them — I used to drink booze. I didn't like to work. 'Did you like to drink?' my Higher Power asked. 'Hell, yes!' I replied. 'Well, then, why don't you?' the sonuvabitch — as I used to refer to my Higher Power — asked. 'Because drink is killing me,' I replied, informing him of something I was pretty sure he already knew. 'So you want to live, to really live?' he asked. 'Hell, yes, again!' I said, thinking that was an awfully stupid question for a Higher Power to ask. 'Then work the Steps,' came the reply: 'Why do you think I helped you remember how to count to twelve with your shoes on?'

" 'Because my feet stink?' I suggested, hoping he would take the hint and leave me alone. But he didn't leave, so I asked another bright question: 'Which ones?' 'Why do you think I helped you remember how to count to twelve with your shoes on?' came the question again. 'Okay,' I said, 'where do I start?' 'Why do you think I helped you remember how to count to twelve with your shoes on,' he shot back yet again. 'So I have got to start with number one and work all of them, then — like once through, right?' 'Right!' came the answer: 'once through each one, until you are doing it perfectly.'

"Now I am smarter than you may think, and I was even then. 'Perfectly!' I said. 'Aw, c'mon Higher Power: you know me better than that!' 'Right!' he said again. Then, 'Look, Ben, I have got to go now, because I get pretty busy keeping this whole world together what with all the alcoholics in it. But I'll tell you what: if you ever need me, anytime, just call. I'll be right there. And the first thing I am going to ask you is what Step you are working on. Got that? So you have an answer ready for me, okay?'

"Well, I sort of wanted to get that conversation over with

anyway, so I agreed: 'Okay.' And I started working those Steps, so I would have an answer ready to that question in case I ever needed him. You know what? Since I have been trying to work those Steps, I have not had to call for him. It's not that I don't need him: it is rather that I discovered that I find my Higher Power, each day, for me, in those Steps — and especially in the one I am working on."

That is, of course, only a part of Ben's story. But it is the part that has been — and that I want to make even moreso — a part of my own sobriety. When I first heard it, I must also confess, I was perhaps a bit prissier than sobriety finds me today. After that meeting, as I thanked Ben for his story, I dared to suggest to him that referring to his Higher Power as "that sonuvabitch" could be offensive.

Although, today, I feel stupid for having made that comment, I am glad that I did. For Ben looked directly at me with those eyes I find it impossible to describe — eyes that held and beamed both pain and love — and asked, very slowly: "What Step are you working on?"

I savor my memory of that moment, now, as I again experience the mixture of pain and love that, over time and many other meetings, Ben taught me is sobriety. I have bought into Ben's "insurance," I hope. For I suspect that so long as I ask myself, each day, "What Step are you working on?" it is very unlikely that I shall take a drink that day. It seems possible even that, on the wings of Ben's question, I shall grow in sobriety.

23

It has often been said of A.A. that we are interested only in alcoholism. That is not true. We have to get over drinking in order to stay alive. But anyone who knows the alcoholic personality by firsthand contact knows that no true alky ever stops drinking permanently without undergoing a profound personality change.

— Bill W.

"AMBIVALENCE" SIGNIFIES MIXED FEELINGS; "ambiguity," mixed being. Both lurk at the deep core of Alcoholics Anonymous.

On the one hand, the primary and indeed sole concern of Alcoholics Anonymous is the alcoholic. A.A.'s example of accepting essential limitation (powerlessness over alcohol) is what renders its message so powerful. By accepting limitation, A.A. affords a model that inhibits grandiosity and enforces humility. We are just a bunch of drunks, now gratefully sober, who have only the experience, strength, and hope of our own alcoholism to offer. Nonalcoholics can accept us because they need not fear us — we have no expertise that might menace their own turf. Alcoholics can accept us because they can identify with our need: as much as when drinking we needed alcohol, in our recovery we need alcoholics. If it is not true that in A.A. "we are interested only in alcoholism," it is true that as A.A.s we are interested only in alcoholics.

On the other hand, however, despite all the later justified wariness of the term *the alcoholic personality*, we do recognize that alcoholics are persons — human beings whose lives have a wholeness. The attempt to deny that, indeed, characterized our active drinking. We thought we could be who we were even though we drank differently than did others — "normal drinkers." Alcoholic progression slowly but completely chipped away that illusion. No part of one's human life can be compartmentalized — parenthesized in an isolation that attempts to deny the wholeness of our human be-ing. And so, just as our alcoholism spread and pervaded every aspect of our lives from job and career to family and loved ones, just as our alcoholic drinking affected us physically and mentally and spiritually, so also our recovery necessarily and inevitably heals into wholeness what our drinking had tried to fracture into parts.

The main reason why A.A. is not interested only in alcoholism is because A.A. is interested, profoundly, in all of the alcoholic. It has to be, for alcoholics come only as a whole.

That alcoholism affects the whole person of the alcoholic is perhaps A.A.'s greatest insight. Alcoholics Anonymous, then, can never be interested only in alcohol or the drinking or the abuse thereof. Our boredom with the issue of Prohibition — an issue on which many others, then and now, harbor strong feelings both for and against — our boredom with the topic, our conviction of its irrelevance, signals that insight and the nature of our true interest: not alcohol, nor even alcoholism, but the alcoholic.

Because alcoholism profoundly impacts the whole person of the alcoholic, so must recovery from alcoholism. Because both alcoholism and recovery have to do with the whole person, we know better than to look only at alcohol use — we look to life use. We have learned that alcoholism is neither physical disease nor mental aberration nor spiritual disability: it is neither/nor because it is all three at once.

The vocabulary of his time, I suspect, trapped Bill W. by affording no terms more adequate than "alcoholic personality" and "personality change." But the context of those phrases — the implications of "knowing firsthand" and "undergoing profound change" — make clear that what Bill was thinking and talking about was less "personality" as a psychological category, than "person" as an existential reality.

The term *existential reality* is hardly better. Each generation of A.A.s, each member of our fellowship, must come himself or herself to his or her own understanding of the profound truth suggested by the paradox that we live. Stated most baldly, the question that each of us must ask is: "What is the relationship, the connection, between my being an alcoholic and my being a human being?"

We answer that question, of course, less with words than by

our lives. Within Alcoholics Anonymous, we answer it by choosing and living a "way of life." Those blind to that way of life, those who see only alcoholism and ignore the alcoholic, will never comprehend either alcoholism or Alcoholics Anonymous. Formerly, for example, at the time Bill wrote the letter that provides the opening selection in *As Bill Sees It*, that indictment was true of most outside our fellowship. More recently, A.A.'s success has enabled many more to come to such comprehension, to such understanding of the paradox that, ultimately, all human beings share.

For this, I believe, we should be most grateful to Al-Anon. That Twelve Step program, when lived by a nonalcoholic, perhaps teaches some truths more clearly than we as alcoholics are capable of doing.

But whatever the sources — and they have been diverse — of the wider acceptance of the insight given to us by A.A., we should be grateful. Grateful first that we have found the truth of our wholeness, the truth that has saved our lives; grateful second that others — those who suffer manifestations of the dis-ease of humanity other than alcoholism — are also available to enhance our sobriety. Nonalcoholics cannot aid us in being alcoholic, but they can help us to be human.

24

Now this, brethren, is the Aryan Truth about the Origin of Suffering: It is that Craving that leads downwards to birth, along with the Lure and Lust that lingers longingly now here, now there: namely, the Craving for Sensation, the Craving to be born again, the Craving to have done with rebirth.

And this, brethren, is the Aryan Truth about the Ceasing of Suffering: Verily it is utter passionless cessation of the giving up, the forsaking, the release from, the absence of longing for, this Craving.

— Attributed to Buddha

EITHER MY HIGHER POWER IS GETTING VERY tricky, or someone else made a mistake, but last night I went to the wrong meeting. I wanted and expected A.A.; I got and accepted Narcotics Anonymous. By the time I arrived at the meeting, there was no place else to go.

The N.A.s understood, perhaps better than I, the confusion in the directions I had received. They also warmly welcomed my presence — especially after learning that although I regard myself mainly and primarily as an alcoholic, I had played prescription-drug roulette in the latter stages of my alcoholic demise.

So I stayed. As the meeting began, noting a few differences in the opening routine, I wondered about "identification." I need not have worried. At least the way that group last night bit into the topic — and I do not think it was done especially for my sake — they invited hearing *alcoholism* and *addiction* as almost synonymous. And they did that not by discussing the terms technically or abstractly, but by organizing the discussion in light of the Serenity Prayer — surely good, solid Twelve-Step program practice.

The main key to my ability to identify last night, I suppose, was the key to all identification as it happens in A.A. itself. I listened to and heard primarily what went on inside — the feelings and the thinking that were described. I do not know much about addiction. But the difference in the ways of thinking that were described last night, the difference between "what we were like" and "what we are like now": that I could and do identify with, even though my main mood-changing chemical was alcohol.

Those speakers described me; they detailed my way of thinking. On that deep level, their stories fit me like a glove. And when they linked that understanding to the Serenity Prayer, no way could that not be a good meeting for me — and that does help my growth in sobriety.

I focus on "way of thinking" this morning because the fact that it was an N.A. meeting that I accidentally attended last night teaches me something about my attendance at A.A. meetings — something to which, I fear, I have too often been stupidly blind. In A.A., when someone who identifies himself or herself as I do, as an alcoholic, mentions taking also other drugs, I seem to identify too readily with that mere external similarity, and therefore I tend to miss the layers of deeper identification.

What happens is not dissimilar to what can occur in A.A. when we hear the story of someone who did drink "what" and "where" we ourselves did. We too easily forget that that surface identification is not the healing identification that we really need, the identification with the inside, gut-level thoughts and feelings that alcoholics — and perhaps lots of addicts — share. Superficial similarities can mask the deeper need: the need to touch and to identify with and to examine precisely those thoughts and feelings that, most of the time, we find it so difficult to talk about directly because they are anything but superficial.

What captured my identification last night was something very simple: how, as alcoholics or as addicts, we insist on demanding that reality outside us change, and thus fail or refuse to realize that it is we who must change. Gene put it well: "Addiction is the belief that when there is something wrong with me, something outside me can fix it." As little as I know about addiction, that is as good a description of alcoholic stinking thinking as I have ever heard. At least it well describes my own.

I also liked the way Sue pointed out how that understanding fits in with the Serenity Prayer. The Serenity Prayer is of course far richer: there are some things both outside ourselves and within ourselves that we cannot change, and so we seek serenity to accept them. And it takes as much, maybe even more, courage to change the things inside us that we can change as it does to change those outside us. But if we want to attain the deeper wisdom that the Serenity Prayer seeks, knowing the things in myself that can be fixed from the outside and those that cannot be so fixed seem a pretty good place to start — at least for this alcoholic.

Frequently when drinking, I turned to alcohol or other drugs as a way of changing something inside me — how I felt, or as a "pick me up" or a "let me down." But often, what was really bothering me from inside should have been either lived with — rather than changed — because it had to be lived with for the sake of my very humanity; or else, if perhaps it should have been changed, that change, in order to be lasting, needed to come from the inside. Something inside me had to change. In short, I myself had to change.

Personal experience, although painful to recall, illustrates the depth of that truth. Before finding A.A. and in sobriety marrying, I courted often, but not well. At times, the breakup of those relationships hurt. So like any good incipient or active alcoholic, I turned to alcohol to drown the pain. Needless to say, that did not work. Drowned pain still haunts. Perhaps inevitably I tried to drown myself in alcohol. That did not work either, but it led to my finding A.A.

Several years later, after I had been in A.A. for a while, I again began courting. In fact, one of those efforts became the ultimate courtship — marriage. But before that, although I was not drinking, it again happened that my "intended" decided to call it quits. That was probably a wise decision on her part: although dry, I was not very sober, and my side of our relationship was very immature. Still, her rejection hurt. But this time I realized, with the help of some good A.A. support, that some pain has to be lived with, at least for a time — it is part of growing up. And I also learned, in trying to apply the A.A. way of thinking to the experience, that if I wanted to change that hurt, to get beyond and outgrow it and perhaps even prevent it from happening again, what I had to change was myself — my immaturity that had provoked the rejection that led to the hurt.

The point of that example is the same as the point made in the discussion last night: there is a lot of hurt in being human. The question is not whether we will have pain, but how we will handle it. As Bill W. reminded alcoholics ever more often during his long sobriety: "Pain is the touchstone of all growth."

It almost hurts even to realize that. On the one hand, I do not like that idea. When I hurt, I want to feel better, not to be told that "pain is the touchstone of all growth." But on the other hand, when I am able to remember that truth, well, then that idea can itself make me feel better, because it seems to connect with the reality of being human, or at least of being an alcoholic. Perhaps that is the key: in sobriety, we learn that it is more important to feel better than it is to feel good.

Both the meeting last night and the train of thought it has engendered this morning remind me of something I read recently: "From the fact that we are sick it does not follow that we can be cured." That certainly applies to the pain inherent in being human. But as last night's discussion revealed, it need not apply to the dis-ease of alcoholic or addictive thinking. That is a matter we can do something about, if we are willing to change ourselves, willing to pray the Serenity Prayer.

I needed that reminder: the reminder that it was the craving to experience life without pain that had so much to do with my alcoholic demise. I still do not know why my Higher Power chose to guide me to an N.A. rather than an A.A. meeting to hear it. Perhaps because there it was put so clearly that I did hear it. Perhaps it was only chance. Help me, then, to be grateful for truth, wherever I receive it — and especially to be grateful for the healing truth that inheres in all Twelve-Step programs.

25

As laudable as it is to live one's life for others, to live it as others think it should be lived is sheer folly.
— Bill W.

OFTEN, IN THIS JOURNAL, I CATCH MYSELF TOO glibly using, or too self-consciously trying to avoid using, the words *good* and *bad*. Those terms grate on modern ears: they reek of crass manipulation and unjust condemnation. Rightly, I think, we have grown wary of too readily passing intellectual or moral judgment.

But it also seems to me that as feeling beings, a big part of our life — and maybe a bigger part of our alcoholism — has to do with the kinds of efforts we made and make in trying to feel good. And that, it seems, itself has to do with how we understand and react to feeling bad.

The topic arises today because of Betty's story, as she told it at the meeting last night. Betty framed her tale in terms of her ceaseless search for some reality that would make her feel good. She told how she turned first to drugs, and that part of her story helped me realize how very difficult life can be for an alcoholic woman. Men usually live in an environment in which being a hard drinker can seem a good thing: sometimes, it even wins respect. But our society is a lot harder on women, when it comes to drinking. Small wonder so many of them turn to pills. Many women eventually discover, of course, what men generally learn with much less stigma: that booze seems the best chemical for what we think ails us. But most women have to be secret about their drinking from the very beginning. And knowing how they are drinking undermines their self-respect and leads to more self-loathing more quickly than with most of us male alcoholics — or at least it seems that way to me, from the women's stories I hear.

Of course, male or female, we all end up in the same alcoholic boat pretty fast. Still, I am grateful that the different angle taken by Betty in telling her story last night made clear how much feeling bad and wanting to feel good can be involved in our boozing. She repeatedly emphasized those words, and thus upon returning home, I looked them up in my unabridged dictionary.

The word *good* comes from the same root as do such words as *gather* and *together*. Its root idea signifies "to be joined or united in a fitting way." We feel "good," in other words, when we fit in, appropriately — like a shoe is "good" if it fits my foot, or a meal is "good" if it suits my appetite.

The word *bad*, even though it derives from a completely different language family, has an origin that implies its root meaning to be "unable to fit in or to join appropriately."

Thus the idea of fitting in, of belonging, of being able to unite or to join "appropriately," seems the key to our concepts of good and bad. Something is good if it fits; something is bad if it does not, perhaps especially cannot, fit.

I find that fascinating, for the understanding itself seems to fit both my drinking of booze and what I find and learn in A.A. I often drank alcohol in order to fit in, to feel I belonged, especially in uncomfortable situations. Of course, I also drank alone — but often I did that to drown feelings of not fitting in. I drank, in other words, because I felt bad; or I drank because I wanted to feel good: and the original meaning of both words well fits my drinking experience.

But they also fit even more, perhaps, in A.A. Alcoholics Anonymous is a place where we alcoholics fit in — no wonder we tend to feel so good at meetings. It is not because we feel virtuous or that we are doing what we should be doing: we feel good in A.A. because we fit in there. That is where we belong. That understanding of "good" and "bad" thus helps me to appreciate more deeply one very large difference between what I was like and what I am like now. It has to do with where and how I try to fit. And I guess what happened was the discovery that booze no longer, at least on balance, made me feel good, while A.A. did and does.

That insight also helps me understand a bit differently a trait of which, in sobriety, I usually tend to be wary — my tendency to rate A.A. meetings, and at times even A.A. speakers. The quick answer to "What is a good meeting?" is, of course, "One that you don't drink at." But there is something else buried in that classic truism. A good meeting is one that fits my sobriety. Because any sobriety I have is founded on not drinking alcohol, the truism always holds — and that should never be forgotten.

But as we grow in our sobriety, as we have our ups and downs even in our efforts at truly sober living, some meetings more than others — or the things that are said at them — will better fit what we have to hear just then, based on how much we have grown, on the progress we have made. That, I suspect, is what I really mean when I say, usually almost thoughtlessly, "Now that was a good meeting."

As I read over what I have written, I find that I am still uncomfortable about the idea of rating A.A. meetings. Am I forgetting about "You get what you need, not what you want"? Might not looking for supposedly good meetings get in the way of that? It seems to me that too much of still clinging to the driver's seat can creep in. If we take the Third Step honestly, and really do turn our will and our lives over, how can we claim the right to rate meetings of A.A.?

Recalling a bit of my own story may help shed light on that. When I first came around A.A., and even for quite a time after I finally stopped drinking, I did not own a car. Some of the meetings I attended, I chose because they were accessible by public transportation. But most were chosen for me by my sponsor, who would pick me up in his car and take me to whatever meeting he was attending. As nice a guy and as great a friend and as helpful a sponsor as Phil was, however, he was still not my idea of "God as I understand Him."

The point I am struggling toward, I guess, is that in taking the Third Step, we rarely turn our lives directly over to our Higher Power. In general, our turning over is more a letting go. And letting go, although it first involves stopping our own efforts at manipulation, also means accepting that what we need might come to us in ways other than through our own will to power. If our Higher Power can guide and provide for us through others, might not that same Higher Power guide us by means of our own intelligent preferences, so long as they flow from our honest sobriety?

I am not sure that this is strictly A.A., but one thing they told me in treatment was that as I got truly sober, I would become able to trust myself. Not trust *in* myself, but trust a body and brain free of chemicals as I had never been able to trust those parts of me when they were sotted with booze. I like to think, then, that in getting rid of the booze from inside me, I made room for my Higher Power there.

In deciding what is good and bad for me, then, I would like to think that so long as I remain free from the delusions imposed by chemicals and open to the guidance available from others who sincerely seek "through prayer and meditation to improve [their] conscious contact with God as [they] understand Him," I can trust the promptings of the Higher Power whom I seek "to improve [my] conscious contact with" in the same way.

Given my track record when drinking, that enterprise may prove tricky. Yet, as I read the Promises as they appear on pages 83 and 84 of *The Big Book*, one of them assures me: "We will intuitively know how to handle situations which used to baffle us." To me, that implies that, if we are truly sober, we can trust at least some of our intuitions.

For I do believe, and I think my experience in A.A. supports that faith, that once I got the booze out of me, my Higher Power could live within me. I cannot force that, and I dare not claim it. But if I make room for that possibility, neither can I refuse its occurrence. One gift of sobriety, it seems to me, is that I can know what is good and bad for me — not perfectly, but surely more accurately than I ever did or could when I was drinking.

26

Dread is . . . both a turning away from, and a confrontation of, the self. . . . our turning away reveals that from which we are turning away.

— Martin Heidegger

THERE ARE TURNING POINTS IN EVERY HUMAN life. The term has become almost as hackneyed as the ancient concept from which it derives: conversion.

I prefer "turning point" to "conversion." It seems better to capture the sense of a change of direction. *Turning point* is thus a dynamic term: it implies motion, both before and after. We define a turning point, it seems to me, by describing both the direction from which we arrived at it and the different course followed after it.

But perhaps motion is less important than perspective. That would seem, at least, to be Heidegger's insight. When we turn, we gain a different point of view and therefore, perhaps, a different vision itself. A different point of view, that is to say, tends to reveal new facets of even a reality already perhaps too clearly seen.

"Dread" well captures my own experience of hitting bottom. The affinity between what is too glibly termed existential thought and the insight of A.A. has often been remarked. Whatever the validity of that larger insight, Heidegger's vision of dread as the turning point, and A.A.'s story format of "what we were like, what happened, and what we are like now," seem perfectly parallel — at least if one accepts, as in my own story, that what happened was hitting bottom.

Hitting bottom is a turning point. As such, it signals not only a new direction but a new perspective. The main new perspective I attained at that turning point was on myself. There remain few things that I would have said of myself while drinking that I would say of myself now. I am still me: Ernie, an alcoholic; but beyond the fact that "I-Ernie" stood, momentarily, at the turning point, few things about "me-Ernie" are still the same.

The chief difference, of course, has to do with the change of direction. Because human life is a process, a progress, the direction in which we are moving seems to determine who we are. I suspect this metaphor will limp a bit, but here goes. In New England, a bird flying south in October is recognized as a member of a migratory species, perhaps a goose. A bird flying north in October is recognized as a nonmigratory species, or perhaps a deranged goose. It seems important to remember that birds do not fly south because they are migratory; rather, we classify them as migratory because they fly south.

In my own case, in the case of me-Ernie-the-alcoholic, so long as I drank alcohol, I was self-destructively and other-destroyingly sick. As far as I am concerned, I did not drink alcoholically because I was sick. I was rather sick because I drank alcoholically. In sobriety, after the turning point of substituting A.A. for alcohol in my life, I do not go to A.A. because I am sober; I am sober because I go to A.A.

Is that merely play with words? I think not. In some strange way, we *are* where we are headed. Insofar, then, as a turning point means a change in direction, to pass through a true turning point signifies a change in oneself — a real difference in one's self. For there is a real difference between Ernie-the-drinking-alcoholic and Ernie-the-sober-alcoholic.

A philosophical truism holds that any real, true difference must make a difference. That is the only way difference can be recognized, verified. If that is so, it would be difficult to conceive of any greater difference than that between a drinking and a sober alcoholic.

That difference is between "what I was like" and "what I am like now." "To be like" is an expression, a concept, with which to conjure. It implies similarity in form but difference in substance. Its root is best preserved, among English-speaking peoples, in the Scottish dialect that employs the term *lich* to signify a corpse, a dead body. Someday, perhaps, friends will gather in a funeral parlor to look at my dead body and say, "That looks just like Ernie." Saying that acknowledges that the dead body, that corpse, is not Ernie. Death is a turning point.

My turning point of hitting bottom seems the mirror image of death's turning point. Perhaps a deeper question lurks there.

Which is the reality and which the mirrored opposite? For now, as one who yet lives with the sense of living anew within A.A., I will exercise the choice of naming as real the turning point of which I can see both sides.

Occasionally, I run into an acquaintance who knew me only when I was drinking. Sometimes, such a person will walk up and say, "You're Ernie, aren't you?" I always reply, "Yes"; but sometimes I wonder how accurate is that answer. I may look like the person they once knew, but in a sense I am not that person, and sometimes I hope for the opportunity to allow them to see that. My brief answer, "Yes," then seems to serve the purpose of truth in the same way as does praising a child's drawing for the effort rather than the result.

Perhaps my life is also a child's drawing from my Higher Power's perspective. Because I know my Higher Power mainly in and through A.A., I seem to be learning to esteem myself according to efforts rather than results; I try to live soberly. But I judge myself, and therefore esteem myself, first on the basis of how well I succeed in not taking the first drink, one day at a time. That teaches me, I suppose, to accept small results. It is, of course, out of such small results that large results are made — although rarely by ourselves. Is there a Higher Craftsman at work, using my life as tool? The tool, of course, never knows.

I sense that I am rambling. Does the idea of *turning point*, with which I started, somehow bind all this together?

Perhaps, in this very simple way: except for hitting bottom, I would not know — because there would not be — the differences in my thinking and my life that have led me to the practice of journaling itself. I know that today, in and through A.A., I am headed in a different direction and therefore am in some sense a different person. I know, too, that the perspective I have today, not only on myself but on all reality, allows me to see and to understand much more beauty than I ever knew existed before I had reached my turning point.

For that, then, I am profoundly grateful. And I think that makes this a good journal entry: gratitude fits sobriety.

Should my Higher Power, who has a unique perspective on my turning point, ever ask the question, "You're Ernie, aren't you?" my answer will be: "Gratefully."

27

Society has become just as sick as we are. People of all kinds and of every class, collectively and individually, are hipped on the pursuit of money, prestige, and power as never before. The demand for these things is utter and terrifyingly absolute. What once were normal instincts are now keyed up to such a compulsion and consuming pitch that they have become juggernauts in collision — man against man, society against society.

— Bill W.

ALTHOUGH I USUALLY TRY TO AVOID SUCH events, last night's meeting was a first-birthday celebration. Perhaps because I did most of my own drinking quietly and alone, I prefer quiet, ordinary meetings. Perhaps because of wariness of the concept "special," I eschew special events even if held under A.A. auspices. In any case, I did attend a first-birthday meeting last night, and today I am glad that I did.

The honored speaker, an A.A. with over a decade of sobriety, chose as his theme: "I am grateful to be an alcoholic." The birthday celebrant, in his own response, told of hoping to grow to that acceptance, but admitted that: "Today, I am grateful for just being able to say that I am grateful to be sober." The after-meeting informal discussion over cake, then, concentrated on that aspect of our gratitude: thankful as we all are for sobriety, in what sense is it possible for any of us to claim that we are grateful to be alcoholics?

Several insisted that since no nonalcoholic ever wants to be an alcoholic, such expressions of gratitude indicate more accurately thankfulness for A.A. — gratitude for the knowledge that one is an alcoholic and for the understanding of alcoholism and of recovery afforded by A.A. As one of this group put it: "When I say 'I am grateful to be an alcoholic,' I mean that I am grateful that I know what is wrong with me, and that there is something that I can do about it." Or, as another chimed in: "Without denying the seriousness of alcoholism as disease, I am glad to be an alcoholic because, if I were not an alcoholic, there would really be something wrong with me: I'd be crazy."

Expressions of that kind of gratitude, it strikes me, are good — especially in such settings as last night's. Newcomers need very much to be able to identify with such positive and healing perspectives, and it does not require much sobriety to feel — deeply and truly — the kind of gratitude thus described. We all, in Alcoholics Anonymous, I think, discover and continue to experience that gratitude — thankfulness that we now know what is wrong with us.

But there is, I believe, a far deeper gratitude occasionally signaled by the claim: "I am grateful to be an alcoholic." We do not talk about it very much, I suspect, for two reasons. First, because we rightly concentrate on living and expressing the gratitude with which newcomers can more readily identify. Second, because we find it difficult to speak easily about something so profound. Such deeply personal parts of our worldview, of our understanding of ourselves, flourish best in silence. They sort of grow within us as they shape us, but they seem to emerge into conversation — or perhaps even into our direct consciousness — only rarely. In a way, they run so deep and are so precious that we find it difficult to examine them directly.

Still, it is perhaps good to try to do that once in a while, for example in meditation or in conversation with one's Higher Power.

I thought last night of a letter Bill W. wrote in 1954 to the condemned murderer, Caryl Chessman, whose case was a *cause celebre* at the time. As I understand it, that correspondence affected Bill profoundly. He had just finished writing the *Twelve and Twelve* and was preparing for the celebration of A.A.'s Coming of Age convention in 1955, so he was in the very midst of examining his own program — his own understanding and living out of the A.A. way of life.

> Society has become just as sick as we are. People of all kinds and of every class, collectively and individually, are hipped on the pursuit of money, prestige, and power as never before. The demand for these things is utter and

terrifyingly absolute. What once were normal instincts are now keyed up to such a compulsion and consuming pitch that they have become juggernauts in collision — man against man, society against society.

Thirty years later, I find it intriguing and perhaps a bit frightening that Bill's diagnosis seems, if anything, even more true. We haven't learned much, have we? Or at least the world does not seem to have learned very much from A.A. — which is, I guess, not too surprising.

But the true point of Bill's words is that they offer perspective not on others, but on self. I do not know about most people, or even about most other alcoholics: but I am very certain that if I were not an alcoholic, I would have that other sickness that Bill describes. It is a contagious, culture-borne dis-ease — a true sickness because it destroys our real humanity. Put very simply, the disease of our times is that we tend to think that we are God, and therefore we demand or presume the prerogatives of divinity.

If I may strain a medical metaphor, I understand my disease of alcoholism as a kind of vaccination that protects me from that more serious disease of thinking that I am God. Vaccines work by inducing a mild version of some disease, so that antibodies will be produced that protect the person from the ultimate ravages of the full-blown disease. I understand my alcoholism, in a way, as my vaccination that protects me from the disease that Bill describes, from the demand for divinity that seems to be so destructive of our own — and others' — humanity.

The metaphor limps, of course. For one thing, the fever induced by a vaccine is generally very transient — one recovers from it quickly. The "vaccinated" condition of alcoholism is more permanent: we spend the rest of our lives recovering from it.

But the metaphor also has its strengths. Just as the vaccine used by a physician induces the body to produce antibodies that ward off the major disease, it seems to me that our alcoholism — at least if we bring it and submit it to A.A. — helps our minds to produce a new way of thinking that leads to the A.A. way of life, which protects us against and wards off the really diseased thinking of the claim and the demand to be God.

Although it is dangerous to mix medical and moral metaphors, let me try to state the point in yet another way. If I were not an alcoholic, I fear not so much that I would be crazy as that I would be evil. Or, as Pete, my pigeon, once put it so gracefully: "If you will pardon my putting it this way: you may have your shortcomings and your defects of character even as an alcoholic, but if you weren't an alcoholic, you would be a real sunuvabitch. Being an alcoholic keeps you from being something worse."

Can you imagine the havoc alcoholic thinking would wreak on this poor old world if the alcoholics in it did not incapacitate themselves by drowning in booze? When I think of the kind of things I tried to use booze to help me do, I do not think it mere grandiosity to fear that if I had not gotten too drunk to do them, there might have been real trouble.

Bill's quotation speaks of juggernauts. A juggernaut is a terrible, irresistible force; and the word comes from a practice wherein human beings were crushed by the idol of a god. It seems to me that A.A., in a way, does not so much teach the alcoholic that he or she is not God: A.A. simply points out the obvious reality and blatant truth already explicit in the alcoholic's drinking behavior — and then teaches the alcoholic how to live with that reality, with that truth.

In other words, we alcoholics come to A.A. and accept the A.A. way of life because we have discovered that we are not God. If that is so, then it is, at root, our alcoholism that cures us of the larger disease of thinking that we are God, or at least of demanding the prerogatives of divinity and therefore running amok over all other reality and especially other people.

A.A. teaches us, as I see it, how to live with that truth, that reality. And therefore, of course, our gratitude to A.A. is immeasurably greater and more profound than any gratitude we may feel simply for being alcoholic. But, at least for me, that other gratitude is there, and it is real. As I look around this old world and see the havoc caused by those who make absolute demands because in one sense or another they think they are or they are trying to be God, I thank God for A.A., but then for being an alcoholic. And so I am grateful for being an alcoholic — and not least because if I were not an alcoholic, I would never have found the A.A. way of life in which for the first time in my life I am discovering serenity.

28

A.A. should always give full credit to its several wellsprings of inspiration and . . . should always consider these people among the founders of our Society.

— Bill W.

ONE FRINGE-BENEFIT OF THIS NINETY/NINETY, or at least of the way I am going about it, is that I am getting reimmersed in A.A. literature. It seems good for my sobriety for me to read and to reread not only *The Big Book* and the *Twelve and Twelve,* but also the other A.A. literature like *Living Sober* and *As Bill Sees It* and *Alcoholics Anonymous Comes of Age.*

Sometimes, however, I have questions about my reading. Whenever I think of reading, for example, it seems good to remind myself that I did not get sober by reading — even *The Big Book.* A.A., for me, was and is the meetings: sober alcoholics sharing their "experience, strength and hope" with each other. I hate to admit it, because I am in general such an avid reader, but I did not get too much out of *The Big Book* when I read it while still drinking. Of course, when I did that, I hardly even looked at the stories — I was mainly trying to analyze the program as it was described in the first 164 pages. And that, of course, did not work. Or at least I kept on drinking then. Also I guess, I did learn that there might be a solution to my drinking problem — that A.A. was out there, if I should ever decide to go find it.

Eventually, of course, I did just that. And then I reread *The Big Book,* and it made a lot more sense — or I did. After I had been in the fellowship for just about a year, someone suggested that maybe I should try to work the program, and gave me a copy of the *Twelve and Twelve.* I loved that book — I think it is still my favorite reading, especially whenever I am not feeling good about myself. It pulls me back to the basics, to "First things first," back to the Steps that are the A.A. program.

But when I am not feeling bad — on my sobriety's ordinary days, if there are such things — I really like to read over A.A.'s own story as it is told in *Alcoholics Anonymous Comes of Age*. It is so easy for me, sometimes, to take A.A. for granted. Reading its story then, is very good for me, and maybe especially how A.A.'s Twelve Traditions were hammered out on the anvil of experience. There are a lot of stories in that history. And because an alcoholic is an alcoholic, I can really identify with some of those experiences that led to the A.A. traditions.

One reason that I know that reading A.A.'s history is good for me is that I always come away from it with profound gratitude. There are many pitfalls, even in sobriety. But the A.A.s who went before us, and especially the very first ones, seem to have discovered just about all of them — probably because they were alcoholics. Reading their story of how they finally succeeded in marking out those pitfalls so other alcoholics might stand a better chance of avoiding them — that helps me grow in sobriety, because I am identifying with their growth in sobriety.

Reading A.A. literature is also good for me because it reminds me that reading is like thinking: doing it *about* something doesn't do much good, but doing it *from within* surely helps. I know it has helped me over the years, and that is why I keep reading *The Big Book* and the *Twelve and Twelve*, and why I try to go to at least one Big Book or Step discussion meeting each week.

You do not have to read to get or to grow in sobriety, but our program does revolve around a book — "the basic text for our Society," as it says in its preface. And so it seems to me that for people like me, at least, people who like to read, indulging that habit in the right way can be a great help to growing in sobriety and especially to progressing in sober thinking.

But "reading from within" can have different meanings, and on this topic I am constantly impressed by the breadth as well as the sensitivity of A.A.'s wisdom. Although, because of our wariness of controversy, most A.A. groups rightly stay with and display and promote only official "Conference-approved" literature, many individual A.A.s cast their nets more widely.

One of the joys of sobriety, it seems to me, is being able to share with others who are trying to grow in it the things we have found helpful to our own growth. And much that is not officially approved A.A. literature falls into that category.

The most obvious example of this is the *Twenty-Four Hour* book. I was introduced to it in my A.A.-oriented treatment program, but since then I have heard many who have good sobriety without ever being in treatment recommend it highly. They and I have surely found it useful. That certainly demonstrates, it seems to me, that one can "read from within" the A.A. way of life even in literature not officially approved by the General Service Conference of Alcoholics Anonymous.

Let me try to explain what I mean, using a familiar phrase: "Stick with the winners." Who is a winner within A.A.? Is it not someone who, by sharing his or her experience, strength, and hope, wins the respect of fellow A.A.s so that they try to learn from his or her sobriety?

The same kind of leadership, it seems to me, emerges out of all the helter-skelter of books, pamphlets, and tapes available. Some A.A. members discover that they can identify with and learn from them, and so they pass the word on within A.A., and the test is in the results. If sober members of A.A. find something helpful, it is helpful.

Official A.A. literature of course remains the safest, the surest, for those of us who seem to have to read and who seem able to learn in that way. In a way, that literature is official mainly because it has been screened by the largest number of A.A. members or at least through their chosen representatives. But it impresses me that A.A. has never condemned any literature, even though — God knows — there is some pretty weird stuff out there. The membership decides, by its living, what works in promoting sobriety. In a way, for each one of us A.A.s, there can be nothing that is more official than another A.A. whose sobriety we admire suggesting something as possibly helpful — whether it be a meeting, a practice, or a piece of literature. That is why, I suspect, we have such a variety of helpful but unofficial literature circulating among A.A.s, even if this is not always available at A.A. meetings.

Whatever works for us, we share — freely and with enthusiasm. To me, it is a tribute to A.A.'s genius that it has so little official literature, as it has so little official anything else. That seems implicitly to encourage those members who want to read more to do so widely, testing whatever works for them, so that all members of A.A. have the widest possible chance of identifying and learning. Like all other reflections of A.A.'s great tolerance, that seems to testify eloquently to the genuineness of A.A.'s living out its primary concern — "to carry its message to the alcoholic who still suffers," and to do so by using any and every means available.

29

Rarely have we seen a person fail who has thoroughly followed our path.

— Alcoholics Anonymous

THIS MORNING, AT LEAST, I CAN DO NO BETTER than record a story I heard at the meeting last night. Although I cannot claim to identify with all its details, I do identify with its substance most deeply — even if in ways that I cannot exactly explain. Let me try to capture what I remember of it; for it is in such memories, I am convinced, that I will continue to find my own sobriety.

My own story is engraved in the fiber of my being. It is perhaps carved so deeply, however, that sometimes I find I can tap parts of it best — if not only — by identifying with the stories of others. I try to record such stories — not on tape, but in my own words. Such, then, is the story that follows.

Tonight is my A.A. birthday — and, as some of you know and as I am grateful, it is not my first birthday in Alcoholics Anonymous. Usually, when I tell my story, I seek balance: "what we are like now" is to me far more important than "what we were like" or "what happened." But this past week another birthday celebrant asked me, in conversation, to recall my hitting bottom. It has been a long time since I had recalled that, and I found the experience good. Because it was good for me, it may be good for you.

Many of you would call me, in this program, a winner. When I first came around, I hated that word, because I was so sure I was a loser. It is difficult, when you have proven yourself a loser, to identify with a winner. In a way, I never have succeeded in doing that. So tonight I want to tell you the story of a loser — to tell you that part of my story you perhaps have too seldom heard because I certainly have too rarely remembered to tell it.

I want to begin by reminding you — and myself — of the

importance of honesty as the foundation of our program and therefore of our sobriety. We all know how frightening that first paragraph of "How It Works" can sometimes be. When I first came around A.A., I did not even try to stop drinking, because I knew that I was utterly unwilling — and perhaps even unable — to be honest.

So when I first heard "How It Works," I was pretty sure I was one of those unfortunates — you know: "constitutionally incapable of being honest with myself." In any case, I was not even really interested in stopping my drinking, because I was just going through the motions in A.A. For, though I used to be a professional, I was literally a bum then, and A.A. was a way of getting off the street in bad weather for at least an hour or so. Knowing that I was going to be sleeping outside again that night, I was ready to take just about any warm, dry place I could find. Even an A.A. meeting.

After a few meetings, I met the priest who ran the church where those meetings were held, Father Mac. Even though he was not an alkie himself, Mac seemed intuitively to spot my dishonesty, and he called me on it. He spent time with me, trying to help me to talk about the things I could not talk about because I could not face them. And he plugged me into a couple of sober A.A. members with whom he thought I might identify. So I had lots of pressure to get honest.

Well, I was too smart for them, of course. But I guess it all helped, because the proverbial straw that broke this camel's back was added one night when, right after Mac and the others had helped me with some decent clothes and a real chance at a job that I actually wanted, I got bombed and got in a fight and landed in jail. None of them — not one of them — came to visit me there. I remember thinking that they must be lousy friends, if they were going to let a little urine and vomit keep them away. Because . . . well, I don't know about the new city jail, but that's what the old one was made out of: urine and vomit and boozy sweat.

Anyway, when I got out, I went crawling back to those "friends," despite all my resentments. Where else could I have gone? So I crawled back, even though I was walking upright. I expected either anger or the cold shoulder. I had blown it, and I knew that I had blown it, but I also realized that I was desperately afraid and ashamed that I had also blown whatever slim chance I might have had for having any real friends. Strange, I felt that way although I doubt that the word *friend* was in my vocabulary at the time.

Well, the guys I saw at the meeting when I first walked in acted cold and angry. Oh, they gave me the usual perfunctory smiles and "good-to-see-you-back" crap, but then they turned away to talk to somebody else or to get more coffee or whatever. They clearly had no more time for me. I slumped into a chair in the back of the room and tried to listen, but I realized that I was fighting off tears.

Now I am not a crier, and I never was one, even during my worst boozing. I was always either a fighter or unconscious. And remember, I was dry: they did not serve booze in the city lockup where I had been for ten days, and after they'd let me out that morning, I had not had a drink. That in itself was a sort of miracle, I guess, but I knew that I wanted to be with Mac and the other guys at the meeting that night, even if only to chew them out for not visiting me, so I had stayed dry.

Deep down I knew that I had blown it, that I had destroyed and lost not only the one good thing in my life, but certainly my only chance ever to stop drinking. It was all over, and it was my fault, and I knew it, and — in a funny way — I didn't care.

Now most of you know that I still do not have much religion. And I will tell you, if you don't know, that despite all the missions and all that, there is not too much religion in the guys on the street. But somehow, maybe just going to so many meetings, if even dishonestly, these words seemed to wrench themselves from my gut: "God, help me." Well, it didn't do any good. There was no flash of light, no feeling of warmth, no voices or any of that stuff that I have heard others describe — even if there had been, I doubt that I would have or could have believed.

So I just sat there, hurting, convinced that I had blown my last chance and seeing in the averted carelessness of the others' eyes proof of my conviction. Probably, I was listening to the speakers that night in a different way — partially because I was hoping one of them would look at me and see my pain, but mainly because deep down I was thinking that that was my last A.A. meeting. I had lost my last chance, there was absolutely no hope, and I was pretty sure I would never be back. Wise people, I believe, refer to the condition I was in that night, at that meeting, as "absolutely hopeless and absolutely helpless." If those terms have any meaning, that was me, for that hour.

Well, the meeting ended and nothing changed. The others clustered around the coffee and each other — not ignoring me, but just not noticing me. I suddenly felt that I had to get out of there: my last A.A. meeting was over, *I was over*, so why bother hanging around? I headed for the door.

I guess I will never know what happened — maybe it was the way I threw my head back and started marching out. Mac just grinned, in later years when I asked him about it and said something about "his sponsor, the Holy Spirit." Anyway, just as I got to the door, there was Father Mac, standing in front of me. Remember now, he is not an alkie; but he always comes to the open meetings, and he sits there, and he listens, and somehow I am sure he identifies, mainly because he loves us alkies. Well, suddenly there he is, standing in front of me, blocking the door. I will never forget the exact words that he said, nor the indescribable look on his face as he spoke, never taking his eyes off of mine.

"Leo, you haven't had a drink today, have you? Does that mean you are finally sick and tired of being sick and tired? You are here. Does that mean you are finally ready to try it the A.A. way? Now shut up! Don't answer me yet, because I have one more question. Are you finally ready to get honest with yourself, do you really want to get honest with yourself, so that you are willing to go to any length to get honest with yourself? If you are not, come on up to my office, and we'll talk about it — maybe. But if you are, don't talk to me: go over and talk to one of those sober alcoholics you heard speak tonight. Because if you are ready to get honest with yourself, they have what you want: the tools to help you do that. Okay, Leo, which will it be — a nice cup of warm coffee and maybe a new pair of old shoes and a flop-pass for the night from me? Or the beginning of a really new life from one of those guys who knows exactly how you feel and what you are thinking, because he was once there himself? Which, Leo? Because from looking at you, I think both you and I know that this is probably the last chance you will ever have to make that choice."

I guess I don't have to tell you what I did. I turned around and without even saying "Thanks" to Mac for his offer, I tried to find the speaker who had said "hopeless."

It is good for me to remember where I came from and how I got here. Now some of you may be sitting out there thinking, "You've come a long way, baby." Maybe, in some ways, I have: these are my own clothes, and I have a job and a clean place to sleep tonight, and — most important — I have not had a drink this twenty-four hours.

But in a more important way, I have not come any way at all. What I described took place in an A.A. meeting and this is an A.A. meeting. And we are all here for the same reason I was there that night: without A.A. we are helpless, we are hopeless. If I have come a long way, it is because I have stayed put — stayed put not in a place, but in this fellowship and this program. And I have stayed put because I know that, if I ever leave, I will be back in the place I was before I found A.A., before I was found by you people and your friends like Father Mac.

Thank you for being here, because — if you weren't — well, you have just heard where I would be, if I was lucky.

30

The guilty man is eminently suitable and is therefore chosen to become the vessel for the continuing incarnation, not the guiltless one who holds aloof from the world and refuses to pay his tribute to life, for in him the dark God would find no room.

— C. G. Jung

In a time so filled with methods and techniques to change people, to influence their behavior, and to make them do new things and think new thoughts, we have lost the simple but difficult gift of being present to each other. . . . Simply being with someone is difficult because it asks of us that we share in the other's vulnerability, enter with him or her into the experience of weakness and powerlessness, become a part of uncertainty, and give up control and self-determination.

— Donald McNeill, Douglas Morrison,
and Henri Nouwen

CARL JUNG'S THOUGHT REMAINS LARGELY A mystery to me. Often, I value his insights and feel privileged that such a great psychiatrist and profound thinker holds such a special place in the history of A.A. "The foundation stone upon which our Society has since been built," Bill W. called Jung's truly historic conversation with Rowland H., who carried his message to Ebby T., who in turn carried it to A.A.'s co-founder. Surely Dr. Jung, with his sensitivity to the spiritual, has much to teach me.

But when I try to read Jung, I tend to get lost in the complexity of his thought. His penchant for irritatingly mysterious expressions frustrates me. "Vessel for the continuing incarnation," I might have enough residual Christianity left in me to be able to understand. But "the dark God"? I suspect that there is something important here: my very resistance seems to signal that. Still, what an arresting, almost weird term.

Clearly, Jung does not mean here to signify "the force of evil." That does not fit the context; and surely Jung, with his world view, would never have termed "the force of evil" any kind of "God." No, "the dark God" seems rather to refer, here, to that aspect of ultimate reality that knows and is pain, suffering, loss . . . all the agonies and dis-eases that afflict the human condition.

In identifying those realities with the dark God, Jung seems to be saying that such experiences are as real as their opposites. The book is titled *Answer to Job*, and its subtitle makes clear with what Jung tries to deal: "The Problem of Evil: Its Psychological and Religious Origins." His inevitable failure to solve the problem of evil should not blind me either to the courage that lay behind his effort or to the insights available in it.

Jung published his book in the early 1950s. I wonder if, given his experience with individuals such as Rowland H., he was mindful of alcoholics in writing it? I would like to think so; and perhaps in this passage I find reason for thinking so. The concept of guilt always confuses me, but the alcoholic is certainly one who does not "hold aloof from the world" nor "refuse to pay his tribute to life." It seems to me that, in a way, we try to consume the world in our alcoholic drinking of booze; and that in our bending the elbow and hoisting good cheer, we pay such tribute to life that we come — literally — damned close to losing our lives.

Does that help me to understand the dark God who seems to be the lord of pain and suffering, of agony and loss? If we are, as alcoholics, in Jung's term, *guilty*, for what are we suitable and chosen? The concept of "chosen" reminds me of Philip Rieff's powerful passage in *The Triumph of the Therapeutic*, where Rieff is examining what he sees as the key to Jung's therapy:

> There is no feeling more desperate than that of being free to choose, yet without the specific consolation of being chosen. . . . Gods choose; men are chosen. What men lost when they became as gods is precisely the sense of being chosen, which encourages them, in their gratitude, to take their own subsequent choices seriously.
>
> . . . In the last analysis, a leap of faith may be necessary, if one is to be free to choose — and to choose because his

> knowledge, being personal, compels him thus. The hardest lesson to learn is not how to choose but rather how to acquire that passionate knowledge which will permit us again to be chosen.

Perhaps that is our gift, as alcoholics who are members of A.A. — the passionate knowledge that allows us to be chosen. For we have been given the gift of choosing: one day at a time, with help, we can and do choose not to take the first drink. We recognize that as gift because once we surely did not have it. But how did the gift come to us? We received it, I believe, because in some sense we have been chosen.

But the sense of being chosen can be dangerous: it verges close to the claim of being special, and therefore it can too readily reflect the self-centeredness that is the root of our troubles. Yet, as Rieff intuited, "in the last analysis, a leap of faith may be necessary." How and why were we chosen? Because of our pain, our hurt. We are chosen, that is, because we lack good, not because we possess it. We find healing preeminently because we need healing. Healing, then, is the only reality for which we, as alcoholics, are suitable.

"The guilty man is eminently suitable," Jung proposed. Suitable for what? The second quotation helps me to find the answer. It comes from a book titled *Compassion*, an essay that affords a more familiar and conventional perspective on the problem of evil. One of its authors, several years ago, wrote another work titled *The Wounded Healer*. At that time, as an alcoholic new to the program and fellowship of A.A., I identified with the concept of "wounded healer." It seems to me that that is what we are to each other within A.A. We can heal — can make whole from — alcoholism, because we share the same wound. Our very wound becomes the source of our healing — both of others and of ourselves. That is the meaning of the Twelfth Step.

If the problem of evil is understood as the question of suffering, then the answer is "compassion," which means "suffering with." Is that not what we alcoholics do for each other in the fellowship of Alcoholics Anonymous? We do not join A.A. in order to suffer. We come, instead, trying to escape suffering — the suffering of our alcoholism. But we do not escape: we transcend. We remain alcoholics. And we cease suffering from our alcoholism only because others are there, waiting and wanting and needing to suffer from our alcoholism with us.

Within A.A., then, we transcend our alcoholic suffering by being ready, by being there, to suffer with another's. That is why the Twelfth Step is an essential part of our program. That is also why any A.A. group dies if newcomers do not approach it.

That is difficult, I suspect, for those outside A.A. to understand. We seem to feed on suffering, to suck it in — even, perhaps, to seek it out. And we do, if it is the suffering of alcoholism, which we all know so well. It is for that that we are suitable, for that that we have been and know ourselves chosen: to heal others and ourselves by suffering with the alcoholic who still suffers.

There are those who would term this understanding "unhealthy." Yet, in it, we find healing. Perhaps, then, alcoholics — at least those of us who are recovering within the program and fellowship of Alcoholics Anonymous — are "eminently suitable" and "therefore chosen" for something else besides. Our existence and the way of life to which we witness by our recovery signal to anyone open-minded, honest, and willing enough to learn from us — signal the reality, the beauty, and the power of compassion — of the suffering-with that finds healing by healing.

Many would be made whole, but few are willing to suffer with. To be sober in A.A. is to learn — and to teach — the profound truth that it is impossible to have the one without embracing also the other.

31

In the animal kingdom, the rule is, eat or be eaten;
in the human kingdom, define or be defined.
— Thomas Szasz

THERE ARE, WITHIN A.A., DIFFERENT UNDERstandings of anonymity. Where I came from, but not where I live now, it was customary to close meetings with the reminder: "We *are* 'Alcoholics Anonymous': we ask you, then, to remember what you heard here, but not whom you saw here." Most groups operate on a first-name-only basis. Yet some speakers insist on using their full names in introducing themselves, often justifying the practice by saying: "Everybody knew I was a drunk — I don't care who knows that I am sober."

A.A.'s guidelines on anonymity are precise but narrow. They apply anonymity not to our being alcoholics, but to our membership in Alcoholics Anonymous. We acknowledge A.A. membership, in general, only at meetings and on Twelfth-Step calls. We do so only to help ourselves or someone else attain sobriety. Even for that purpose, however, we do not claim A.A. membership and use our full name "at the level of press, radio, and films." We treasure anonymity as "the spiritual foundation of all our Traditions," and we cherish and seek to learn from its "ever reminding us to place principles before personalities."

Few A.A. members violate those guidelines. But what about those occasions on which some, although not claiming membership in A.A., present themselves publicly as alcoholics? Let's be honest and face reality: largely because of A.A.'s outstanding success, just about everybody in our culture realizes that when someone comfortably and perhaps even happily refers to himself or herself as an alcoholic, he or she must be a member of A.A. We are the only ones who can do that. That may achieve much good, perhaps, especially because of the message it implicitly sends to active alcoholics still mired in denial; but is it not some sort of a violation of A.A.'s tradition of anonymity?

The obvious answer offered by A.A.'s own history is: "No." Alcoholics Anonymous Tradition, as made clear both in the *Twelve and Twelve* and Bill's telling of that Tradition's history in *Alcoholics Anonymous Comes of Age,* is applied strictly to claiming A.A. membership in the media listed — with the modern addition of television. Early A.A. history and experience reveal the reason for that understanding. The tradition of anonymity affords especially two protections. In the first place, it protects all of us from the weirdos among us: we have them now as they had them then. But more important, it protects A.A. members from rationalizing the tendency to grandiosity that lurks ever within us. If anonymity is the spiritual foundation of all our Traditions, it is because humility is the spiritual foundation of all our sobriety.

That consideration might seem to afford a simple answer to my earlier question. Saying that one is an alcoholic rarely scores points for pride: it does not usually win praise or admiration, especially when done on the personal, one-to-one level. To acknowledge that one is a recovering alcoholic is necessarily to admit that one was, once, an active alcoholic. Society's stigma remains: no one wants to be an alcoholic, nor to be thought of as alcoholic. The stigma may, for some, reinforce denial; but for more, I suspect, it supports sobriety by serving as a useful antidote to pride. Even among friends and sympathetic acquaintances, to admit alcoholism is to focus attention on one's defects, on what one cannot do.

But that answer is too simple, despite all the potential usefulness of such an approach in educating others and as a reminder of humility for ourselves. For one thing, humility does not come that easily. Because I am always mixed as well as too often mixed up, my motives cannot be otherwise. There are times when admitting that I am an alcoholic can be a coy seduction or a subtle plea for admiration. We rarely attain humility by striving directly for it; we never gain in humility by being ostentatiously humble.

For me, then, it seems more helpful to think not on my humility, but about A.A.'s. There is a stroke of genius in A.A.'s very name: "Alcoholics Anonymous" — a genius I too easily forget when I focus on "Anonymous." In A.A.'s earliest days far more than now, "alcoholic" was a disparaging, derisive label. Because we live in a world where names and labels are important, people who feel themselves stigmatized generally go to great lengths to change society's perception of them by changing what they are called. Many obvious examples come to mind, from "gay men and women" to "exceptional children."

Those are praise-worthy efforts: we need all the help we can get in reminding us to treat all human beings humanly. But perhaps A.A.'s greatest claim to exceptional historical status is that it did not do that, nor even try to do it, by jettisoning the word *alcoholic.* The early members of our fellowship accepted the label *alcoholic* almost joyously, and that at a time when many regarded "inebriate" as the more genteel and scientifically correct term.

Two things strike me as especially relevant both to their choice then and to my sobriety today. In the first place, those early alcoholics who shaped A.A. were so happy to hear that there was hope, that they really did not care much what anyone called what it was there was hope for. In fact, by embracing the term *alcoholic,* which came usually conjoined in the all-too-true expression, "hopeless alcoholic," they signaled that they knew what they were talking about and that their program promised a kind of miracle. The name itself suggested that there was hope for the hopeless.

But more deeply, they suggested more — a truth and a reality too often overlooked by those who focus attention on what they are called, on how they are named. To quote one perceptive commentator on the modern scene:

> If a change of terminology does not reflect a real change in the way we conceive of and act towards the realities to which the terminology refers, it simply results in the new word coming to have the old meaning. Thus when medical terms replaced moral ones referring to "madness," the medical terms became charged with moral overtones — "sick" came to be a term of condemnation.

I sometimes fear that the "disease concept" may have hurt some alcoholics because — in the modern culture in which we live — "sick" has become an epithet of derision. It amazes me — or, more profoundly, it fills me with admiration for the intuitive wisdom of the early A.A.'s — that they knew that. And so they concentrated their efforts not on what people called those whose lives were being destroyed by booze, but on how people thought about that phenomenon.

Their effort was directed, of course, primarily and even exclusively at their own members, at themselves, at me. I suppose holding to that term was a part of hitting bottom. The drinking alcoholic, nearing bottom, cannot help but wonder, "What's wrong with me?" A.A. suggests bluntly: "If you can identify with our powerlessness over alcohol, you are probably an alcoholic."

"Oh no, anything but that!" most drunks instinctively reply. And A.A. says back, in effect: "Yes, that! But look, we are alcoholics, too, and we are serene and sober or at least progressing in those qualities. So maybe what you have to do is understand differently what it means to be an alcoholic. If you want what we have, try to be an alcoholic the A.A. way, and see what happens."

And of course we know what happens, at least often: another self-loathing drunk becomes a self-esteeming A.A. member, and soon he or she is carrying the same message to yet another drunk.

There is, of course, a lot of surrender in A.A. — to reality, to the wisdom contained in the Twelve Steps. But as far as the outside world is concerned, our surrender is a sort of judo-like maneuver. We accept the label but change our thinking about it. And, because we do live in that world, we are also changing the world's thinking about it. That's why today, when someone says publicly, "I am an alcoholic," under N.C.A. (the National Council on Alcoholism) auspices, for instance, it tends to win admiration for courage rather than contempt for weakness.

The problem with that maneuver, with that success, is that any success can prove very treacherous to the alcoholic. It seems to me that if any alcoholic goes public in order to win admiration, both he or she and we are in big trouble. That, of course, is the reason for that Eleventh Tradition. And that is one reason, too, I believe, why the role of the N.C.A. is so important. The N.C.A. is of course in no way affiliated with A.A. Alcoholism and alcoholics are two different spheres of interest. Except, of course, that alcoholism does not come in test tubes: it comes in alcoholics. So N.C.A. does what A.A. cannot do; and thus far at least, probably because Marty Mann knew us so well, it has done a pretty good job of screening alcoholics who go public.

Some in A.A., of course, still do object. They may have a point, but in a way it is their own sobriety that has created the situation that N.C.A. chooses to see as opportunity rather than problem. Those who go public never say that they belong to A.A. If most people in our society today assume that anyone who says comfortably, "I am an alcoholic," must be a member of Alcoholics Anonymous — well, that is their assumption. Implicitly, at least, it is a tremendous tribute to A.A. Still, mindful of the prevalence of that assumption, we in A.A. must be very careful. And I, for one, think it remains always best to risk erring on the side of caution.

Still, I have to admit that this whole topic and the phenomenon it reflects do sort of tickle me. Doctor Thomas Szasz has suggested that: "In the animal kingdom, the rule is, eat or be eaten; in the human kingdom, define or be defined." If he is correct in that perception (and I think that he has glimpsed a significant truth about our modern world), then I delight in feeling, deep down, not so much that we alkies are a pretty cool bunch, as that our founders, the people who devised this program and designed it especially for us, have been proven wondrously wise. And for that, I am, as always, yet on a still deeper level, profoundly grateful.

32

fun-da-men-tal: 1. of or forming a foundation or basis; basic; essential; 2. relating to what is basic; radical; 3. on which others are based. . . .
— Webster's New World Dictionary

THE GROUP WHOSE MEETING I ATTENDED LAST night has an interesting little sub-tradition. Invariably, after the reading of the "Preamble" and "How It Works," the chairman opens the discussion with the question: "Anybody here want a drink today?" He or she then waits a full half-minute before going on to the more usual question, "Okay, anybody here have anything at all they want to talk about — anything that has to do with drinking booze or living sober?"

Curious about the origin of such a custom, I asked, in the conversation after the meeting, whether there might be a story behind it. "How did this group happen to start asking that question?" I queried one of the apparent oldtimers.

"It's been going on for about twenty years," he replied. "I wasn't here then, but I'll tell you what they told me about how it got started. Everybody tells pretty much the same story about it, so I guess it is probably true."

The story was brief. It seems that meeting had been started close to thirty years ago as a "Step and Tradition" discussion meeting, where each week they would read and then discuss one chapter of the *Twelve and Twelve.* One evening in the mid-sixties, that week's chairman, after reading the "Preamble" and "How It Works," began the discussion by saying: "Okay, tonight we are here to discuss the Fourth Tradition. . . ." One of the off-and-on members, invariably described as "that goldanged fifty-five-year-old hippie," suddenly broke in and pounded his fist on the table and almost in tears blurted out: "Damn the traditions! I want a drink of booze!"

"Well," the oldtimer told me, "the group's regulars insist that that was the best meeting those good old boys ever had."

Anyway, ever since that night, that group's own specific purpose and sense of identity as a group has been shaped by that visitor.

Every A.A. member in this district knows that there is one meeting you can go to, and be sure of hearing that question asked — "Anybody here want a drink today? — and know that he or she has twenty-nine seconds to get up the courage to mumble, "Yeah," and be welcomed as a gift rather than greeted as a problem. Maybe it is because of that that those externally rough-hewn and occasionally foul-mouthed farmers have a reputation that extends, in A.A. circles, across the whole state — a reputation for simple honesty infused with tolerant, understanding love.

I do not recall ever hearing any of them talk about it around the table, at least when a visitor like me was present, but just about every member of that group has taken some very sick and usually very citified alkie into his home for a time, given him or her some healthy outdoor chores to do and a bit of self-respect to ponder while working on A.A. In fact, the odds are that that young and pale newcomer sitting there last night was there for that reason — I would guess that he is staying with one of those A.A.s in what just might be the most effective treatment program you will find in this part of the country.

Thinking upon it, last night, I found the story of that group fascinating. This morning, on further reflection, I seem to find in it also profound insight into the riches of "Keep it simple" and why A.A. works. There seemed to be a special kind of sobriety, if there is such a thing, in that old shack last night. Perhaps because I am, at heart, a "sophisticated city-slicker," the very atmosphere of rough-hewn love penetrated the defenses I raise against more effusive expressions of warmth.

I really like the idea of a meeting opening with that question: it seems one sure way of reminding everybody why they are there. Yet as I was listening to that story for the first time last night, I wondered why that did not become just another formality, losing its meaning over time. But now I see the answer. Because of the group's reputation as well as because of their old-time in-home twelfth-stepping, very often there is someone present who desperately needs to speak to precisely that question.

But the group's larger secret, if that is the right word, seems to me to be how it keeps it simple without ever lapsing into just being simplistic. They know that the A.A. way of life must begin with "Don't take the first drink, one day at a time, and go to meetings." But they also know and live what must grow out of that if Alcoholics Anonymous is to become truly a way of life. The sense that I came away with last night is that in that particular group, each of its meetings is a kind of Twelfth-Step call.

Sometimes, these days, it seems to me difficult to make the old-fashioned Twelfth-Step call. I realize that that is a mixed bag, and mostly good: having formal treatment available not only saves lives and much grief by offering the help earlier, it also enables A.A.s, if they carry the message into those settings, to have maybe the best possible atmosphere for a Twelfth-Step call.

But sometimes, it seems to me, we almost forget the middle phrase in that Twelfth Step and our fellowship's history of seeking out alcoholics in order to keep ourselves sober and to grow in our own sobriety. I think that it is great that we have treatment facilities to which to take active alkies: the people there, for example, can cope with medical complications that we would almost certainly mishandle. But, if that can be part of a Twelfth-Step call, it is still only part: real twelfth-stepping doesn't end with referral or drop-off.

I learned that for myself many moons ago, and I almost learned it the hard way. Once, when I was having a really rough day, I could not seem to find any of my A.A. friends at home. Then I remembered a drunk I had dropped off at the hospital two weeks before and forgotten about since. Well, I marched myself over there and walked into his room and sat down and said: "Joe, I'm here to talk with you because *I have* to talk with you. I don't know if you even heard me, the day I brought you in here, when I told you I was an alcoholic; but today I am afraid that I might go out and get bombed . . . not just take a drink or two, but get plastered. And the only way I know how not to do that is to talk to another alcoholic, and you are the best I can come up with today."

I will never forget the look on his face, until it slowly dawned on him that I was serious. Well, neither of us had a drink that day. But that day's sobriety I owe to the kind of thinking that I found in that group last night, and I am grateful for that reminder. They have the fundamentals, without being fundamentalists: they know where it starts; they also know where it has to go, if dryness is ever to become sobriety.

For whatever reason, it seems to me that at precisely this point in my ninety/ninety, I need that reminder, both sides of it: remembering the fundamentals is important, but it is what comes after them — how I live them — that gives them meaning.

That group last night, with their question about wanting a drink today, brought me back to fundamentals. And from the example of sobriety that they build on that foundation, I just might learn more about what I need right now than I would at any number of "sophisticated" discussion meetings.

33

"Think" and "thank" are kindred roots, and the German word an-denken *— literally, "to think on"' — means* to remember: *hence, for Heidegger, think, thank, and remember are kindred notions. Real thinking . . . is at once an act of thanking and remembrance.*

— William Barrett

FOR A LONG TIME, WHEN I FIRST CAME AROUND A.A., the ready ease with which members said "Thanks" irritated me only slightly less than their constant prattling about gratitude. Over the years since, I think and hope that I have grown in both acceptance and understanding of that A.A. hallmark. This morning, reflecting not only on last night but also on this ninety/ninety thus far, two things strike me about that growth.

The first is the realization that how I have just phrased it is correct: in gratitude, acceptance comes before understanding. We do not know gratitude so long as we fight it — in ourselves or in others. That is, perhaps, the first clue to its deep relationship with sobriety.

It impresses me, second, that, like sobriety itself, gratitude is something we gradually grow in. We seek — or perhaps claim — not perfection but progress in our thankfulness.

It helps me, then, to recall how I thought and felt at the very beginning of that road, the moment when I first came to A.A. Two things, I recall, especially used to bug me then. People in A.A. said "Thanks" so frequently and so easily that I found it difficult to believe that they meant it: it seemed too automatic. And second, my own pseudo-highbrow aversion to "stupid cliches" led my nerves to jangle whenever I heard the phrase, "The attitude of gratitude." It seemed just too cute.

I recall also how and when I at least began to think differently. For many months my sponsor's saying "Thanks" as he dropped me off each night I was sober enough to get to a meeting really annoyed me. It seemed the epitome of thoughtless cliche or merely ritualistic gesture, especially given the fact that I was not making much apparent — or real — progress. "What the hell is he thanking me for?"

Sometimes, important things happen in strange ways. One night shortly after I had finally put the cork in the bottle for what even I did not then know was the last time, my key jammed in the door for a moment. I began talking to myself out loud, and therefore maybe for the first time heard my own question. We had had a fairly good conversation that evening about the A.A. slogans. I suddenly realized that it was a conversation, and that therefore I had contributed to it.

There came a sort of instantaneous revelation: knowing Phil and his constant effort at honesty, and hearing again in my mind the tone of his voice, I realized that he really was grateful — that his brief and almost offhand "Thanks" was not cliche or ritual but a deep and real and heartfelt and almost half-embarrassed clumsy expression of honest gratitude. I must have been really dumb to learn something that obvious so slowly, but I also suddenly realized that all Phil's other "Thanks" had been as honest: seeing what my continued drinking was doing to me was surely helping him to not take the first drink, one day at a time.

I thought quite a bit about gratitude after that incident. And I began to realize that part of my revulsion at hearing "Thanks" was rooted in the fact that, when I was drinking, I also had said "Thanks" fairly often. Far too often, in fact, for my "Thanks" had been just about always insincere — a part of my people-pleasing and feeling worthless or an attempt to con someone into giving me "more" . . . usually, more booze. I came to realize that I still carried around a lot of resentments, that I was fighting sobriety by adopting a pose of cynicism. It seemed to me that in my earliest A.A. days, not only did I not say "Thanks" very often, I even made a point of not saying it. Those drunks kept telling me they were helping me for their own sakes, so why should I thank them — that was how I, if you will pardon the expression, thought.

In time, after that revelation, further understanding dawned. Probably because I was getting sober, I began to feel genuine, honest gratitude for perhaps the first time in my stunted life. So I began saying "Thanks," but very carefully. The echo of my too-easy, dishonest "Thanks" while drinking still haunted my memory.

As so often with so many things in A.A., that worked. The more I said "Thanks" honestly, the more honest gratitude I discovered myself feeling. But beyond noticing that, and being grateful for it, I never really thought very much about gratitude. Thus, what seems to be happening on this ninety/ninety is a kind of second revelation to me — a revelation about gratitude.

Last night, for the very first time, I really heard the meaning implicit in the phrase "the attitude of gratitude." Perhaps it was the tone of the speaker's voice; more likely it was the way she stood as she said it, but I suddenly realized that an attitude is, of course, a posture or a position, especially of the mind. When I got home, I looked up *attitude* in the dictionary to check on that. Not only was my memory of its deeper meaning correct, I discovered, but *attitude* has the same root as and is related to *aptitude*. It implies an appropriate posture that enables one to do something. The phrase, "The attitude of gratitude," then, itself reflects my own experience with "Thanks." Being grateful leads to being more grateful, because gratitude is an attitude.

And it is, of course, an attitude that permeates A.A. — not just on the surface, but deep down at the very foundation of all true sobriety. A.A.s are people who have known the depths of "hopeless" and "helpless." Now they have both hope and help. Realizing that they got that from A.A., how can they not be grateful, especially each time they walk into an A.A. meeting? Many don't always express it well, perhaps, but that is why gratitude is almost an atmosphere in A.A. meetings. There is so much of it in the room that some of it just has to spill over.

That fits well, it seems, with the A.A. practice of telling stories. If all "thinking on" is remembering, then there is an intrinsic connection between telling my story and being grateful. Those who tell their stories are necessarily grateful, and those who are grateful necessarily tell their stories. The very idea of gratitude begins to overwhelm. Let me rest, then, in being grateful: not only for A.A. and for sobriety, but also for the ninety/ninety and its journal. I have never seen more clearly that the A.A. way of life involves not only a way of thinking but also a way of thanking.

34

Man killed God because he could not bear to have anyone looking upon his ugliest side.

— Friedrich Nietzsche

UNTIL RECENTLY, I FOUND IT DIFFICULT TO identify with a woman's story — especially about drinking. That began to change about the time I decided to undertake this ninety-day journey, and last night's meeting helped to nail down that change. I think I am beginning to see a deep truth about living sober: in recovery, an alcoholic is an alcoholic; and the growth we are engaged in, because it involves progress in being human, is neither male nor female. If anything, the very difference between men and women — and especially between society's expectations of us — can help me understand better the nature and implications of true sobriety.

Something seemed to be trying to break through, last night, as I pondered my day-end inventory. The lead speaker's story kept echoing in my mind. When Patty first stood up and introduced herself, I must confess, I thought of her mainly as an attractive woman. By the time she finished, I identified with her as a struggling yet joyously sober human being. I can hear her even now — every word of her story — for as much as it was Patty's story as she told it, it is also Ernie's story as I see myself in its light. Patty's words touched my humanity, and I want to record them now, as I remember them, because I hope to preserve the clear vision they afforded me of one area in which my own sobriety requires growth.

"My name is Patty, and I am an alcoholic," the speaker introduced herself. "But maybe, because I am still an alcoholic even though I have not had a drink of alcohol this twenty-four hours, maybe it would be better to qualify by telling you what my friends used to call me when I was still drinking — a name that reflects a personality trait that still clings to me, and I to it, as a day at a time I try to grow in sobriety. Just as I was, and still am, an alcoholic, I used to be and still too often am, 'Little Ms. Fixit.'

"The story of my drinking and the story of my life, you see, seem to be the same: whenever anything goes wrong, Perfect Patty just has to fix it.

"Let's start with the drinking years. Whenever a party seemed to be lagging, whether I was the hostess or not, I just had to fix it. I tried to do that, usually, by pushing or pouring more booze. And of course, since it was important to set a good example, I always made sure to pour a good portion of that booze for Patty.

"Pardon my calling it 'booze' by the way. Those were polite drinks, but they were alcoholic drinks; and I got here not because they were polite, but because they were booze. I may have taken cocktails and sipped sherry with friends, but at least toward the end, when I was drinking by myself, I was swilling booze. 'A rose by any other name may smell as sweet,' but calling alcohol anything other than booze did not save me from becoming an alcoholic. Seeking pretty names for alcohol only served my denial, so now let me embrace that ugly name — booze — that you beautiful sober alcoholics have taught me. Its honesty may help to keep me sober.

"At those parties, of course, as well as when I was drinking alone, the main thing I was trying to fix was myself. There really were not that many parties: I certainly cannot blame my alcoholism on the obligations of my high-class social life. What I was really trying to fix, I am sure all of you in this room realize, was something inside me: a gnawing discomfort, a strange and empty uneasiness, a sneaking suspicion that Patty was not good enough — not only not good enough as a party-goer, but not good enough as a person, as a woman, as a human being.

"And so poor, not-good-enough Patty turned to chemicals, and especially to the soothing joys of alcohol, in order to fix that pain — the pain that was Patty, the pain that Patty more and more became as she drank more and more alcohol. It never really worked, as I am sure you all know: the chemicals wore off, and Patty was still Patty and still not good enough, and now increasingly in ever more pain, because 'nice girls' didn't drink like that — secretively, alone, sobbing, and then sick.

"Eventually, poor Patty came to A.A. — less to stop drinking than in hopes of feeling less sick, less to get sober than in hopes of feeling good . . . feeling good about Patty. And in these rooms, these halls, around you people, that happens. As you promised me, it works. Here, Patty is 'good enough'; here I have learned what it means to be truly sober. But here Patty also learned another important lesson: life is not an A.A. meeting. And I am also learning, one day at a time, that that is not life's fault — it is rather Patty's problem, in the beautiful sense you people have taught me: the sober awareness that in every problem lies the opportunity and the invitation to be human, to progress ever more in the wonderful adventure that is sobriety.

"And it is an adventure. Let me try to tell you what I mean, to share with you my 'experience, strength and hope' as a sober alcoholic who still tends to be Little Ms. Fixit, but who is beginning to realize that that gets in the way of truly living sober.

" 'Progress rather than perfection,' it says in *The Big Book*. I like to think that I accept that, that I find freeing relief in it. For myself, I seem to; but as far as things outside myself are concerned, I still have much progress to make. I seem, on the surface, tolerant of my own imperfection, but all too often I am pushed by the need, and I push the demand, to be surrounded by perfection. Whether it is the way the pictures are hung on the wall (perfectly evenly), or the top of my desk at the office (perfectly neat), or my expectations of those with whom I work (perfectly polite), whatever my eye falls upon must be perfect. Is that perhaps because, deep down, underneath my apparent joy in sobriety, I remain very unhappy with my own imperfection?

"What seems to be rearing its treacherous, ugly head — even in sobriety — is my old need to be in control, in absolute control of everything around me. I seem unable to feel okay unless everything around me bears my perfecting touch. It seems that I must leave my imprint: little touches of perfection must mark my trail — they say not only that I was there, but that I was in control. And so I seem to invert A.A.'s beautiful service motto: 'Whatever happens, I must be responsible.' After all, won't everybody judge me if anything goes wrong?

"I try to tell myself, sometimes, that this is just the reflection of my acceptance of full responsibility as a human person who happens to be a woman. It would be nice to be able to believe that, but would I put up with such behavior in a man? No. I suspect you all, male and female, recognize what is going on here: the big I of ego. Why do I, why must I, seek and even demand perfect control? Because even in sobriety I can, at times, play at being God.

"Somebody once wrote that man killed God because he could not bear to have anyone looking at his ugliest side. I am killing myself, with my self-imposed demands for perfection, for the same reason. If Patty is surrounded by, clothed in, perfection, perhaps no one will look at Patty's own continuing imperfection.

"But I am imperfect — that is why I am here. You do not look at Patty the Perfect: you see Patty the Alcoholic. For Patty is an alcoholic. That is why she comes here, to these meetings, and stands here, pouring out her not-so-sober heart at these tables. And what does this experience teach me? That you accept, and see, and listen to, and love not Patty the Perfect, but Patty the Alcoholic.

"Just like each one of you in this room, I want to be loved — I need to be loved; and that means being seen for what I am rather than looked at even for what I might want to be. Here I find that life-giving love, that identification — find it not because I am perfect, but because I am alcoholic. And that is one thing that I know I cannot fix. I know, in fact, that I would not fix it even if I could, for then I would no longer share in the loving identification that is these meetings.

"And so, thank you. Thank you for being here and for loving me by seeing me and listening to me, but thank you especially for letting me in, for listening to me, for loving me precisely because I, Patty, am so imperfect as to be an alcoholic. With your love, in these meetings, perhaps I will learn to grow in my own love for Patty — to love her enough so that she will no longer have to be Ms. Fixit."

I think I know why Patty's story so struck me: there is, in it, a message of freedom for me, for the "Mr. Fixit" that I still harbor.

Especially when I am with a woman, it seems, I have this need to be in charge — isn't that, after all, the role of a real man? Social life, in sobriety, can be treacherous. Not only because of the alcohol that always seems to be around to lubricate it, but because of the presober thinking into which there are even more invitations to fall.

I have always wondered about the differences between men and women, between how they think and the ways they feel. In A.A., listening to the stories told by alcoholics, both men and women, I seem to be learning more about those differences — and those samenesses — than I ever dreamed of knowing before. If we are alcoholics, we are human; and if we are first and foremost human, we are more alike than different in our joys and our sorrows, our fears and our triumphs. I am learning in A.A. to be honest — honest about what I think and how I feel, honest with both myself and others. And I am learning also to invite and to listen to such honesty from others, for only by doing that can I grow in my own.

Patty's story last night taught me much. I pray that it may continue to teach me; but even more, I ask that I may become more willing and more honest and sufficiently open-minded to be able to learn from any human being, to be able to see myself in every alcoholic. Hearing and identifying with Patty's story gives me freedom — and for that I thank you as well as her.

35

For a story truly to hold the child's attention, it must entertain him and arouse his curiosity. But to enrich his life, it must stimulate his imagination; help him to develop his intellect and to clarify his emotions; be attuned to his anxieties and aspirations; give full recognition to his difficulties, while at the same time suggesting solutions to the problems which perturb him.

— Bruno Bettelheim

LAST NIGHT MARKED ONE OF THOSE RARE occasions when Sam (my sponsor) and Pete (my pigeon) and I met together for coffee and ice cream after the meeting. Afterwards, at home, I tried to think on what we had discussed about sponsorship. That effort bore little fruit, for what had lodged in my mind was what our conversation had covered on the topic of "pigeons."

Pete brought up the term, and I sensed that he was sort of appealing to Sam over my head. "It is a small point," he began, "but I hope you can help me get cleared up on it — because now, as when I was drinking, it is not the big crises that mess up my thinking and my life: it's the piddly, small things that seem to undermine my sobriety unless I get honest with myself, and I do that by talking about them, talking with other A.A.s. And what is bothering me right now is that I do not like being referred to as a 'pigeon.' I feel that that is a stupid and derogatory word."

I laughed, although a bit embarrassed: I do use the word *pigeon* glibly and also unthinkingly, forgetting how the term had irritated me when I first came to A.A. Then, I had felt, calling newcomers *pigeons* seemed to violate everything A.A. stands for — that with just one day or even one hour of not drinking, you can respect yourself at least for that. I felt that being called a pigeon infantilized me.

Sam, meanwhile, was laughing. Perhaps he too was recalling my earlier outburst on the topic. "Yes, but newcomers have always been called pigeons," Sam chided. "Didn't you (glancing at me) even once go through the trouble of looking that up — 'researching it,' as you say?"

I had done that, and oldtimers I interviewed were enlightening. The term *pigeon* had originated primarily as an expression of affection, but with the built-in reminder to "handle with gentle care" lest the terrified newcomer become skittish and fly away.

Hearing that had helped my acceptance of the term. Because of a bit of my own family history, the term *pigeon* suddenly seemed to me very appropriate for what happens in Alcoholics Anonymous. My father, as a boy, had raised pigeons — real ones — and I recalled his telling me, when I was a young child and would chase the pigeons in the park, how to catch one. You had to walk slowly and directly toward the pigeon, he claimed, rather than making any sudden move or seeming to be trying to entrap it. And if you ever caught one — which, as you can imagine, I never did — you had to hold it firmly but gently, enveloping it with the warmth of your hands until it became calm, and perhaps even making a cooing sound so that the pigeon would accept that you identified with it and meant it no harm.

My dad did not say "identified," of course, but that surely does capture the idea of what he meant, as I remember it. And I do know that recalling that image and that memory helped me overcome my own aversion to the term *pigeon*, although I am not sure it much helped Pete last night.

Sam took us off in another direction then, reminding both of us that if "pigeon" can be an at times misunderstood word, so also, and perhaps ever more so, can the term *sponsor*. In most non-A.A. settings, he pointed out, a sponsor is someone who proposes you for membership, vouching for the uprightness of your character. That was not, Pete and I allowed to Sam's chuckles, exactly how either we or most other A.A.s we met had become members of Alcoholics Anonymous.

Yet, I was reminded, a hint of that understanding did inhere in at least one aspect of A.A.'s original use of the concept and term *sponsor*. Back in the early years, especially in Akron and Cleveland, some A.A. groups saw that a drunk needing hospitalization received it. That was in the days before treatment programs and even health insurance as we know it. And, of course, given the financial condition of most active alcoholics by the time they hit bottom, hospitalization was available only when someone promised to pick up the bill — someone other than the alcoholic. The people who ran the hospitals were not dumb.

And so the idea and term *sponsor* came into use because some already sober A.A. member who was in good enough financial condition to do so would stand the bill for treatment, hoping to get repaid those dollars after the newcomer finally got on his own feet economically. None of them, of course, was very well off in those years. It was the era of the Great Depression, and thus, what the economy was suffering added to the burden of those early alcoholics' own pasts when it came to trying to get jobs even after they got sober. In such circumstances, the sponsor tried to be very sure that someone who asked for help really wanted it — truly was "willing to go to any length." The earliest sponsors thus served a sort of screening function, although the screening had more to do with getting into the hospital than with getting into Alcoholics Anonymous.

But there is yet another and a more profound way in which sponsorship, as it has evolved within A.A., differs from the usual understanding of the term. In most other groups, sponsors retain a kind of responsibility for the behavior of those whom they have proposed. Because the sponsors chose the members, that responsibility can at times become a burden. In A.A. the exact opposite holds true: it is the newcomer who chooses his or her sponsor. Any member is always free to choose another sponsor, and the sponsor takes on that responsibility primarily as a way of keeping himself or herself sober. Those understandings combine to render A.A. sponsorship more of a joy than a burden.

With sponsorship as with sobriety itself, A.A. tradition holds: attraction, not promotion. Sponsors are guiding beacons — they do not push, they pull. And perhaps that understanding sheds further light back on the image inherent in the correlative term, *pigeon*.

In a way, it strikes me that training pigeons — at least, carrier pigeons — is not unlike sponsoring alcoholics. Alcoholics, especially in early recovery, are easily distracted; their courage can too easily flag. Further, recovering alcoholics also have, in a sense, two homes. When we were drinking, we always solved our problems or celebrated our joys by flying toward booze. That urge, however latent, remains always with us, even in sobriety.

But sobriety within A.A., in a way, means learning that we have another home, a different place where we truly belong: A.A. As newcomers, then, we are sort of in training: we must learn about our new home, Alcoholics Anonymous. And sponsors help us do that — not so much by training, but by showing the way, by helping us to find and to feel at home by their own example.

Living in the middle — having both a sponsor and a pigeon — offers many occasions for growth, for deepening my own understanding of sobriety.

36

. . . Grant that I may not so much seek to be consoled as to console; to be understood as to understand; to be loved as to love; for it is in giving that we receive. . . .

— The St. Francis Prayer

I THINK AND FEEL THAT SLOWLY I AM BEGINNING to learn something very important. Yet I am finding it difficult to put into words. It has to do with understanding, and especially with my own sense of being understood.

Countless old cartoons and not-really-funny jokes immediately rush to mind — the bleary-eyed drunk telling a bored bartender or stunningly vacuous companion: "Nobody really understands me" or "My wife doesn't really understand me." That scene is deemed funny, it seems to me, because it lays bare in caricature two human tragedies: that of the alcoholic, and that of the human being.

The bite of the drinking alcoholic's pathos is that no one can understand, at least not in the sense of the word that the active alcoholic demands. No one understands alcoholism. But that "understanding" is what the active alcoholic thinks — albeit unconsciously — that he deeply wants. We crave understanding of our alcoholism when we are drinking, I believe, because our deepest fear and the thing we seek at all costs to avoid is ourselves being understood.

The human tragedy is that to be human is to need understanding. I seem to recall someone once describing "what it was like": "I sometimes think that life is nothing but a generally futile search for at least one other person who really understands." The tragic aspect of that need is that the pressure of its claims tends to confuse us as to its meaning. To need understanding means first not the demand to be understood, but rather the requirement inherent in our being to understand. We need to understand — perhaps especially to understand ourselves.

Let me try to come upon this from another direction. We want and need not so much to be understood as the sense that we are understood. But the only way to attain that sense is by ourselves understanding. And we achieve understanding not of ourselves, directly, but by seeking to understand others — others with whom we identify.

Identification opens the door to two-way understanding; and two-way understanding is the only understanding, for understanding is by its nature mutual. Although the cliche only begins to capture the truth hidden here, as with so many of life's most precious realities, "you can't have one without the other."

One facet of A.A.'s bountiful genius appears precisely here. The alcoholic comes to Alcoholics Anonymous hoping to be understood. At first, of course, often to his or her surprise and frustration, A.A. does very little listening to the newcomer. The newly-arrived alcoholic rather is told, "Don't take the first drink, one day at a time, and go to meetings." At those meetings, the alcoholic hears the stories of other alcoholics, and hears also the frequent reminder, "Identify, don't compare."

What happens within the newly dry alcoholic as he or she tries to do that? It seems to me, from my own experience, that two processes are going on within us during those first few weeks or months. Both involve head and heart, and the relationship between them — but in a way that strikingly reverses what some outside observer might imagine to be taking place.

First, I think that inevitably and perhaps even instinctively, we begin listening with our heads — "comparing" in the sense that we look for external things that we hope will signal that the speaker might understand me. "After all," we think, "how can anyone who has not lost wife or career or done whatever I have done understand me?" Slowly, over more or less time, but certainly, through hearing many stories that describe tellingly "what we were like, what happened, and what we are like now," slowly we begin to understand that what we are really listening for and hoping to hear are not occurrences or events, but feelings. We move, then, to listening with our hearts more than with our heads — to the identification with feelings that marks the beginning of true identification.

But that, I think, is only the first phase of the beautiful process that is A.A.: identification by telling our stories. At the same time or slightly later but on a far deeper level, we are moving in a strangely opposite yet parallel direction on our pilgrimage toward sobriety. What I mean by that, I think, is that although we begin identifying in the hope of finding understanding in the sense of being understood, slowly the feeling develops within us that we are among people who can — and do, perhaps — somewhat understand us. The deepening of the initial acceptance, "I am an alcoholic, just like them," seems to signal this phase of our beginning passage from mere dryness to true sobriety.

But that is only the beginning. It seems to me that as our hearts find warmth, as our deepest feelings begin to become engaged in the ongoing process of identification, our minds at some point suddenly leap back into action: we attain what some psychologists term "the Aha! experience."

The "Aha!" — I think — consists of the insight, usually sudden but always profound, that the point of all this identification is not the sense, "I am understood," but the realization, "I understand." We see as if brilliantly lighted the two-sidedness of the understanding that we have always craved. And we embrace in that vision the reality that, in a way, our whole active alcoholic lives had been devoted to denying: one gets understanding by understanding. We attain the sense of being understood, that is to say, by being understanding. And that means, it seems to me, that we discover through experience the vital connection between head and heart.

I doubt that I have set down well here what I both feel and think on this topic of understanding. But I think that my idea — what I am at least reaching for — involves the profound reality so elegantly set forth in those familiar words we know as part of The St. Francis Prayer.

> . . . Grant that I may not so much seek to be consoled as to console; *to be understood as to understand;* to be loved as to love; for it is in giving that we receive. . . .

37

. . . The consequence of willing what cannot be willed is that we fall into the distress we call anxiety . . . . drugs offer [relief from anxiety by providing] the illusion of healing the split between the will and its refractory object.

— Leslie Farber

LAST NIGHT'S MEETING TOPIC WAS "FREEdom." Freedom is, we are told, the great gift of the A.A. way of life. But what does that mean? How does the A.A. way of life free us?

Obviously, freedom has to do with choice. I have today a freedom to choose that I did not have when I was drinking: I am free to choose not to drink alcohol. Every member of A.A., everyone who has ever experienced the obsession or compulsion to drink, knows the glory of that freedom.

But how free, ultimately, is my choice? I know that I am not free to choose to drink alcohol safely. The story told last night by that returning slippee reminds me that I probably am not free to stay sober without going to meetings. I have learned, over the years — and that learning certainly is being reinforced now in doing this ninety/ninety — that I must make some correct choices, if I am to preserve my freedom to choose and perhaps even to grow in it.

What are correct choices? The experience of alcoholism and recovery seems to teach that a choice is correct if it opens up rather than closes off opportunities for further human choices. If I should choose to drink alcohol, I may begin with a choice between scotch and bourbon, but that will be the last choice I will be capable of making for some time — perhaps forever. If I choose to attend an A.A. meeting, my choice opens up further choices in such areas as honesty, caring, and sharing.

The nature of choice, the significance of freedom: these concepts have baffled philosophers over the centuries. They involve the meaning of human will. Thinking about recent reading I have done, my experience of sobriety within A.A. seems to fit the understanding of human will set forth by Dr. Leslie Farber.

According to Dr. Farber, there are two realms, two areas or arenas, in which my will, and therefore my choice, operates and can have impact. In the vocabulary of A.A., there are the things I must work on and the things I must let go. The distinction seems reflected in the Serenity Prayer: it is the difference between what I can change directly, with courage, and what I cannot change directly and therefore must in some way accept.

In Farber's terms, those two kinds of reality are "the realm of objects" and "the realm of directions." I can choose objects directly. I can, for example, choose to use pen or pencil in writing this entry, or I can choose to use one word rather than another in trying to make my meaning exact and clear. Directions, on the contrary, I cannot choose directly. Any attempt to do so, to treat them as if they were objects like pens or pencils, renders them less accessible and perhaps even destroys them — at least such attempts tend to destroy the possibility of my ever attaining them.

Examples may clarify. One that Farber suggests holds special meaning for me: "I can will directly to go to bed, but not to fall asleep." In the early years of my drinking, as now on occasion, I knew and know the experience of going to bed and wanting to go to sleep but being unable to fall asleep. When I was drinking, I turned to booze to help me. One painful illusion of mind-altering chemicals is that they seem to turn directions into objects. In our drinking, we believe that we are able to will, for example, to go to sleep.

That is, of course, not only illusion but almost diabolically treacherous fallacy. Alcoholic oblivion is not sleep. And even to obtain the stupor of unconsciousness, of course, the dosage must be progressively increased. Our bodies seem to know the limits of our wills, even if our minds attempt to deny or strive to circumvent those limits. "Tolerance" and "progression" are not unfamiliar terms and concepts to those who attend A.A. meetings and listen carefully to the stories told there.

Today, freed from my bondage to the false and destructive promises of chemicals and alcohol, I still, on occasion, have difficulty falling asleep. But I know, because I have learned the hard way, that the solution to that situation is not to try to fall asleep. Trying directly to will myself to sleep is the surest way I know to remain wide awake. Instead, then, I choose to exercise during the day and to relax just before going to bed. Usually, that indirect willing of direction rather than object proves sufficient, and most nights I fall asleep promptly.

On those occasions when I do not, I sometimes think of the A.A. parallel to Farber's "two realms of the will." We do not "take the pledge" in Alcoholics Anonymous — sobriety, too, is a direction rather than an object. I can will directly not to take the first drink, one day at a time; I cannot will directly to attain or to grow in the A.A. way of life. I can choose directly to go to a meeting or to work on the Sixth Step; I cannot choose directly to eliminate my defects of character, as the wording of that Step itself reminds me.

It seems, in brief, that I can directly will dryness, but not sobriety. If I choose sobriety, then, it is by choosing to live the way of life that leads in its direction. And I do that by willing the "objects" that do that: going to meetings and talking with other A.A.s, continuing to take personal inventory and when I am wrong promptly admitting it, engaging in prayer and meditation, and especially seeking out opportunities to carry the message to other alcoholics.

But I cannot directly will sobriety, any more than I can directly choose sleep or love or wisdom or virtue. The best things in life, it seems, if not exactly free, do come only by letting go. At times, of course, we can even try too hard — too directly — to let go. It is not mere truism to observe that "letting go" means "letting go," as I suspect anyone who has worked on the Sixth and Seventh Steps will agree.

I was reminded of that the other day, while watching a four-year-old at the county fair with his father. Several children had obtained balloons apparently filled with weak helium: they rose barely, almost imperceptibly, but they did rise if loosed gently. Soon a game developed among the children, a sort of slow-motion balloon race — each child blowing or fanning upwards, trying to make his or her balloon rise faster and farther than the others.

The boy I noticed caught my attention because he saw the fun and wanted to join in, but as a latecomer, he was starting at a disadvantage. To make up for that, he tried to play catch-up by throwing his balloon into the air. His very effort of course defeated his own purpose. Each time he hurled his balloon upwards, the resistance of the air pushed it back at him. The harder he tried to throw it, the quicker the bright green sphere rushed back at him.

"Were entirely ready" and "humbly asked," read the operative words of A.A.'s Sixth and Seventh Steps. When I forget that, I become far more foolish than that little boy. He, after all, was only four. And I . . . will I ever learn?

38

The mediocre teacher tells. The good teacher explains. The superior teacher demonstrates. The great teacher inspires.

— William Arthur Ward

LAST NIGHT, I RETURNED TO THE GROUP whose adherence to basics has so inspired me several times previously during this ninety/ninety. "Rough-hewn rustics shaped by profound sobriety," I had once rhapsodically characterized them: "dedicated to the fundamentals, but knowing and living that the fundamentals are but where you begin."

Sometimes, my self-image as intelligent and sophisticated can get in the way of my sobriety, so I guess my main gratitude to that group is that I always come away feeling that I have learned so much from them. I walk in expecting and needing A.A. love. I get that love from that group. But it seems to me that the most important thing I usually get from their meeting is some new and fruitful way of looking at and thinking about our shared journey in sobriety. I really love those guys, but I think I love and respect them most of all because they teach me so much, so well.

Last night's lesson was not exactly a new one, as A.A. topics go, but it somehow became new for me. When old John launched forth in his deep, weather-beaten voice, extolling the importance of becoming teachable, just about everybody in the room, no matter how often they might have heard that before, seemed to get drawn into a unique kind of identification with him.

John is simple in the best sense of that much maligned word. He doesn't just elicit identification: he seems to suck identification out of each listener, to create not only an atmosphere of sharing but the sense that you can almost see the bonds of healing identification stretching across that table.

Perhaps because I have been a teacher, the theme "becoming teachable" rarely impresses me. I must confess to having too often felt, on hearing that topic, that I already knew all about it. In one sense, I did: John did not impart any new information to me last night. Yet somehow, John managed to say more than everything I had ever heard before about that wondrous quality, "being teachable."

A.A. is more than learning: but because its way of life involves and expresses a way of thinking, we need to be teachable if we are to live and to grow in that way of life. It is all too easy, I suspect, for teachers to wax eloquent about being teachable. John's eloquence was of a different sort: his very presence at meetings, obviously learning even as he exudes profound sobriety, seems to make everyone who sees him as well as those fortunate enough to hear him want to learn more about thinking and living the A.A. way.

What was it he started with last night? The discussion topic was the difference between accepting responsibility for our difficulties and blaming them on others. "Alcoholics like to play 'falling leaf,' " one of the earlier contributors had observed. "The wind or something else is always moving us around. And we have a way of all too easily discovering that we need what we want." Then John lumbered into the discussion, describing how even though he had never needed a reason to drink, he had always seemed to find one.

"Well," he went on, "when I finally became teachable, which I learned by sitting around these tables and listening to what you people said, I learned that you were trying to teach me that I, John, and my drinking — John's drinking — had an awful lot to do with causing most of what I thought were my problems. You taught me that John's main problem was John — John who drank like an alcoholic, John who thought like a drinking alcoholic, because that's what John was, an alcoholic.

"Now I didn't like that very much. No siree, I did not like hearing that at all. If anybody else had tried to tell it to me — as in fact a few had, before I found A.A. — well, I just figured that anybody who said that did not really understand poor old John and all his troubles. But you people taught me that in a sneaky way. You did not try to tell me about John; you told me about yourselves, as alcoholics, about Tom and Mike and Ken and Angie and Margaret and Frank. And somehow, your telling me about you made me teachable about me.

"Never in my life have I believed what anybody else told me about me. Maybe that's why I never got very smart. It seemed to me, all my life, because it still seems to me, that anybody who tells me what I need is either trying to sell me something or to get me out of their own way. Now I don't exactly think I am paranoid — it just seems clear to me that that is how this world works. Beware anyone who tells you what's good for you.

"And so it was fortunate for me, for my sobriety, that you people did not try to do that. Instead, you told me what was good and bad for you. I do not know how it worked, except that, of course, it is part of "How It Works," but your doing that made me for the first time in my life teachable. That's what A.A. means to me: becoming teachable, and especially teachable about John. Because it seems to me that sobriety's great task is the same as life's own adventure, now that I am sober: getting to know John and learning about John and maybe even learning to love John instead of trying to run away from him or to drown him in booze."

John's excursus on being teachable reminded me of another word: *docile*. It is sad, I think, that no one would ever think of referring to crusty old John as docile.

"Docile" is another of those words that have been stolen from us . . . like "sober" and "virtue" and so many others. There seems little room in a society that expects chemicals to solve its problems and to make life worth living for terms that signify strength that is not oppressive or letting go that is not cowardly.

It sometimes seems to me that in A.A. we recapture a precious heritage — perhaps precisely the one that we ourselves most squandered by our own alcoholic drinking. We lay hold of the healing ideas that we scorned while drinking and that even most nonalcoholics seem to reject. Words transmit healing ideas because they embody the way of thinking that helps to make us whole. The A.A. mottoes especially seem to do that, in all their simplicity. "Easy does it" and "First things first" are less truisms than reminders of profound truths generally lost.

And of those truths, of course, John's lesson last night most importantly teaches and reminds me that "Keep it simple" seems to heal me best. Simplicity is perhaps the most basically important concept generally scorned and therefore too often utterly lost. To recognize the depths of wisdom in A.A.'s simplicity is, I sometimes think, the first real sign of true sobriety.

That lesson, that truth, is very important to me because of the error I once fell into, the mistake that so many outside A.A. or very new to its program stumble over — trying to match minds in order to promote identification. Too often, since I have been in Alcoholics Anonymous, well-meaning friends who knew of my background and interests encouraged me to go to meetings attended by people whose interests were as intellectually aimed as my own. And for far too long, when I first came round, I lapsed into that too-ready trap.

But now I am learning the deeper truth that I long suspected: if the identification that heals us comes on the level of our being alcoholics, then we find that identification best by not cluttering up our sense of sharing with such accidental things as education or life-style. If anything, especially for someone like me, I best find what my drinking lost — my very humanity — in the humanity of others who are superficially very different from me. That surface difference better serves the deeper identification. I now also understand an oldtimer's comment that puzzled me when I first heard it — Ben's musing that, at times, he could learn more about the A.A. way of life from truly sober young people than from wizened and wise oldtimers who were too much like himself.

What I seem to find growing in my own "becoming teachable," just now, is my ability to learn from many different A.A. groups, from many varied expressions of the A.A. way of life. But there is more even to that. An ancient proverb admonishes: "If you would learn, teach." Alcoholics Anonymous is of course the ultimate teacher of the way of life to which we aspire. But because we ourselves *are* Alcoholics Anonymous, I must give at those meetings if I am also truly to receive from them. There are no observers in A.A.: we participate, or we die. And so I do participate: I do try to give. I only hope that I do it — that I teach — one-tenth as well as John.

39

I don't know who he was, but I wanted to thank him.

— Cliche often remarked about the Lone Ranger

SOMETHING RARE OCCURRED LAST NIGHT — two things, in fact: an actively drinking alcoholic crashed our meeting, and there fell to me the task of calming a dry newcomer's upset over that fact.

By "actively drinking," I mean actively drinking: "Bub" or "Bob" as he tried to call himself, had a pint in his pocket; and, as the meeting progressed, he took swigs from it. The group, I thought, handled the situation well. But at least one other visitor obviously disagreed with my assessment. Partially because everyone else was fairly busy, partially because carrying the message means many things to me, but mostly — I suspect — because my Higher Power saw an opportunity to teach me something, I suggested to Dan, the shaken newcomer, that we stop and chat over coffee on the way home.

Dan was more than willing. He also proved far soberer than I had guessed, at least after he calmed down. Thinking back on our conversation, I suspect that I have still more to learn from it. Let me, therefore, set it down as best as I remember its main points.

"That was something I had never seen before, nor even imagined," Dan exclaimed as we were served our sherbet. "I can hardly believe that someone would come to an A.A. meeting not only drunk but drinking. Why, he had a pint in his pocket!"

"Yes," I acknowledged, "he sure did. And that brown bag brought back some memories. But tell me, what did you think of how the group handled the situation? Let me make that two and maybe even four questions: what did you think and how did you feel when it happened; and what do you think and how do you feel now, a couple of hours later?"

"Good questions," Dan said and paused. "My first reaction when that drunk walked in, I have to admit, was revulsion, anger, resentment, and perhaps even some fear. My first thought, very honestly, was that I wanted to see him thrown out, because he did not belong at an A.A. meeting. I am still not sure that I was wrong on the last point: after all, isn't the only requirement for membership a desire to stop drinking? It is hard for me to believe that someone carrying a jug has any desire to stop drinking. That drunk just did not belong at an A.A. meeting in his condition."

"Didn't he?" I asked, trying to sound wiser than I felt. "It was an open meeting, Dan. That means, I think, that one does not have to be a member to attend. What is the purpose of open meetings? Don't we have them, at least partially, so that some who are unsure whether or not they want to join A.A. can learn more about us, and therefore about themselves?

"In fact," I continued, "I find it hard to believe that any drunk does not belong at any A.A. meeting. What were any of us, the day we first walked through that door? Oh, sure: most of us had enough pride and sophistication — and probably denial — that we tried to come at least fairly dry. But to say that a drunk doesn't belong at Alcoholics Anonymous? I will never buy that. For one thing, as I am sure you have heard, we in A.A. cannot promise to stop someone's drinking, but we sure can promise to louse it up.

"I think that means that no matter how resistant most of us are when we first come around, somehow we do hear something that sparks at least a scintilla of identification. For many, that is the first tiny step that enables at least the beginning of getting honest. But I am firmly convinced that no alcoholic who has ever been exposed to Alcoholics Anonymous by hearing our stories as we tell them on Twelfth-Step calls and at meetings can ever again be or think in exactly the same way as before that experience."

Dan had listened patiently. Why must I get so preachy? I thought. "You are right, of course," he acknowledged. "But let me turn to your second question — my feelings. I mentioned feeling revulsion, anger, resentment, and perhaps even some fear.

"I realize now that although I felt the revulsion and fear deeply, those feelings were good for me. The very presence of that drunk hit me right between the eyes with 'Remember when.' I have never come to an A.A. meeting that drunk, but I did get that drunk — and when I did, I know I did quite a few things worse that going to an A.A. meeting, not to mention the things I do not remember doing. And even when I did go to A.A. meetings dry, at times my thinking was as stubbornly stinking as that poor drunk's boozy body was tonight.

"I guess, in a way, that my revulsion and anger and fear were directed at myself — and not so much at what I was like in the past as at what I would become if ever I try to graduate from A.A. In fact, if — God help me — I ever do try to graduate, I only hope and pray that I live long enough and have even the drunken insight and courage to do what that drunk did tonight — drag my butt back to A.A. in any way and in any condition that I am lucky enough to be in."

Dan's last comment hit me squarely. There I was, playing "older, wiser, soberer," when obviously he had identified with the meeting's unexpected visitor better than I had thought of doing. With newcomers especially, we talk a lot about a sort of upward identification: the less sober identifying with the more sober. But I suddenly realized that downward identification might be even more potent. In fact, thinking on it, I sort of wonder, looking at A.A., which is more miraculous, more beautiful: that a drinking alcoholic catches a glimpse of himself in a sober alcoholic, or that a sober alcoholic recognizes himself in a drinking alcoholic? That too, after all, is the identification that keeps us sober; and clearly Dan had received more of it than I at the meeting we had just left.

"In hindsight," my new-found teacher interrupted my reverie, "in hindsight, at least, I am grateful. You know, I think even my brief flare-up of resentment was directed at myself: how could that drunk dare to come to A.A. in that condition, when I had never done so? I guess I did think, momentarily, that his presence might ruin my meeting. Would that all my resentments were so quickly turned around.

"Anyway, tell me: what happened to him? I saw him stagger in, just as the meeting started, and I saw one of the home members of that group look as frightened as I felt for a moment, but then guide him to a chair. Maybe he should have stayed with him, because as soon as that member left to perform some chore or other, the drunk began first to mutter out loud and then to talk back to the speaker.

"But what happened then, after the others came over to the drunk and took him away? I know they did not throw him out, because I still saw him sitting at the table with that small group when we left. What were they doing and what will they do now — take him to a hospital or something? I guess he must have driven to the meeting, but I cannot imagine anyone in that group letting him drive home by himself — at least not until they and their loved ones are all safely in. I wonder what a cop would think if he picked that guy up for D.U.I. and the drunk told him he was on his way home from an A.A. meeting."

Dan's last concern caused me to chuckle. I refrained from telling him that I had recognized at least four police friends in the meeting. Instead, I assured him: "To start with your last worry, most of the police around here know quite a bit about A.A., so you don't have to worry about our image. But that won't happen, because you are right: no one in his right mind would let that drunk drive.

"I honestly do not know what they will do, Dan. You saw the cluster at that table: apparently they were ready to sit up with him right there all night, if that seemed indicated. As always in tight moments in A.A., the group conscience will guide them. They may choose the hospital: Ray, who was sitting there, works in that program. Or they may try to take him home, if he has one; or they may just sit up with him so long as he seems to need that kind of care. All I am sure of is that whatever they do, they will do it out of identification and compassion, because as good A.A.s they identify with and truly care for all alcoholics, drinking or sober, hurting or happy."

"But how would a group have handled that in different circumstances, a smaller meeting or a smaller room?" Dan asked.

By now, I was comfortable pleading ignorance — up to a point. "I really do not know, Dan: except that I am pretty sure that there are very few, if any, A.A. groups whose 'group conscience' would allow them just to throw a drunk out. Our first obligation, of course, is to the meeting — to those recovering alcoholics gathered to grow in their own sobriety.

"A.A. groups may decide differently how to carry their message in such a circumstance, but I am pretty sure that if it is an A.A. group, that principle will guide its members. Tonight, I think, was a pretty good example."

It had gotten late; it was time to go. I doubt that I will ever forget that A.A. meeting, that visitor, and the conversation with Dan afterwards.

And then we went our separate ways. Today, I still feel gratitude — not only to Alcoholics Anonymous but to that poor anonymous drunk who literally graced our meeting with his presence, and perhaps especially to Dan, who helped me to discover depths of gratitude in an experience that I might, by myself, have seen as mere curiosity or spectacle.

40

The Sacred is revealed to us in the experience of our failure. Religion is indeed the awareness of human insufficiency, it is the lived admission of failure.

— Leszek Kolakowski

The chiefest [sic] sanctity of a temple is that it is a place to which men go to weep in common. . . . Yes, we must learn to weep! Perhaps that is the supreme wisdom.

— Miguel de Unamuno

SO OFTEN, THE WORD *RELIGION*, OR WORDS having to do with religion, make me bridle. I suspect that the problem lies within me rather than with them. My mind seems to light on those words, almost as if seeking combat. Serenity, if it means anything, would seem to suggest that I be more open-minded.

The above quotations help, and I think they are related: each sheds light on the other. In the A.A. fellowship, through the program that is the A.A. way of life, I have seen the depth of the riches of the beauty enabled by "the awareness of human insufficiency" and especially by "the lived admission of failure."

As members of A.A., even if we have taken only the First Step of the A.A. program, we acknowledge our insufficiency, our failure to be able to drink alcohol safely, as some others do. A.A.'s genius sometimes seems to me to lie in the fact that it condemns neither the alcoholic nor alcohol, despite our insufficiency.

A.A. does not condemn the alcoholic because A.A. is made up of alcoholics. Our awareness of our insufficiency, our lived admission of our failure, is thus for us the mainspring of hope rather than a source of shame or guilt. Many others, before A.A. came into being, had the same insight. But in their acceptance of and love for the alcoholic, they often condemned alcohol.

That did not work, it seems to me, mainly because it ultimately denied human insufficiency and failure. No one feels insufficient and thus comes to realize human insufficiency because he or she cannot drink carbolic acid safely. We need, if we are to live the profound admission of human failure, the reminder that others do succeed where we fail. A.A.'s approach of not condemning our culture's use of alcohol confirms the reality of our failure.

For we are failures, at least in the sense that to be human is to fail. Sartre wrote: "Man is the being who wants to be God." But we are not God. And because we are limited, because we are failures, we weep. How does that — and the quotation from Miguel de Unamuno — relate to Alcoholics Anonymous? The A.A. fellowship, after all, is not a sad place: it offers far more laughs than tears. Still, Alcoholics Anonymous does afford us a place to go when, as we all sometimes do in one way or another, we need to weep — when we need to know that there are others who understand and share our hurt, when we need to be with others who are aware and accepting of our human insufficiency because they participate in the same insufficiency, in the same "lived admission of failure."

There is weeping in every life. Sometimes, I think the greatest difference between "what we were like" and "what we are like now" has to do with the things we wept over then and those that we weep over now. And with whether we weep alone or, as Unamuno suggests, we weep "in common."

When I was drinking, I always wept alone, even if others were present. I remember what it was like when I wept — or, more accurately, bawled and blubbered — alone, when I was drinking: I sniveled in rage, in frustration, and most of all in self-pity. Perhaps that is the greatest penalty as well as the greatest pain of weeping alone: the certainty that no one understands because, if we weep alone, how can anyone understand?

Today, I do not weep often. But when I do, when I need to, I am grateful that I can truly weep rather than only childishly bawl. That I can weep at all, Unamuno reminds me, is a precious gift. An even greater gift is that, when I do need to weep, I need not do so alone.

Every member of A.A., it seems to me, has discovered the two truths signaled by those quotations. We daily live out their reality — by whatever name. Religion and weeping are not, for many of us, pleasant names, pleasant words. That is not, I suspect, the fault of the words. As valuable as all my experience, strength, and hope are to my sobriety, not all of my experience contributes to the growth in sobriety that the A.A. way of life requires. At least it does not unless I reevaluate that experience from the perspective of that way of life.

Within A.A., I have learned to think differently about many realities concerning which I used to think, when I was drinking, that I already knew everything. Sometimes, that means thinking of things by different names: what used to be righteous indignation, for example, I now recognize as resentment; what I used to term my people-skills, I now more often than not call the manipulation that signals alcoholic stinking thinking. And, I suppose, in some sense and to some extent, I now call spiritual at least part of what I used to reject as religious; I am also still uncomfortable about weeping, but I have learned the importance of being honest about my feelings of pain.

Is that enough: name-changing? Perhaps; it does seem to help and to work. But might there be more, more that might work better in helping my growth in sobriety, if I asked for help in letting go of my character defect of being a narrow-minded know-it-all on some topics — and perhaps especially on the topic of religion?

Because this journal is turning out to be a kind of meditation, and because I therefore try in thinking and writing it to be open to the presence of my Higher Power, the answer seems clear. As I once heard a fairly sober A.A. member challenge a potential slippee: "What is a nice controlled drinker like you doing here, at a meeting of Alcoholics Anonymous?" My Higher Power seems to be saying to me now: "What is a really smart know-it-all like you doing here, meditating on quotations about religion and weeping?"

I am almost glad that I have no easy answers, that I seem to have to wrestle with such topics. That which is valuable does not come easily. Clearly, however, I need to be more open-minded, and on a wider variety of topics.

Recently, I rediscovered the meaning of "being teachable." Within Alcoholics Anonymous, I think, I am teachable — but A.A. is a way of life more than it is a series of meetings. It seems, then, that I still need to become teachable. And so I hope and pray, if it be my Higher Power's will, that my ninety/ninety be used by my Higher Power to help me grow in that quality.

What does it say in the appendix of *The Big Book* — say in flaming italics? *Willingness, honesty, and open-mindedness are the essentials of recovery. But these are indispensable."* The time has come, I think, to apply the Sixth and Seventh Steps of what I sometimes too glibly call "my program" to this topic, lest I lose my program, and thus fail in my recovery.

41

What is real or unreal to us is a matter of practical, rather than philosophical, commitment; the real is what people really crave for.

— Leszek Kolakowski

SOMETIMES WHEN PEOPLE IN A.A. TALK ABOUT the difficulty they have in accepting "a Power greater than ourselves," I find it difficult to identify. At other times, I seem to understand perfectly what they mean.

Most of us, when we were drinking, had a profound faith: a blind belief in the power of alcohol to solve our problems. What, after all, is "a Power greater than ourselves" or a "Higher Power"? Is it not that to which we turn for help in times of difficulty? And did not alcohol at one time, however briefly, hold that place in our lives? For many of us, booze was our higher power. And we did believe — with an awesome faith: how else can we explain those final, tortured months when we turned to booze no matter how it had turned on us, when our denial blinded us to its all-too-evident destruction of our very humanity? If all faith is terrible, our belief in alcohol was surely a true faith.

I do remember when. As an adolescent, I was painfully shy. But a drink allowed me not only to ask a girl for a date: a few more drinks even turned my stumbling clumsiness into dance-floor wizardry. Or, at least, so I thought; but at best, that perception was only partially true.

A bit later in my life, after graduation and entry into the work force, a drink helped me when I had to meet new people or confront a difficult situation. And after work, another drink or two helped me to relax. Booze . . . my miraculous helper. Today's advertisements furnish an effective reminder of the power of my higher power of alcohol. One might almost think, watching the television commercials shown during sporting events, that all sociability and friendliness derive from booze.

Somewhere along the line, of course, at least for those of us who are alcoholics, booze as a higher power turned on us with a vengeance that makes the Puritan preacher's portrayal of the wrath of God seem mild indeed. Booze proves this theological truism: That which saves can also damn. And just so our higher power of alcohol did damn us to the living hell of alcoholism.

But then what happened? One of two things, it seems: and it is because there can be two understandings of the source and therefore of the nature of our sobriety that confusion seems to reign whenever we try to talk, soberly and seriously, about our Higher Power.

For some of us, it was "the true God" — a real Higher Power — that saved us from our alcoholism. For others "salvation" came when we realized that no power could save us from the reality of ourselves, that living life meant seeking neither refuge, nor escape, nor help from chemical crutches.

Can these two diverse points of view, these two very different understandings of sobriety, be reconciled? Ultimately, probably not; but must we think in ultimates? We seem to have a tendency to demand ultimate answers. A.A. recognizes this, and helps us to overcome it by teaching us to live "one day at a time." Another apt reminder might run: "one truth at a time."

It seems to me that there are two more proximate truths on which we can agree — two more immediate realizations on which we can more practically found our sobriety. They have less to do with what our Higher Power is than with what any power greater than ourselves is not. As such, these truths are simple — even obvious. But the A.A. way of life seems to suggest that we need to be reminded of them and to think on them often. Perhaps that is why it seems appropriate that the ultimate question about the existence of God can never be answered within A.A. If it could, then we would lose an effective, constant reminder of those other two very important truths.

The first truth, one with which I trust any member of A.A. will agree, is that booze — alcohol — is not our Higher Power. Its capacity to save us is destroyed. We know and admit and accept alcohol's power over us, but doing that renders us free from its domain rather than subservient to its sway. As sober A.A.s, we neither honor nor dread booze: we simply no longer need it, in any way. With that simple knowledge, we shatter the myth of its power over us. A Higher Power that is not needed is no Higher Power at all.

The second truth on which we all agree is a trifle more complex: it has, in a sense, two parts. Most baldly stated as witnessed by our membership in A.A., I am not my own Higher Power, because I do need some reality outside of myself — the fellowship of Alcoholics Anonymous — in order even to be myself. As *The Big Book* reminds us, we liked to play God when we were drinking. "First of all," then, "we had to quit playing God" (p. 62). Many, of course, have said that. It is in the sentence immediately following that A.A.'s genius shines: "It didn't work."

We used to think that we were in control. The very concept of "alcoholic," as set forth by Alcoholics Anonymous, shatters that falsehood — the myth of self-control. How do we differ from at least some outside the A.A. fellowship? We know that we are not God. We have had the privilege of proving that fact.

A deep truth lies hidden in the lesson we have learned: power has to do less with control than with need. Our Higher Power, then, is not that which controls us, but that which we need. "The real," one modern philosopher has suggested, "is what people really crave for." The ultimately real, then, is that for which all people ultimately crave: and that is "spirit," however understood, rather than "spirits," however distilled. We need some reality that is somehow outside and beyond the self rather than self however extended or glorified.

Any addiction — alcoholism, for example — is spirituality . . . perverted spirituality. Our problem, when drinking, as Dr. Carl Jung knew, was not lack of spirituality but its perversion. Nor is "perversion" too strong a term for the phenomenon — the experience — of needing that which destroys our very being. The difference between "true" and "false" spirituality is very simple: does what we need fulfill or destroy our humanity?

We all need something. To be human is to need. In the fellowship of Alcoholics Anonymous, through the A.A. program, we learn to recognize and to evaluate our needs according to that criterion. In a sense, we choose our Higher Power whenever we admit and embrace our need. To need, then, is to have a Higher Power. Our choice as human is not whether or not we will have a Higher Power, but what that Higher Power will be. Because we are human, of course, there are false as well as true higher powers. Embracing a true Higher Power means acknowledging that we need that which we actually do need.

Members of Alcoholics Anonymous have understood, do understand, and will understand their Higher Power differently. It is one aspect of the genius of A.A. that its program invites and encourages that diversity. For the important points to learn, as alcoholic or as human, are that there are false higher powers and that we have to know how to recognize them. That which does for me and to me what booze did for me and to me is a false god. That which does for me and to me what my participation in Alcoholics Anonymous does for me and to me is a Higher Power worthy of my humanity — however I conceive of Him, or Her, or It.

42

Nietzsche had discovered the shadow, the underside of human nature, and he had correctly seen it as a side that is present inescapably in every human individual. But he converted this perception into a kind of romantic diabolism; it amused him to play at being wicked and daring. He would have been prepared to meet his own devil if this devil had appeared in some grandiose form.

Precisely what is hardest for us to take is the devil as the personification of the pettiest, paltriest, meanest part of our personality. Dostoevski understood this better than Nietzsche, and in that tremendous chapter of **The Brothers Karamazov** *where the devil appears to Ivan, . . . it is not in the guise of a dazzling Miltonic Lucifer or a swaggering operatic Mephistopheles, but rather of a faded, shabby-genteel person, a little out of fashion and ridiculous in his aestheticism — the perfect caricature of Ivan's own aesthetic mind.*

— William Barrett

BACK IN THE MISTY DAYS OF A.A.'S ORIGINS, when the first "One Hundred Men" still referred to themselves as "the alcoholic squadron of the Oxford Group," the same word was used to describe what later generations of A.A.s distinguish as "telling my story" and "taking my Fifth Step." That word was *sharing*.

Within the Oxford Group, members did differentiate between "sharing for witness" and "sharing for confession." Witnessing, of course, was story-telling, and confession involved the less public activity captured by A.A. in the Fifth Step of its program. But an important lesson lies buried in the earlier vocabulary: how the two practices of telling one's story and taking one's Fifth Step are related.

That relationship — that connection — is important. For as different as are the evident purposes of the two practices, a less obvious benefit also flows from them. Both teach an important lesson: the deep truth of the banality of all evil, and especially of our own evil.

A very wise person who has devoted much of his life to working with alcoholics mired in denial once observed that the problem of especially the intelligent alcoholic "is not that he feels, 'I am a worm'; nor that he thinks, 'I am very special'; the alcoholic's main problem is that he is convinced that 'I am a very special worm'."

That may sound clever: it is also profound. One aspect of alcoholic grandiosity, and perhaps the most perverse manifestation of human pride, consists in the conceit that one is able somehow to be uniquely wicked. There is nothing *mere* about any alcoholic. Alcoholics, as Bill W. often remarked, are "all or nothing people." Or at least we try to be and claim to be, even in what we recognize as our evil.

Sobriety — recovery from alcoholism — involves rejoining the human race. For most alcoholics, that is not an easy task. Because of the way alcohol affected us, we were different. No merit devolves from denying that. For whatever reason, probably some quirk of our biochemistry, alcohol affects alcoholics differently than it does nonalcoholics. That is simple, plain reality — whatever agonies we had to undergo before finally accepting that bald, bare fact.

In a sense, the drinking alcoholic attempts to deny his or her difference from nonalcoholics. The pitfall assumption that underlies that attempt seems to be the conviction that "different" somehow means "better" or "worse" — "more" or "less" — rather than simply "different." An alcoholic is simply a human being who reacts to alcohol differently than other human beings. That fact does not make the alcoholic better or worse any more than it makes him or her taller or shorter, smarter or dumber, sexier or plainer.

For the problem is not difference but comparison. Precisely as human beings, we are different — diverse in sex and sexuality, in height and skin color, in mathematical ability and musical aptitude and physical stamina. To be human is to be a unique combination of a virtually infinite congerie of innate abilities and disabilities, of environmental impacts, of choices made by ourselves, our parents, and others. But our differences as human beings have nothing to do with our value as human beings. Ultimately, each of us is simply human: in our very humanity, there are no differences.

This is perhaps the most profound lesson of being human. We pass a lifetime learning it, and some learn it only at the moment of death — the ultimate equalizer. One privilege of alcoholics, it seems, is that we are given the chance to learn it earlier. And, in the A.A. practices of telling our stories and taking our Fifth Step, we have powerful reminders of that truth first glimpsed when we hit bottom.

Those reminders work like this. Sometimes, outsiders visiting our speaker meetings or even potential members attending them complain that A.A. storytellers seem to engage in a contest of "Can you top this?" If one speaker tells of demolishing two cars, the next quietly describes three total wrecks — and perhaps one of them a truck or a train. Or the sequence of "bottoms" detailed might run from losing one's job to losing one's family to being jailed for theft to being imprisoned for a crime of violence. At some meetings, at times, one almost perversely longs to hear what new depths the next speaker might have plumbed, had not the meeting time expired.

But is this merely "Can you top this?" — garrulousness reminiscent of alcoholic drinking? I think not. In fact, I suspect that what really is going on is clarified by the related sharing that takes place in the practice of A.A.'s Fifth Step.

Imagine an experienced but in the ordinary sense simple A.A. Fifth-Step hearer. A relatively new member comes to him to "take his Fifth" and tells how, in the final four months of his drinking, he had stolen three cars. The veteran member senses a touch of awe in that confession, and so what ensues might run something like this:

— "What kind of cars were they?"

— "Oh, two old Chevies and a fairly new Pontiac."

— "Y'know, I heard a Fifth Step once: in the last two months of that guy's drinking he had hot-wired and cracked up six Caddies and a couple of Lincolns. Yeah, and he's sober today: still working on his Ninth Step, I'd guess, but not drinking and happily sober."

That is not "Can you top this?" It is rather the puncturing of the "very special worm" balloon with the artful dart of the banality of evil. The lesson of A.A.'s Fifth Step is the same as the message we hear if we listen attentively and with identification to A.A. stories: we are not very special because of anything we have done. We find, rather, that whatever we thought special about ourselves, if we will share it, we will find to be shared. Sharing inoculates against feeling special.

The word *sharing* has become debased in recent usage, but in terms familiar to the early members of Alcoholics Anonymous, because the practice of sharing punctures the illusion of specialness, it is the royal road to rejoining the human race. And that is the meaning of sobriety.

Today, in my own sobriety, I tend to prefer discussion to speaker meetings — perhaps because our common, shared humanity seems most evident around those tables. But once in a while, especially when I travel, my sobriety also gets nourished and polished on the occasions when I attend a meeting that features speakers.

"Remember when" means many things. It is good for me to remember the first meetings I attended, when identification came hard and comparison came all too easily. I learned to identify, partially, because the rich diversity of the detail of the stories I heard soon rendered comparison impossible. I learned, that is, that the point of listening could not be to judge better or worse: there had to be something else. That something else is what I have now — sobriety. It is good to be reminded of what I share with all other A.A. members . . . and to remember that I got there only by sharing.

43

Few people have been more victimized by resentments than have we alcoholics. . . . Anger, that occasional luxury of more balanced people, could keep us on an emotional jag indefinitely. These "dry benders" often led straight to the bottle.

— Bill W.

THE TOPIC LAST NIGHT WAS A PERENNIAL ONE around the tables at A.A. discussion meetings: resentment. We know that "Resentment is the Number One offender" in getting the alcoholic drunk again — *The Big Book* tells us so. And if we doubt that authority, there is usually someone around who has tested and proven its truth — and been fortunate enough to live to tell about it. We know also, from our own experience, that repressing anger led many of us on drinking bouts during our years of active alcoholism. "How dare they treat me like that? I'll show them!" That pattern may not have been all-pervasive, but it strikes a strong enough resonance in many of us that identification comes easily.

Well, at times, "they" still treat me like that. The changes in my way of thinking since I have been trying to live A.A.'s Twelve-Step program help. The imagined slights are fewer, and so are the kinds of treatment that make me bristle. And that is a big help. Still, as my working the Tenth Step and Eleventh Step makes me reflect on the defects of character and shortcomings laid bare in the Sixth and Seventh Steps, I wonder about the path I have yet to travel in handling my tendency to resentment.

Some injuries are real, and some treatment meted out to me by other human beings is unjust. If I am not perfect, neither are they. And so they, as I, can cause pain; and pain hurts. An honest program seems to require that I do not deny that pain, that hurt. Again, I realize and remember all too well that dishonesty and denial also used to play into my active alcoholism. "Those s.o.b.s don't bother me," I would lie as I poured my pain-killing triple.

One of the first things I learned in A.A. was that dishonesty never works.

But what then? If even justified indignation endangers my sobriety, and if denying honest feeling is an even more treacherous pitfall, does that mean that I must never feel anger? Since A.A. promises spiritual progress rather than spiritual perfection, I doubt that. To be human is, at times, to feel anger; and sobriety, after all, is quite simply to be truly human. Still. . . .

Last night, at home after the meeting, I tried to talk over that confusion with my Higher Power. As always in such conversations, I tried to listen as well as to speak. So, after setting out my confusion pretty much as I have here, I rested my mind and opened my heart as best I could. The incident that provoked my meditation, however — an impatient rage at a store-clerk's trivial misunderstanding that led her to accuse me of dishonesty — still gnawed in my memory. An echo insisted: "Why me?" Here I was, sober and trying to live soberly. Despite all the chicanery I used to engage in while drinking, my honesty had never been challenged then — why now? Why me?

Now, when I listen while meditating, I do so carefully, because my Higher Power usually whispers. Last evening, however, the answer boomed: "Why not?"

I guess it is appropriate and important to write down my scintillating response to that "Why not?" It was, as I recall, "Huh?"

But then, slowly, painfully, and prayerfully, my mind and my heart — my brain and my guts — seemed to get into sync. Why *me*?" . . . "Why *not*?" "*Why* me?" . . . "*Why* not?" "*Why me*?" . . . "*Why not*?" However the accenting changed, the rhythm remained the same. And slowly, I began to understand several things.

Who am I, the thought emerged, to ask "Why?" Reality — even the reality of insult and anger — simply is. My task, the Serenity Prayer teaches me, is to change it if I can and to accept it if I cannot. Wisdom consists in knowing that difference — not in dissecting its causes. If I had remembered that at the time of my upset, I might have reacted better to it.

Why must I ask — nay, demand to know — "why"? That question may not be as foolish as it sounds: why "why"? Or at least its very foolishness might help me to gain perspective on myself. Some "whys," it might help me to see, are appropriately asked. When I was drinking, the answer to "why do I get drunk" was "because I drink alcohol." Why did I drink alcohol in that way? Because I am an alcoholic, I have since learned. Why am I an alcoholic? . . . Why not? I begin to see that "Why" questions are okay: it is the petulant "Why me?" that must ever escape my grasp, that can only be answered, "Why not?"

For the root answer to "Why me?" can be only this: as human, I both am and am not. To be human is to be "someone," and therefore to be both not-nothing and not-everything — not "nobody" and not "God." The feeling of anger, and the incidents that rouse that feeling, simply reflect that basic truth.

Injury, insult, and anger are never pleasant — but they are important reminders of who I am . . . and who I am not. If I can learn to remember that the flip side of every "Why me?" is "Why not?", perhaps even those painful hurts can help me to live more humanly and therefore more soberly.

When I first came around A.A. and learned what an alcoholic was, I often moaned, "Why me? . . . Why do I have to be an alcoholic?" In time, through attending meetings and not taking the first drink one day at a time and identifying rather than comparing, my "Why me?" shifted from latent resentment to explicit gratitude. There are thousands of alcoholics out there who are still drinking and still dying: why should I have been fortunate enough to find Alcoholics Anonymous and through it the joy of sober living?

As with the other "Why me?", the only answer is again "Why not?" And realizing that sharpens and deepens my gratitude. And so there is another lesson here, I think: for every "Why me?" that cries out from pain, there is another "Why me?" that wonders at love.

My task, when oppressed by one, is to find the other. For a time still, I am sure, occasional anger and tinges of resentment will continue to surface even in my A.A. way of life. But that way of life has also taught me something about handling such moments. When I catch myself asking even validly "Why?", I need to be alert to the possibility that that question carries buried within it the dangerous "Why me?" Wisdom, I need to remind myself, consists in knowing the difference between what I can and cannot change — not in dissecting the cause of that difference.

And when I hear that "Why me?" sneak into my thinking, it will help my serenity to recall not only its obvious flip-side — "Why not?" — but also to remember that in my sober life, there are other "Why me?"s for which I can only be grateful. On balance, sobriety offers more to be grateful for than it does to resent. Perhaps the answer to "Why must I always ask 'Why?'?" is that I need that reminder.

44

Boredom is the feeling that everything is a waste of time; serenity, that nothing is.

— Thomas Szasz

ONE DIFFERENCE THAT STANDS OUT, IN MY own case, between "what we were like" and "what we are like now" has to do with my relationship to time. Before finding the Twelve-Step program of A.A., I lived only in the past or in the future: my present alternated wildly between sheer boredom and frantic agitation. Serenity means to me living in the present, calmly.

"The alcoholic," Bill W. once wrote, "has no present tense." How well he knew me. For this active alcoholic, now was never good enough — it was always a waste of time. My attention focused on the past, which I either resented or regretted losing. Or I projected imagined futures, fearing and fighting them or fantasizing successes that had to render any present pallid. No one knows the nature of time, the philosophers tell us. Alcoholics seem determined to prove that insight.

Irony lurks in the phrase, "a waste of time." How can we waste that which — strickly speaking, if we stop to think about it — has no existence? Ultimately, time is a comparison. And precisely in that lay our problem as active alcoholics: we knew only how to compare . . . we never allowed ourselves simply to be by identifying with our only reality, our present now.

Time is a waste if we become captured by comparison. For comparison, like boredom, is never restful. Comparison agitates; boredom refuses to see. "Refusal" signifies "pouring back" — a rejection of that which is given. In rejecting time-as-now, boredom refuses life itself. For, with apologies to Mr. Luce, time is life: we are the moment that links our past with whatever potential we have, as the practice of telling stories plainly reveals.

To be bored is, in a sense, to refuse one's story and therefore to reject oneself. No wonder boredom kills. For one who is bored, time drags because life is a drag. Such a life is not lived. Is there any nonentity more "non" than the unlived life? The unlived life is not a paradox — it is a contradiction. Boredom is less a waste of time than a denial of life.

Which brings me to *serenity.* Serenity, it seems to me, is best understood as an embrace of life. And to embrace life is to embrace time. In that embrace there can be no waste. The nature of the present — of time, of now — is such that we embrace it wholly, or not at all. Time is not a prostitute but a loved one. We do not buy time's dalliance; we are time's constitutive other half. That is why each moment is precious, and every now is nothing more than each moment.

What is this now that is all that we have? Philosophers and scientists, artists and poets: each point of view suggests its own vision. For me, the relevant vision involves a contrast rather than a comparison — a contrast between *being* and *nothingness.*

The active alcoholic or using addict, the chronically disabled person who lacks the way of life enabled by a Twelve-Step program, has no now and therefore has nothing. How can one have nothing? Ask any alcoholic: it is not easy, but we achieved that paradox. And because any void is painful, we tried to fill that nothing with booze or whatever. Is it too much to claim that it was because we had nothing and lacked a now that we tried to fill our void with booze? If that hunch has any validity, it uncovers the most vicious cycle of our alcoholic experience: the emptier we felt, the more we turned to booze; and the more we turned to booze, the emptier we felt and were.

The A.A. way of life substitutes sobriety for booze by replacing nothingness with now. What did Alcoholics Anonymous first give me? It offered me my now. I remember those so simple, so wise, slogans that first caught my eyes and ears: "One day at a time" and "First things first." To someone who has no now, those cliches are a profound and elegant gift.

Having my now, the very phrase "waste of time" is meaningless. Even if absolutely nothing else were going on at this moment, at the very least I am not drinking. For an alcoholic, not drinking is not a waste of time. But, of course, something else is going on — my life, as moment by moment I live the Twelve-Step program. And because, each moment, I can live that A.A. way of life, no moment can be or can be thought of as waste.

When I was a young man, a mildly ribald joke asked: "What part of a woman's anatomy is her 'now'? . . . You know: as in 'I wonder who's kissing her now.' " I associate thinking that funny with my drinking years, with my alcoholic thinking. Today, perhaps partially as amends for that adolescent dehumanization of women, I try to redeem the memory by embracing my own now . . . and, through Alcoholics Anonymous, by helping others — male or female — to embrace theirs.

We all need to embrace: we long not only to be held, but to hold; for, in fact, we cannot have the one without the other. In embracing, we are embraced; in being embraced, we embrace. Ultimately, regarding my life, my choice is clear: I embrace my now, or I embrace nothing — and if I embrace nothing, nothingness embraces me. That is perhaps the most profound lesson that my alcoholism and my recovery have taught me. Now is all that I have: this twenty-four hours, this moment. In A.A.'s embrace, I find my now, and thus I discover serenity. "Boredom is the feeling that everything is a waste of time; serenity, that nothing is."

Moments after Bill W. underwent his spiritual experience, A.A.'s co-founder anxiously asked his physician, "Is it real?" Am I sane?" Dr. Silkworth's response finds its moment of truth in each of our lives: "Whatever it is you've got now, hang on to it. Hang on to it, boy. It is so much better than what you had only a couple of hours ago."

Now is infinitely better than nothing. For the chance to live that simple truth, I am grateful — to Dr. Silkworth, to Bill W., and to the fellowship and program of Alcoholics Anonymous.

45

The investigation of any trait in alcoholics will show that they have either more or less of it.

— Mark Keller

SOMETIMES, EVEN THOUGH I INDULGE IN THE practice myself, it troubles me when sober members of A.A. refer to sober nonmembers as "earthpeople." Are we not all, after all, ultimately human? Then I realize that the term *earthpeople* does not question outsiders' humanity, but our own. Implicitly, at least, the term is always spoken tongue-in-cheek.

A quarter of a century ago, a noted researcher reviewed the whole vast scholarly literature on alcoholism and alcoholics and, as the first fruit of his efforts, published "Keller's Law": "The investigation of any trait in alcoholics will show that they have either more or less of it." The time has come, I believe, to revise Keller's Law. Today, some pair of scholarly articles can always be found that will infallibly demonstrate not that alcoholics have *either* more or less of any postulated trait, but that they have *both* more and less of it. Research indicates that alcoholics are both oversexed and undersexed, both dependent personalities and defiantly individualistic, both . . . need I go on?

I would like to suggest and to propose, therefore, "K.'s Corollary" to Keller's Law. In a formulation that might prove especially attractive because of its mathematical — and therefore scientific — format, K.'s Corollary states:

"alcoholic" = HUMAN

Although that may seem a circular truism, let me try to explain its significance. Normal human beings, social-drinking earth-people, nonalcoholics: those are all synonyms for what one person who works in the field terms "being an apprentice alcoholic." His answer to those who impolitely or carelessly ask whether he is an alcoholic runs: "Not yet." People such as him — normal, social-drinking nonalcoholics — share our character defects and shortcomings. Simply from their disabililty of being human, they have as great a need for the way of life embodied in A.A.'s Twelve-Step program as do we. The continuing spread of the Twelve-Step program among nonalcoholics, I believe, supports that insight.

But alcoholics are also apprentice human beings. Our difficulty is not that we are other than human — that we are less than human or more than human, although some of us have tried to be one or the other . . . or both. Our problem is rather that we are all too human. The alcoholic is a no-trump human being, because to be human is to be both more and less than merely human. Alcoholics are uppercase, italicized nonentities who must learn to be simply human, for that is all there is. Humans are human, not HUMAN nor *human*.

Booze seemed to promise us more. It lured us into trying to live in italics or capital letters. But we can no more live that way than we can write or speak that way, consistently. A scream is not a conversation. The damaged light bulb burns most brightly just before it goes out: is that not the story of our alcoholism?

One way of understanding ourselves as alcoholics, I think, is that we have tested the limits of our humanity and not only touched them but also run smack, full-tilt into them. And so we lie there, bruised and bloodied from that encounter — those of us fortunate enough to have made it into A.A. — a reminder to any who take the trouble to notice that to be human is to have limits. Our apprenticeship involves finding our way back from those limits . . . about Twelve Steps back.

For us, as human, there is no higher dignity than being human. That may sound banal — but I suspect that it is the truth that we stumbled over, that we ignored or tried to deny, when we drank alcoholically. The essence of being truly human involves being limited. The very concept of "alcoholic" signifies one who refuses limits, who attempts to deny them. Earthpeople, in this perspective, are simply human beings who have always accepted their humanity. Perhaps, then, we can learn from them.

And they, of course, can learn from us. A.A. history, from one point of view, is the continuing story of more and more nonalcoholics learning more and more from alcoholics. That is its glory. But any glory, if human, also has its darker side. For some A.A.s, at least, A.A. history seems also the story of alcoholics learning less and less from nonalcoholics. Bill W.'s many tributes to nonalcoholics and A.A.'s own concern for the preservation and promulgation of its true history work against that trend. But is it not a trap of thinking into which each of us falls, at times? For myself, the answer must be: "Yes."

Realizing the banality of being human can preserve us from that pitfall. Is that truth not, after all, one deep and constant message of Alcoholics Anonymous? We are warned against grandiosity. A.A.'s way of life teaches us not so much to be ordinary as to accept our ordinariness. At times, that message rankles: something deep inside of us wants to be — and to be thought — special. That we are somehow special rather than just plain ordinary is our deepest denial. Remember the first words out of the mouth of Bill D., "A.A. #3," when A.A.'s co-founders approached him? "But I'm different!" he exclaimed. How often, even in sobriety, do my thoughts echo that fatal denial?

And so, I think, it is time for me to stop thinking in terms of *us* and *them*. I once heard a preacher suggest that the most obscene four-letter word is *them*. Anything that separates me from humanity, that pushes off against any part of humanity, destroys my own humanity.

There are many areas of my life and thought that need that truth. Most basically, my sobriety needs that truth. Because earthpeople — nonalcoholics — can drink differently does not mean that they are different. We are all just plain human; and since that is the only game in town, it might be nice for me to accept that I am in it.

K.'s Corollary revises Keller's Law, but it still presents only half the story. The process of recovery from alcoholism, its formulation suggests, is a more complex and process-oriented equation:

"alcoholic" = HUMAN → "alcoholic" = "human"

Somewhere, I recall, we are reminded that recovery's promise is "spiritual progress rather than spiritual perfection." Someday perhaps, then, we might even get rid of the quotation marks. Meanwhile, it is good to be at least "becoming human."

46

Gratitude is like an itch: it irritates until you scratch it.

— Anonymous

LAST NIGHT'S TOPIC WAS "GRATITUDE." AS it unfolded, the discussion reminded me of something I have often noticed within Alcoholics Anonymous. Sometimes, after people have been sober in A.A. for perhaps four or five or six years, they begin to talk about a lurking, emerging feeling that they are not putting enough back into the program.

The perception is understandable. Most groups assign to newcomers, those in their first year or so of sobriety, such tasks as setting up the chairs, putting out ashtrays, and making the coffee. The peak glamour of speaking at meetings usually occurs between years two and four. At discussion meetings, the dialogue seems to flow most electrically between those who offer the insights of bare months of sobriety and those wisdomed by decades of living the A.A. way of life. Opportunities for Twelfth-Step outreach are always present, of course, but less so for some than for others.

Middlers — those who bring to A.A. years rather than months or decades of sobriety — are sober. One day at a time, they do not drink alcohol and they go to meetings and they try to practice the principles of the Twelve Steps in all their affairs. Why, then, this incipient malaise over putting back in? Whence comes this feeling of not doing enough?

At first glance, those feelings might appear to flow from gratitude. Having cleared up sufficiently to realize how fortunate we have been, we find that sense reinforced as we observe other, later, newcomers who fail to make it in A.A. "They are not ready yet," we tell ourselves, remembering our own long unreadiness and perhaps also uttering a silent prayer that they somehow get ready before they die of their alcoholism. If we have been around for any time, we likely have seen a few who did die, and again our gratitude for our own sobriety overflows. We have been given so much. How can we ever express that gratitude adequately?

These seem, again at first glance, sober thoughts. What could be more healthy, more healing, than the "attitude of gratitude"? Nothing, I suspect; but sometimes I do question whether such thoughts are gratitude. For the answer to the question "How can we ever express our gratitude adequately?" is simple: "We can't."

Gratitude, after all, is for a gift. And a gift is something that we have not earned, nor can we ever pay it back. Paying back is not gratitude: it is the attempt — sometimes, unfortunately, successful — to turn a gift into an item of contract. When we feel that we owe, that feeling is not gratitude. Real gratitude involves a sheer acceptance that arises out of true humility.

Perhaps that is why the A.A. insight reminds us that gratitude is an attitude — a posture of our very being. It is certainly why gratitude is so important to our sobriety. I remember how it used to be when I was drinking. I thought, perhaps, that I wanted gifts, but what I actually craved was the success of my manipulations. At the very least, when someone gave me anything, I was sure to reward the giver by offering a drink. Drinking with someone was my way of saying "Thank you" — and, for an alcoholic, that is not exactly gratitude.

Gratitude is not only not the same as paying back: it is its exact opposite. True gratitude springs from humility because it involves the realization and the acceptance that because we are lacking, something can be given to us. What then does it require to be grateful — how are we to understand the humility that is at the root of true gratitude?

It cannot be self-loathing, for gratitude implies the acceptance that we are good enough to be gifted, good enough to receive a gift. Not good enough to deserve the gift, but good enough to receive it without embarrassment. A gift does not come out of justice, but neither can a gift ever be an injustice.

Nor can self-complacency underlie gratitude. If we must be good enough that the gift we receive not express injustice, we must also be bad enough that the gift supplies some lack, some need. It is impossible to give gifts to those who have everything — to the perfect: at best, our gift to such a one is but a symbol, a token. One who has everything can receive only nothing, and only a Higher Power can find "gift" in our nothingness. We can receive gifts, then, precisely because we are not perfect, because others do have something that we do not have.

When drinking, I suspect, we were incapable of gratitude because we were incapable of receiving gifts. On the one hand, we loathed ourselves so much that any gift that we did not "earn" or "con" seemed blatant injustice. And on the other hand, we played God to such an extent that we denied our needings and our lacks. The active alcoholic receives no gifts — except one.

For somehow, despite the morass of self-loathing and self-complacency in which we were mired, we were "gifted." In a way that no one of us can tell, we were given the gift of Alcoholics Anonymous. A.A. was a gift because we needed it in two senses: we lacked it — it was certainly a way of life that we did not have; and we surely qualified as worthy of it — not deserving, but worthy.

Because A.A. is a gift — something just given us that we did not deserve nor earn — we can never pay back for it. Gifts may entail responsibility; they do not impose obligation, else they are not gifts. So I will be responsible, but I cannot be obligated.

For me, that serves as a healthy reminder. Although it does not much quell my need to express gratitude, thinking about the meaning of A.A. as gift helps me to understand that need and therefore to understand myself in recovery.

Because I am not worthless, I can accept gifts without feeling that justice is violated by my acceptance. If I am good enough for A.A., then I am good enough . . . period. And because I am not perfect, I can accept that I lack and that I need — and that therefore gratitude is an attitude rather than the feckless, proud endeavor to pay back. Gratitude's responsibility involves not paying back but being grateful — being ever-mindful, that is, that I am both good enough to receive and bad enough to need.

An oldtimer once asked me, "What is the most important part of any A.A. meeting?" I had no real answer, although I limply suggested that the after-meeting conversation over coffee seemed most effectively to deepen my identification while, at times, answering some of my lingering questions.

"Good insight," he replied, "but may I suggest that the most important part of any A.A. meeting for you is the moment when you walk through the door into it? It's not what you do here that is important: it is the fact that you are here. Your very being here, if you stop to think about it, is A.A.'s greatest gift to you. And, let me suggest, your being here is also the best way you have of expressing gratitude for that gift."

My deepest need, it sometimes seems, it to be needed. In Alcoholics Anonymous I learn that I am needed and how I am needed — not for my doing anything but for my being there.

47

I have often thought that the best way to define a man's character would be to seek out the particular mental or moral attitude in which, when it came upon him, he felt himself most deeply and intensely active and alive. At such moments there is a voice inside which speaks and says: "This is the real me."

— William James

MANY PEOPLE TORMENT THEMSELVES TRYing to define alcoholism. Others, probably rarer but certainly more intense, agitate for more practical efforts designed to delineate clearly and distinctly "the alcoholic." Sometimes, out of respect for the proven success of A.A. as a program of recovery from alcoholism, such inquirers turn to A.A. seeking help in their quest.

"Tell us," they say, in one form or another, "what you have learned about alcoholism. And tell us especially just what is an alcoholic. Help us to devise charts and questionnaires — lists of characteristics that will enable us to determine exactly who is and who is not an alcoholic."

Those efforts, I suspect, are doomed to failure. Nevertheless, because those who urge them are motivated by good intentions and because we know that open-mindedness is important to our sobriety, we attempt to answer. We begin, perhaps, with a gentle reminder that "A.A." stands for "Alcoholics Anonymous," not for "About Alcoholism." Then, to ease any sting in that observation and perhaps also in gentle self-mockery, we point them toward *The Big Book*, and perhaps especially its second and third chapters, for the latter is titled "More About Alcoholism." But we also point out that the first chapter of that book is "Bill's Story"; and we suggest, firmly, that they not overlook the story section that begins after page 164. Finally, we tell them our own stories.

All but the most open-mindedly honest investigators will feel frustrated at this point. If we in A.A. know so much about alcoholism and alcoholics, why will we not just give some simple, clear answer to their question? Surely after almost fifty years of being Alcoholics Anonymous, we can define the alcoholic: why do we so stubbornly refuse to do so?

This is a difficult point, for the answer is not that we as A.A.s are refusing to, but that we as A.A.s cannot define the alcoholic. All that each one of us can do is to describe *this* alcoholic. We can tell our own story, inviting identification. But "Utilize, don't analyze" represents insight rather than injunction: we simply are unable to subject the concept *alcoholic*, as we come to understand that reality within A.A., to the tools of scientific analysis.

All metaphors limp, but one who tries to know the meaning of "alcoholic" with the tools of analytic science is not unlike the baseball player who would step up to the plate and try to hit a home run with a ping-pong paddle. Some tools are inappropriate to some projects; and the analytic approach of modern science is a tool, and understanding the alcoholic is a project.

A.A. offers a different tool — a time-honored instrument of understanding that comes complete with its own modality, with its own set of instructions as to "how": identification by "telling stories." One comes to understand the alcoholic, A.A. teaches, by identifying with the stories of those who know that they are alcoholics.

Some knowledge — that which is perhaps better termed *understanding* — comes not by objective observation but by the identification that derives from a sense of participation. As Dr. Harry Guntrip has noted, a mother "knows" her baby differently than does a pediatrician. Both kinds of knowledge are valid; each even has its proper scope. Both parent and physician can learn from each other, to the baby's benefit, so long as each does not try to be the other.

And so science and scientists can tell us much about the alcoholic. But who is an alcoholic, only each person can decide for himself or herself. In a way, it seems to me, Alcoholics Anonymous answers that question, "What is an alcoholic?", by suggesting, in effect: "Anyone who can identify with the alcohol-related thinking and behavior — but especially the thinking — of someone who says that he or she is an alcoholic just might be an alcoholic." And so if someone asks me, as an A.A. member,

"What is an alcoholic?", I respond by telling my story, the story of this alcoholic — by inviting identification, if appropriate. As A.A. wisely understands, no A.A. can affirm that anyone else is an alcoholic.

It is good to remind myself of that. Sometimes, in my zeal to help some poor sufferer on a Twelfth-Step call, I have been known to get pushy — almost to try to convince someone that he or she is an alcoholic and therefore needs A.A. That is good neither for that person, nor for me, nor for A.A. Rhetoric has its tricks and there is at times a thin line between persuading and inviting identification. But that line, that difference exists — it is real; and probably no one senses it more clearly than the drinker who is approaching the bottom. And so I have learned, in later years, to tell my own story simply and directly, and then to invite this person to accompany me to hear others tell theirs.

48

As alcoholics progress in sobriety, they apparently begin to differ more and more from each other in their cognitive styles.

— Patricia Kearns Thomsen

LAST NIGHT, A RELATIVE NEWCOMER TO MY home group said that for some time he had avoided A.A. "because he didn't want to be brainwashed" — never mind all the trouble he was in. He hadn't talked long before my mind wandered, and I started thinking about something I had recently read.

A research psychologist tested a number of sober members of Alcoholics Anonymous, seeking to learn what a specific personality inventory might reveal about growth in sobriety. She hoped to isolate common denominators in such things as learning style and habitual patterns of thinking, with the larger hope of helping those who deal with alcoholics in treatment to better prepare their charges for lifelong recovery in A.A.

In undertaking her study, Thomsen, the psychologist, hypothesized that as A.A. members matured in sobriety, they would think more alike. Alcoholics Anonymous, after all, teaches a way of thinking: one might reasonably expect certain patterns of thinking to emerge from long practice of its program and thus to correlate positively with length of sobriety. But the results of Thomsen's research contradicted her hypothesis. The longer their sobriety, her empirical data revealed, the more diverse were the thinking styles of A.A. members.

On first hearing of Thomsen's research, I was both intrigued and delighted. Intrigued, because an overthrown hypothesis seems one of the best guarantees of open-minded research. Delighted, because so many unthinking people — self-styled experts more addicted to opinion than skilled in research — tend to accuse A.A. of brainwashing and of imposing conformity.

But another, more important, insight emerges from her investigation — one that impresses on me a truth important for my own sobriety. In shedding light on precisely what is meant by "growth in sobriety," Thomsen's study helps deepen my understanding of A.A.'s Second Step and especially of one phrase in Step Two that used to trouble me: "restore us to sanity."

When I first came to A.A., after I cleared up sufficiently to begin to understand the Twelve Steps, I had more trouble with "restore us to sanity" than I did with "a Power greater than ourselves" or even with "God as we understood Him." Looking back on my life, discovering the story of my own alcoholic drinking and examining its implications for my recovery, I at times questioned whether I had ever been sane. How could I be restored to something that sober evaluation of my track record indicated I never had? What did it mean, then, to believe that I could be restored to sanity?

Slowly, as I did not drink and went to meetings, one day at a time, an answer emerged. Sobriety, in the sense of accepting A.A. as way of life and seeking to live and to grow in the Twelve-Step program, allowed me — freed me — to be myself. This may be far too simplistic, but it seems to me that I turned to chemicals, and especially to alcohol, because — unhappy with the way I was, and unwilling and unable simply to be myself — I was seeking from them help to be other than myself.

At the time, of course, I did not realize that. I thought that booze, by destroying inhibitions or by quelling pain, was enabling me to be my real self. That, it now seems to me, is alcohol's ultimate deception: it promises precisely what it destroys. For the "real me" enabled by alcohol, even before my drinking became an overt problem, more and more became someone with whom I could not live comfortably without the aid of alcohol. To live without the inhibitions that derive from principled ethical choice, to live without occasional pain and anxiety, is not to live humanly. To be human is to be limited. At times we may test those limits, but limitation defines our humanity.

I turned to booze, it seems to me now, because I was attempting to refuse to accept that reality — the reality that I would feel bad when I violated the limitations that defined my humanity. In that violation, mind- and mood-altering chemicals such as alcohol did not allow me to find the real me. Rather they destroyed the real me by cutting me off from my reality. To be separated from one's reality is the meaning of "insanity." Restoration to "sanity," then, need not mean that we ever accepted reality; the term implies only that our reality was always there.

What does all this have to do with Thomsen's research? Human beings are different — wondrously different. That is the glory of our humanity, the gift by which reality — our Higher Power, if you choose — compensates us for our limitations by making use of our very limitations to lift us beyond our selves.

Those who accept their humanity, those who simply are themselves, will be different. They will think different thoughts and live different lives, even if they embrace the same way of living and the same way of thinking that allows them to do that. In giving us sobriety, A.A. first and foremost gives us the gift of ourselves — of our "self" as we really are: limited and imperfect and therefore needing others who also accept their own limitations and imperfections even as they strive to grow.

It is not those who accept the limitations of their reality who are think-alike conformists. Mindless conformity derives from the refusal of that acceptance of self, from attempts to deny the reality of self. All drinking alcoholics think alike; every sober alcoholic grows in his or her own sobriety by living the A.A. way of life in his or her own unique way. That is why, in the words of Bill W., "Honesty gets us sober, but tolerance keeps us sober."

Thomsen's research, I think, demonstrates the depth of Bill's insight. We know its truth, and nothing has changed in its truth; but I find it nice to have empirical confirmation of what I both sense in myself and see all around me in the fellowship of Alcoholics Anonymous: sobriety gives freedom — and, of all freedoms, the freedom to be truly oursevles is perhaps the greatest.

49

Quality has become quantity: the answer to all questions of "What for?" is "More!"

— Phillip Rieff

A CHANCE REMARK BY A MAN I HAD NEVER seen before at A.A. caught my ear tonight. He was only recently dry. Asked whether he had yet chosen a sponsor, the fledgling replied: "No, I haven't been around long enough to figure out who is the most sober person in this group." I hope he was joking.

"The most sober person in this group": the phrase struck my ears strangely. Might it be a valid concept, on some theoretical level? Certainly there is a "longest dry" member in every group. And the A.A. axiom, "Stick with the winners," seems to imply differences in quality of sobriety just as does the distinction between "dryness" and "sobriety." Indeed, the phrase "quality sobriety" seems explicitly to undergird the understanding that sobriety has degrees.

Because we can grow in it, sobriety does seem to admit of "more" and "less." But something about the idea "most sober" does not ring true. If there is a most sober person in a given meeting, then there must be someone who is most sober in a particular city, in a specific state, in the nation, in the world. What would we do with that individual? Elect him king? Buy him a drink?

If we all had the exact same understanding of sobriety, of course, we would not need an election. Social scientists could devise tests to measure sobriety, and the highest score would simply win. I can see all the world's alkies gathered in a hall to take that test. Somehow, if it ever happened, I think I would suspect that the most sober person, if such existed, was not in that room. Clearly, the idea of "most sober person" both irritates and amuses me. And in so doing, it reminds me of two important things I have learned in my own sobriety.

In the first place stands perhaps the most important lesson: quality is not quantity. "How much?' and "What kind of?" are two different questions. To confuse quality with quantity, to assume that more is better, is precisely to think like an alcoholic. Is that not the exact error we made with booze? Anyone who doubts that "more" is not necessarily "better" should look up the nearest local active alcoholic.

There are, then, some realities that cannot be quantified, cannot be counted: wisdom, love, sobriety. They admit of varieties of depth, of richness; but the attempt to put numbers on them somehow violates their reality. That sense, I think, reflects one aspect of what human beings have throughout the ages termed *the spiritual*. Indeed, it seems to me the most simple and most obvious first meaning of A.A.'s presentation of itself as a spiritual program.

The second reminder is perhaps less obvious. Sobriety is ultimately a subjective judgment. Some aspects of sober living and sober thinking are fairly obvious and therefore in general commonly accepted: humor, humility, patience, tolerance. But like sobriety itself, these qualities cannot be measured. In fact, their manifestations can be so diverse that where I see much of such a quality, some other person may find very little of it. If I value humor as a component of my own sobriety, it may be difficult for me to appreciate the depths of the sobriety of someone else whose way is more appreciative of quiet patience. Where I find humor, another may not see it. Where another finds an opportunity for patience, I may see only passivity.

I am reminded of Bill W.'s practice in choosing sponsors. Bill had many, for his practice was to select some quality — on the basis of his continuing practice of the Sixth, Seventh, Tenth, and Eleventh Steps — in which it seemed he should next make some effort to grow. Having chosen the trait — for example, patience — Bill sought out someone who showed and lived it, asking that individual to be his sponsor. The relationship continued, and Bill worked especially on growing in that quality, not so much until he finally achieved it as until his continuing practice of the Steps indicated that it was time to work on some other trait, the flip-side of some other character defect or shortcoming. The process then began again, almost invariably with a new sponsor.

In those ongoing excursions, it should be noted, Bill did not necessarily seek out the most patient, or the most honest, or the most tolerant person he could find. His practice was rather to choose someone who showed the quality in a way with which he could identify — someone who seemed to have the kind of patience or whatever that Bill felt he himself ought to grow in next.

Sobriety is so rich — so full — that, while we can embrace it, we can never capture it. That is perhaps the deepest reason why, at depth, sobriety is a subjective determination. I can always spot someone who seems to have better sobriety than do I, especially as that sobriety is manifested in some quality in which my own inventory reveals me deficient. At times, I also sense that another sober A.A. is at a place along the way through which I have already passed — again, in some particular aspect of sober living. My task then is, if invited, to try to share with that individual whatever growth I have attained.

But to judge "most sober" or even "more sober" — spare me the task.

50

"Alcoholic's Anonymous"
— Title of first draft of the book, *Alcoholics Anonymous*

ALTHOUGH A.A. IS, FOR US, EASY AND EVEN fun to think about, how does one talk about — and, even more, write about — "Alcoholics Anonymous"?

It is even a problem in punctuation. When should one write "A.A.," and when should one choose "A.A.s"? The starting point, the guideline, is clear: all generalizations about A.A. or A.A.s are false. (Including that one, of course: it is valid to say that "Every member of Alcoholics Anonymous has a desire to stop drinking" — or is it?)

But what about that "A.A." or "A.A.s": what is the difference between them? Most profoundly, there is none; and it is too easy to lose sight of that simple reality. Many members of many groups other than A.A. can claim with much correctness: "We are (whatever)." But the faculty are not the university, any more than are the students or the administration or the library. In a sense, indeed, all faculty members gathered together are not even "the faculty." Annihilate them (only in imagination, of course), and next year this university would still have "a faculty." We belong to groups as we belong to our neighborhoods: this neighborhood remains this neighborhood, even if all its present residents move away. Even if all the inhabitants should move out and no new ones move in, New Orleans would still be New Orleans. We live in it; but we do not — because we cannot — live it.

Alcoholics Anonymous is different. On one level, we live in it, and by it, and through it — not unlike the relationship of the dedicated faculty member to his university or the participation of any conscientious professional in her profession. Yet, however great may be our professional identification, or even our religious affiliation, they are not our human identity. For members of

A.A., that, too, is different. We are alcoholics differently than we are Baptist or Buddhist, printer or physician, Republican or Democrat. If there be a closer parallel of this profound level of being and identity, it may perhaps be found in race and ethnicity. The difference between being an A.A. and not being an A.A. is closer to the difference between being Black and being White, between being an Arab and being a Jew.

No one can speak for A.A., and it is perhaps even more impossible to speak "about" A.A. That is true because, in a unique way, A.A. is its members, and its members are uniquely diverse. The faculty of a university and the profession of medicine exist independently of whether or not any individuals are actually engaged in the art of teaching or the practice of medicine. A.A. could not be conceived of as existing if no one had "a desire to stop drinking." Its members are not only A.A.s: they *are* A.A.

The same ambiguity inheres even more clearly in the unabbreviated term, *Alcoholics Anonymous.* The problem is long-standing. As very many A.A.s know, the prepublication, multigraph edition of *The Big Book* was titled "Alcoholic's Anonymous." That was not, I suspect, mere error, but rather reflects the ambiguity inherent in choosing a name for such a unique group. Its members were unique not because of their drinking experience, but because of how they constituted — were "members of" — this new entity that they were trying to describe.

Recall the setting: the early members of what we so glibly call "Alcoholics Anonymous" saw themselves as a "fellowship" of anonymous alcoholics. In referring to themselves, in the first words of the foreword to the first edition, they identified themselves as "we, of Alcoholics Anonymous . . ."; and they signed that foreword, "Alcoholics Anonymous."

It may seem a picayune concern, but I sometimes like to recall and ponder a question once asked of me. "Is 'Alcoholics Anonymous' the title or the author of that book?" The only possible answer is: both. That is what makes A.A. uniquely worthy of historical study: of what other group of people, of what other book, could that answer be given?

Recalling the early title of *The Big Book*, of course, necessarily opens the question of the possessive form. Should one write, for example, of "A.A.'s program," or of "A.A.s' program"? Historical practice as well as common sense dictate the latter: the program is possessed only by its members. The question immediately also arises, of course: Can the steps we took, which are suggested as a program of recovery be possessed by anyone? I try to practice the Twelve Steps; on occasion, I even comment that someone "seems to have the program"; but I doubt that I would claim, for myself or anyone else, that we possess the program.

Dr. Carl Jung once commented, concerning the truth that he termed "metaphysical," that "One does not possess it: one is possessed by it." Thus it is, I think, with the program of Alcoholics Anonymous — thus it is, indeed, with Alcoholics Anonymous itself.

Do we, its members, belong to A.A., or does A.A. belong to us? The question may at first glance seem arrogant — at least until one remembers that *belong to* signifies *fit.* To belong to is "to have a proper or suitable place." In one sense, at least, A.A. fits me at least as well as I fit A.A. I surely do find "a proper and suitable place" in Alcoholics Anonymous. But the program of Alcoholics Anonymous even more surely finds a proper and suitable place in me. In fact, it seems to me that I could do worse than understand the task of my sobriety to be to fit A.A. as well as A.A. fits me.

To play with words is "to play." But sometimes the meaning and implication of words get lost, and we become impoverished — deprived of a certain richness of understanding. Too soon we become too familiar; too readily we speak glibly. Still, if there be anything worse than playing with words, it is toying with grammar. Again, however, grammar and usage can also become too familiar, their implicit significance unrecognized. It is good, then, at times to toy. I have done it often in this journal: on the one hand, in imitation of many thinkers I respect; on the other hand, because I find in my attendance at ninety meetings in ninety days far more play than work. Perhaps we best grow in sobriety, if we naturally tend to be serious people, less by working on it than by playing with it.

Play need not be childish; it can be childlike. Because, in a sense, my real birthday is my A.A. birthday, I know that I still am in many ways a child. One joy of sobriety is being able to accept this. A greater joy, perhaps, comes from the sense that my Higher Power not only accepts it, but relishes its ironic intensity.

51

You cannot kiss your own ear.

— Old Russian Proverb

Our stories reveal in a general way what we were like, what happened, and what we are like now.

— Alcoholics Anonymous

TONIGHT'S MEETING FEATURED THREE SPEAKers, and listening to their stories moved me again to think about stories — about the rich benefits that accrue to us within A.A. from our practice of telling stories. All three speakers, it turned out, were fairly new to the program: two were speaking for the very first time. Each introduced himself self-consciously, with just the hint of a catch in the throat as he blurted out: "My name is ———, and I am an alcoholic."

To identify oneself as an alcoholic is a momentous step, but it is only the first step. I have met a few people who have taken only that first step, A.A.'s First Step. Most of them are now dead; the others, I fear, soon will be.

To identify oneself as an alcoholic is an awesome thing. Fortunately, within A.A., for most of us, our mere identification as alcoholic is but a moment, a doorway. The identification that matters is our identification of ourselves as sober alcoholics. And that is an identity that by its nature calls for growth.

The process of identification is a marvelous thing. On the one hand, it is rooted in finding likeness: we identify on the basis of similarity. On the other hand, identification also implies difference. We are able to change because we can identify not only with what we were and are, but with what we are not and therefore can become.

All identification involves mirroring: we see a reflection of some aspect of ourselves in some other person. We need such identifications because, in a sense, we cannot identify or even see ourselves directly. The eye cannot look upon itself: it can only see its reflection in a mirror.

Within A.A., three kinds of mirroring take place. When I first arrived, I discovered who I was — an alcoholic — in the mirror afforded by the members' stories of "what we were like." Although that was my own First Step, and as such unrepeatable, it seems to me that I retake it as often as, in later months and years, I see in the mirror of a later newcomer's plight what I myself was like. Our past is always part of our present identity.

But it is only part. In A.A., we come to know what we are not only by embracing what we were but also by understanding who and what we can become. If it be remembered that, in our relationship with others, identification is not comparison, then, in the relationship with ourselves in which we accept our identity, we are freed to grow in that identity. Alcoholics Anonymous is a program of never ending growth: "We claim spiritual progress rather than spiritual perfection."

As the phrase "growing pains" reminds us, growth can be unpleasant. Change frightens, for it involves surrender of the familiar and a leap into the unknown. We also wonder, perhaps especially as alcoholics, can we change? Many of us come to A.A. only after we had become totally cynical about our ability to change. I know that broken promises to myself littered the path by which I arrived. I intuited — correctly, I think — that at least so far as my relationship with alcohol was concerned, I could not change myself.

In sobriety, it seems to me, we learn more about both the depth and the extent of that truth. Not only in our relationship with alcohol but in many other intimate areas of our lives — our shortcomings, for example — we still cannot change ourselves. But we can be open to change, open to being changed, once we acknowledge that there exists power outside of and greater than ourselves. Once we have learned to embrace the identity of sober alcoholic, at least part of that outside and greater power works in us through our relationships with other sober alcoholics. We may still doubt that we can change, but we can see others change. In that mirroring, then, we find the hope of our own change and thus also the courage to be open to that growth.

Using the mirror of identification to look backwards, we discover that we have been changed. Every retelling of our own story reveals that what we are like now differs significantly from what we were like. But what about looking forwards? Hope is not the same as projection. When drinking, I did not hope: I fantasized or tried to manipulate, and that is not hope.

In A.A., I find hope — hope that I can change because I see others change. A sober alcoholic who tells his or her story reveals to me not only what I was and am like, but what I can become if only I follow through on my identification. When I first asked, from the pain of my withdrawal from alcohol, "How can I be like you?', I was told: "Don't take the first drink and go to meetings, one day at a time."

I did, and I still do; and it worked then, and it still works. But along the way, something else began working. More and more, as I grew in sobriety, I continued to ask — in one form or another — "How can I be like you?", and to ask it not only in the hope of not doing something, like drinking, but in the hope of being something, like truly sober. Thus, over time, I have tried to change — more accurately, to be open to being changed — in such ways as developing a sense of humor, learning patience with both myself and others, and a whole host of other qualities that make for true sobriety.

In other words, I learn that I can change, and I get the courage to be changed, because I see changes that have taken place in other A.A. members. At first, those changes were only described: I heard what those others had been like, but I saw only what they were like now. With time in A.A., however, I began to see the changes themselves — the growth in sobriety as it occurs, week to week, month to month, year after year. Seeing others change gives me the courage to be changed, and that is a precious gift.

52

Understanding the Recovering Alcoholic
— Book Title by Kenneth Anonym

OFTEN IN A.A. SERIOUS TOPICS ARE TREATED in humorous and even trivial ways. I find a special value in that: when I was drinking, I customarily approached the most trivial realities with pomposity. We are serious in A.A. — alcoholism is a matter of life and death for us. But we also know enough not to take ourselves too seriously; after all, we are alcoholics.

Tonight's discussion was surely serious. It started when Jerry commented: "I still seem plagued, at times, by my goldanged perfectionism. Something inside me seems to insist that I be perfect — as husband and father, as worker and friend. I keep forgetting that all I am perfect at is being an alcoholic."

After the meeting, I got to thinking. As an adolescent, I wondered whether there could be such a thing as "pure dirt." The phrase was not a contradiction, like "square circle," but somehow it irritated the mind if not the ear. "Perfect alcoholic" has a similar effect, but it agitates more deeply. Is it possible to be a perfect alcoholic? That may seem — and even may be — a silly question, but thinking on it may also serve my sobriety.

Most literally, "perfect" means "completed." When something is perfected, there remains no more work to be done on it. That which is perfect is finished. From that perspective, and understanding "alcoholic" as having to do with a human being's relationship to alcohol, all of us in A.A. are "perfect alcoholics." We are finished with drinking alcohol — our drinking career is finished. Or so, one day at a time, we hope.

In the broader sense, of course, because in sobriety we are in a way reborn in the sense of beginning again, we can never be perfect as sober alcoholics. There is no such thing as perfect sobriety. As drinking alcoholics, then, we are finished, complete, perfect. But as sober alcoholics, we can never be any of those. The sobriety that A.A. offers involves far more than not drinking.

Sobriety is but a synonym for growth as human. And, if I stop to think about that, such growth is completed only at and by death.

Sometimes — rarely within A.A. but often among A.A.s — mild controversy stirs over whether we are "recovering" or "recovered" alcoholics. I like such arguments because they afford the only chance I ever get to identify with Clark Gable: "Frankly, my dear, I don't give a damn."

In a way, what is really being explored in such discussions is one aspect of the question: are we "perfect alcoholics?" I have heard it said by a knowledgeable medical authority who is in the fellowship and who works in the field of treatment, "The only recovered alcoholic is a dead alcoholic." And Russ occasionally will tell stories about alcoholics who thought they were "recovered" and therefore went out and drank again and cracked up a car . . . "and so he became a real recovered alcoholic."

The medical model tends to understand recovery from any disease as involving the regaining of the pristine condition present before its onset. That is why many researchers ignore the experience of A.A. in their drive to prove that the alcoholic can return to controlled drinking. The most obvious futility of such efforts, of course, arises from the simple fact that the nonalcoholic — the so-called normal drinker — does not consciously have to control his or her drinking. To have to control one's drinking, in a way, is already to be a perfect alcoholic. To those who both think medically and accept A.A. assumptions, our claim to be recovered alcoholics will probably always prove confusing.

"Recovering," then, enjoys the advantage of avoiding that possible confusion as well as of emphasizing that sobriety is an ongoing process of growth — that it involves "spiritual progress rather than spiritual perfection." But the term *recovering* can also limp and cause confusion. To some, it seems to imply that at every moment we are on the verge of a drinking binge. In a sense perhaps understood only by us, we are. But I recall the mordant humor of an experience I had after being in A.A. for five years. A professional colleague who had just learned of my A.A. membership (not from me) carefully moved his rather elegant supply of cordials to a locked trunk in his basement before inviting me to dinner — presumably lest the very sight or mere scent of alcohol turn me into a raging maniac! Kind, large-hearted David was respecting my sobriety as best he knew how; but I rather doubt that real sobriety is much aided by that kind of respect.

We talked about the distinction implied between "recovering" and "recovered" that night. And the discussion helped me to learn to be wary of both terms. I know that I am an alcoholic, and I learn more about what that means each time I attend an A.A. meeting. It means first, to me, that I must grow in sobriety if I am truly to live the A.A. way of life that saved my life.

Sometimes, then, it helps to think of myself as a perfect alcoholic. Like Jerry, at times I feel driven by the need to be perfect. Remembering the one area of my life where at least perhaps I *am* perfect can help blunt the pain of that need even as it helps also to put it — and all needs — into perspective, the perspective of the A.A. way of life. As philosophers since Socrates have known, all perspective reveals irony.

"Perfect alcoholic," like "pure dirt," has the benefit of helping me really hear words that I might otherwise bandy about too casually. In late adolescence, I put aside much — but not all — of my tendency to vacuous speculation. In the ongoing adolescence of my sobriety, a similar sensitivity to the concepts behind terms might help me to regain something that my drinking stole from me — a kind of playfulness that is more childlike than childish. My Higher Power, I suspect, would approve of that, for I need often to be reminded that one task of my sobriety involves ceasing to take myself "too damned seriously," as A.A.'s "Rule #62" puts it.

For that reminder, I am grateful to all the perfect alcoholics, whether recovered or recovering, who are Alcoholics Anonymous. Because, for me, to be a human being is to be a member of that fellowship and to live its way of life, which is recovery — recovery not of the ability to drink alcohol, but of the ability to be human and therefore imperfect.

53

The God I worship, I am very, very sure, is a very, very active member of Al-Anon.

— Comment at an A.A. meeting

IF THERE IS ANY ONE TOPIC THAT CAN MAKE soft sparks fly around the table of an A.A. discussion group wherein diverse members know each other well — and each other's sobriety perhaps even better — it is the subject of "spiritual rather than religious." The group I have attended for several recent Mondays seems composed half by those who feel that organized religion failed them when they were drinking and proved of no help in getting them sober, and half by those who find in their sobriety a doorway to fuller appreciation of their Higher Power as revealed to them in their churches. Although there is no necessary contradiction between these two points of view, the dialogue between those two experiences often grows spirited.

Fred's point tonight seemed to build a kind of bridge, at least for some. "I cannot help but think," he insisted to a meeting attended also by the partners of those of us fortunate enough to have loved ones in Al-Anon, "that the God I worship is a very, very active member of Al-Anon. Or let me put it this way: God, when I was drinking, was somewhat like I am now. He didn't like to talk with drunks because he realized how useless it is to try to communicate with an alcoholic who is drinking and not yet ready to give it up. He knew the difference, when I prayed for help, between a promise and a con-job. The God I found — and find — in organized religion treats me as does my sponsor who Twelfth-Stepped me: with tough love. So long as I wanted only what I called 'love,' he sidestepped me, just like my wife did once she found Al-Anon. Well, thank God, I have learned that my sponsor's and my wife's was true love — and so then also was and is my God's."

I like Fred's image. Sometimes, even sober A.A.s hold weird ideas about Al-Anon. I used to think that Al-Anons met to talk about their problem — their problem being their alcoholic. I now know that they meet for the same reason we do: to talk about their problem, yes; but they realize that their problem is how to live the Twelve-Step program so as to grow in their own humanity. Al-Anons seek what A.A.s seek: the freedom to be themselves.

They have to learn that, of course, as did we. When they first come to Al-Anon, most even more than we, it seems, need to be taught by older members just why they are there. Most Al-Anons, I think it fair to say, first approach that program seeking help for their alcoholic: *they* want to help their alcoholic. Al-Anon's First Step, which is the same as A.A.'s, and the experienced tough love of Al-Anon oldtimers recalling them to that Step's meaning, help them to understand that they are seeking help for themselves, that their dis-ease derives precisely from their determination to help rather than to seek help.

I remind myself of that because I wish to indulge in a fantasy: my Higher Power, who had bailed me out of so many jams only to see me drink yet again, arriving frustrated and bedraggled at his first Al-Anon meeting. "I am absolutely at wit's end," my Higher Power tells the group. "I mean, my love is infinite. It really is . . . after all, I am God. If I ever stopped thinking of that lousy drunk, just for an instant, he would cease to exist — gone without even a poof. I have sustained and do sustain every step he has ever taken. I have saved him from things that you — and even he — would not believe! But will he trust me, will he let go to my love? Hah! He has forgotten my Spirit and given his love to spirits. What is wrong with me? How can my love be defective? It can't be, but he seems to make it so every time he reaches out to booze rather than letting go to me."

The members murmur sympathetically. Each had been through this, although most not exactly with such self-assurance about "infinite love." Then one of them points out the First Step. "You are God, of course, and so I suppose you could eliminate either alcohol or alcoholics from existence. But so long as you will that there be both alcohol and alcoholics, God, I suspect that you are, if you will pardon the expression, as 'powerless' as anyone else sitting around this table."

Another member chimes in: "I was watching you, God, when you walked in. I saw you reading over our Steps; and if I read your eyebrows rightly, you had less trouble with the First Step than with the second one. Now, I am not exactly a believer myself, but I think I can understand the problem you might have with that phrase, 'a Power greater than ourselves.' Let me tell you how I understand it, with regard to myself and my own alcoholic. You might be God, but you have the same problem — some call it a sickness — that everyone else in this room has: by your own admission, you love an alcoholic.

"Now, that is not exactly a disease in the medical sense. If it were, I am sure you could fix it up real easy with a couple of simple miracles. But because of the way you made this world, love always involves some dis-ease — because, in a sense, our love is always greater than ourselves. You made us that way, in fact, I am told, so that we could find you. In any case, we are that way, and it is sort of nice to discover that you are too. I find it hard to believe that God can love an alcoholic. But you say that you do, and your being here proves it. Welcome to Al-Anon, God."

I am sure that meeting did not end there, but my imagination does. At best an unconventional believer, I am not sure which idea I find more difficult: "God" or "loving an alcoholic." If I may indulge one last whimsy, the meeting also could not have ended there because I am certain that God's story of his own experience, strength, and hope in loving alcoholics took a bit of time to tell.

But it's time to break off fantasy. In my own case, I married only after some sobriety in A.A. Although she never knew me as a drinker, my spouse attends Al-Anon and gains from it, as do I. My Higher Power, I suspect, like Fred's, also remains "an active member." As profound as is my gratitude to Alcoholics Anonymous, it is good for me also to remember, at times, to be grateful also to and for Al-Anon. Those who love us, if we can believe that any do, need the wisdom of the Twelve-Step way of life at least as much as we ourselves — whoever they may be.

54

[Some individuals seem] never to feel a sense of inner satisfaction at accomplishing something. No matter what one tries or how well it is done, it is never enough. . . . For such an individual . . . awareness of differences between self and other becomes automatically translated into a comparison of good versus bad, better versus worse. . . . Rather than valuing the difference, such an individual feels threatened by it. Hence, in perfectionism, one attempts to be all things rather than simply who one is. The perfectionist has yet to learn that only when we stop trying to be all things do we ever become free to be who we are.

— Gershen Kaufman

TO ATTEND A.A. MEETINGS IS, AMONG OTHER things, at times suddenly to feel that some other person knows me better than I know myself. Often, a speaker's story or a discussant's comment seems to shine a beam of light that penetrates my very being. I have come to call that the MGYTM reaction: "My God! Yes, that's me!"

But Alcoholics Anonymous is generous. The fellowship, if one lives its program, does not hoard that light nor restrict its benefits to its own setting. One of the freedoms bestowed on me by my participation in A.A. is that sometimes in my reading, now, I have a similar experience. Before A.A., I read as I listened — defensively and critically — using my awareness of my own experience, such as it was, only to rebut proffered insights. In other words, before A.A., I never really read, any more than I ever really listened.

The theme I am heading toward is the rich fruitfulness of A.A.'s suggestion, "Identify, don't compare," which we talked about last night. But before I get there, another observation suggests itself as an apt reminder to guide that journey. Because of "what happened" in A.A., there are also differences between what I was like and what I am like now. Some passages that I read, like some stories that I hear, seem most valuable because they help me to appreciate that difference.

The quotation that introduces this meditation is of that sort. When drinking, I was such an individual: sick perfectionist unable ever to find inner satisfaction; whatever I did was never enough; and, because I always compared, anything that anyone else ever did or was led me to feel threatened. I attempted to be "all things," thus squandering whatever hope I had of being simply who I was.

Those traits and that life-style, it seems to me, were intimately connected with my resorting to alcohol and my eventual descent into alcoholism. If active alcoholism is above all a way of life characterized by a certain way of thinking, as I am convinced it was in my own case, then that quotation well describes that way of life and way of thinking, at least for me.

For me, at least, turning to booze signaled an attempt to find inner satisfaction. The warm glow that alcohol's advertising promises, however, is even at best only a shallow mockery — a distorted caricature — of that precious gift. At less than best, of course, as we descend the slope of alcoholism, it becomes more and more a mockingly false promise. Soon, no matter what or how much we drink, it is never enough. That is, it seems to me, the definition of alcoholism.

I remember, as a child, one occasion when I was both sick to my stomach and hungry at the same time. One day at an amusement park, although actually needing real food — a hot dog would have sufficed — I gorged myself on cotton candy. The result was one very sick, and still very hungry, eight-year-old. The frustration of that feeling still echoes: the feeling of being overly full yet also abysmally empty, even as I emptied my stomach of its nebulous, sticky contents. Did that incident prefigure my later alcoholism?

And then there is the matter of comparing. Because of my perfectionism, even as a child I "automatically translated" all "awareness of difference . . . into a comparison of good versus bad, better versus worse." Others' differences always threatened. I could see only "better" or "worse," whether in scholastic grades or social graces, Christmas gifts or athletic skills, parental love or peer popularity. . . . But why go on? I recall, also as a child, being fascinated by chameleons when we studied them in our Nature Science course. Those little lizards supposedly could change their coloration at will in order to fit into their surroundings. Perhaps my fascination with them reflected an unconscious desire to hide, a fear of never being good enough if I were really seen — a fear rooted precisely in my failure to achieve inner satisfaction.

Alcohol, when I discovered it, seemed to allow me to be the ultimate protean being. For many years — in fact, until I had some sobriety in A.A. — I forgot the myth underlying that term, the context of that story. True, Proteus could change his shape into that of any being that he chose, but he did so only when bound fast by chains.

Alcohol forged my chains. Its promise — to enable me to be all things or to quench the pain of not being all things — thus bound me fast into not being simply who I was. And so I never learned, until I found A.A., "that only when we stop trying to be all things do we ever become free to be who we are."

I am an alcoholic. That means that I cannot drink alcohol safely, without risking self-destruction. I learned that I was an alcoholic because Alcoholics Anonymous invited me to identify rather than compare. Yet again, I stand in awe of A.A.'s simple wisdom. There is a connection between the tendency to perfectionism and the addiction to comparison. And of all psychologists, William James perhaps most clearly intuited the nature of that connection — the failure of self-esteem, the rejection of self as not good enough.

James wrote of that connection, however, not in the book beloved of A.A.'s founders, *The Varieties of Religious Experience*, but in his monumental *The Principles of Psychology* and in his more popular *Talks to Teachers* — at neither of which, to the best of anyone's knowledge, any of A.A.'s founders ever so much as glanced. In other words, the insight glimpsed by William James through diligent research and profound thought was arrived at by members of Alcoholics Anonymous in a way that the great philosopher would have approved and applauded — through their own experience.

We in A.A. have paid a terrible price for our wisdom, but if we grasp and cherish and use that wisdom, even that price was worth it. At this point, anyway, we have no choice concerning the price; but we do concerning the wisdom, if we will but recall it.

Kaufman's words recall that wisdom — that way of life and way of thinking that A.A. frees me to embrace. For this thought also, then, I am grateful. But, as always, my deepest gratitude runs toward Alcoholics Anonymous, which, by teaching me and freeing me to identify rather than compare, enables me in my reading as well as my listening to discover: "My God! Yes, that's me!" — and to cherish the difference between what I was like as a drinking alcoholic and what I am like now as I strive to grow in sobriety. "What happened," I need always remember, is that, having paid my dues, I became a member of Alcoholics Anonymous.

55

Alcoholism is not contagious, but recovery is.
— Comment on a television presentation
about Alcoholics Anonymous

BEFORE AND AFTER THE MEETING TONIGHT, members of the group discussed a recent television portrayal of A.A. All agreed that it was tastefully and adequately done, presenting A.A. in accordance with our traditions. I also had seen the program, and one passing comment offered during it sticks in my mind, perhaps because I have ambivalent feelings about it: "Alcoholism is not contagious, but recovery is."

We should know better, but the medical model still on occasion haunts us. The weight of scientific evidence, at least for today, seems preponderantly inclined to acknowledge that there exists a physical, physiological component to our malady. Although I should know better, that acknowledgment warms me.

I should know better because the program of Alcoholics Anonymous amply verifies the threefold nature of our malady. We are, the testimony of others and our own experience make clear, afflicted physically, mentally, and spiritually. Although the depth of the ravages of our alcoholism varies in each of these areas, all of those areas are affected in the life of any alcoholic. We have but one life. However we may distinguish facets and aspects of our being, we are — ultimately, at least, even if tenuously — in some sense whole and one.

I am an alcoholic: neither my brain nor my hormones, neither my body nor my emotions, neither my imagination nor my spirit can make that statement. Oh, there is alcoholic thinking and alcoholic behavior, there are alcoholic resentments and alcoholic grandiosity; but only I can say, "I am an alcoholic," and "I" is an inseparable unity of the physical, the mental, the emotional, and the spiritual.

And so I have mixed feelings and diverse thoughts about that apparent truism: "Alcoholism is not contagious, but recovery is."

On the one hand, it contains and teaches an important truth. On the other hand, however, it can open the door to dangerous misunderstanding. Because I prefer to end with the positive, let me begin with the negative.

Because alcoholism is so complex, because our malady ravages our lives in so many ways, because also no man is an island and alcoholics almost always reveal the strange circumstance of being loved, there is a sense in which our dis-ease is contagious. That is why Al-Anon exists. That is why, although the discovery's one-sided emphasis marks it as probably a passing fad of this moment's generation, groups of adult children of alcoholics find bonds of affinity. If recovery from alcoholism involves a way of life characterized by a way of thinking, then alcoholism itself must be a way of life, a way of thinking. And ways of life, if not exactly contagious, yet have a way of profoundly impacting those even inadvertently caught up in them.

Thus, although "alcoholism is not contagious" sounds cute and clever and even superficially profound, I suspect that any member of Al-Anon, on hearing it, would raise an eyebrow and begin thinking of appropriate distinctions and necessary qualifications. We alcoholics are, in one sense, carriers of highly contagious dis-ease. It may be painful for us to admit, but at least in my own story, my Fourth and Tenth Step inventories, my Sixth and Seventh Step confrontation with less pleasant aspects of myself, my Eighth and Ninth Step advertence to amends — all reveal that I have injured others, loved ones, by having drawn them into the maelstrom of my sick alcoholic way of life. Alcoholism, the physical disease, may not be contagious; but alcoholism the disrupter of mental and emotional and spiritual serenity is highly transmissible and pathologically communicable. Anyone who doubts that should visit Al-Anon and simply listen.

One should do the same if he or she doubts that recovery is contagious. And that is, of course, only one-half of the positive side of our quotation. It is, after all, good to remind others as well as ourselves that alcoholism is not leprosy nor plague nor cancer nor herpes.

Every age, it seems, makes some disease into metaphor. If you want to know what any generation or culture most feared, study not only its labeling of sin but also its attitude toward sickness. The history of medicine reveals more concerning our ideas about our essential humanity than the histories of religion and philosophy combined.

Our era's paradigmatic disease is cancer. Most people accept that most cancers are not contagious. Most of those same people nevertheless also shun — or are at least highly uncomfortable in the presence of — one who has cancer. The very existence of the disease of cancer threatens some of what we would like to hold as cherished assumptions about ourselves: that we are in control; that more is better. The very existence of the phenomenon of alcoholism threatens the same assumptions.

And so the truism that alcoholism is not contagious, at least in the usual understanding of those terms, is an important truth. If nonalcoholics could learn not to shun and fear and stigmatize alcoholics, they might learn something from us about themselves. At least that seems the experience of many nonalcoholics who have been open to such learning and such discovery — from Dr. Benjamin Rush and William James's Jerry M'Auley before A.A. to Dr. Silkworth and Dr. John Norris and Professor Milton Maxwell and literally innumerable others today, under the guidance of Alcoholics Anonymous. It is good, then, good both for alcoholics and nonalcoholics, to spread the knowledge that, in strict medical terms, "Alcoholism is not contagious, but recovery is."

But the more important accent falls on the second half of that truism.

Usually, in A.A. itself, we miss an important experience. Very few drinking alcoholics attend our meetings. Al-Anon is substantially different. At a good number of their meetings, an Al-Anon group harbors both those whose loved ones are in A.A. and those whose loved ones are still practicing their alcoholism. In such a setting, it is easy — and beautiful — to see how contagious recovery can be.

We do see some of that in A.A. itself, of course. Sobriety is contagious. Because we learn and grow and indeed become by modeling, the fellowship and its program suggest that we "stick with the winners." The serenity of true sobriety is always attractive: if and when we see it, we want it. Because we are alcoholics, we also need it. And so we search out models for growth and sponsors who will guide growth, even as we learn also bits and pieces from just about everyone else who is also trying to grow in sobriety and serenity.

For many long centuries, physicians practiced an art more than a science. As part of their art, they thought in terms of atmospheres and auras. That holistic approach understood certain settings to be healthful or unhealthy in themselves. The atmosphere of a rocky island engendered health no less than the miasma of a dank swamp induced illness. Our colonial forebears, insofar as they were able, rigidly controlled the temperature and humidity and especially the circulation of air in their sleeping chambers.

Today, we have more accurate knowledge of the etiology of such diseases as malaria and pneumonia, arthritis and dyspepsia. But there are few of us who would choose to live near a nuclear reactor or to work in an asbestos-lined office. More profoundly, as the modern science of medicine learns more and more about the phenomenon of stress, the concepts of aura, environment, and atmosphere are beginning to make a respectable recurrence in medical literature.

A.A. is different, but it is an atmosphere. To walk into one's own A.A. group's meeting is to feel at home — to relax and to enjoy calm acceptance of one's acceptance. To find an A.A. meeting when one is traveling in a strange city is to discover the same feeling, for it is sobriety that not only creates but itself is that atmosphere.

Some medicines we taste or swallow, others are injected or otherwise violently intruded into our bodies. Alcoholics Anonymous, it seems to me, we inhale or, better, absorb — not through our nose or our pores, but with our very being.

Recovery is contagious because sobriety — the A.A. way of life — is contagious. More than any other reality in my experience, to know it is to love it. Perhaps that is ultimately why "alcoholism is not contagious, but recovery is." There is nothing more unknowable and unlovable than a drinking alcoholic; there is nothing more knowable and lovable than the way of life lived by those who are sober in Alcoholics Anonymous.

56

. . . When "to explain is also to inventory," then the act of recounting is once again justified.

— Paul Ricoeur

Taking inventory is not the same as keeping score.

— Anonymous

THE SPEAKER AT TONIGHT'S MEETING touched off one of my sober addictions — playing with the different meanings of simple words. Instead of "telling" her story, Peg noted, she would "recount" it, for that term helped her remember the kind of story that it was.

Peg's use of "recount" struck me, because I believe it sheds light on the connection between two practices very familiar to members of Alcoholics Anonymous: taking inventory and telling stories. Recently, I found the same connection hinted in a non-A.A. source — the French philosopher, Paul Ricoeur. Investigating the relationship between quantification and narrative style in historical exposition, Ricoeur suggested an essential relationship between *re-counting* in the sense of "counting again," and *recounting*, which seems "to relate, to bring forth by telling in detail." In A.A. we do both.

The simplest and best answer to how A.A. works, the answer more recounted than described by *The Big Book* and its famous fifth chapter, is: "by telling stories." "Rarely have we seen . . . . Our stories disclose . . . . Here are the steps we took . . . ."

Story is narrative — a recounting of one's experience that brings it forth by relating it in detail. Stories have meaning because they convey context. Context means not only external setting, but the internal relationship of the incidents and events involved in the story itself. Events are not the raw material for stories, as if the storyteller artificially linked together freestanding events to devise a story that had meaning. The story and its meaning rather come first: any event in its becoming is part of at least one story, and any event is defined only by the stories of which it is a part.

Let me try to illustrate, although the only way to do so adequately would be by telling my whole story. But, for the sake of illustration: angry at being rejected in love, I once went out drinking and totalled my car by broadsiding a trolley. That incident led me to attend my first A.A. meeting. The accident is an event in the story of my love-life, my drinking-life, and my recovery-life — not to mention my life as a vehicle operator in one commonwealth and my ongoing relationship with the gendarmerie of a certain municipality. The same event is also part of the story of the trolley-operator and of the emergency personnel who extracted me from the wreck. It is also a part of the story of the police officer who did not charge me because, as he said, "I have a few too many sometimes, too." Years later, I met him again — at an A.A. meeting where he told my event as a minor incident in his own story.

Newspapers and casual conversations inform us of events. We learn to listen to and for stories only when we are truly and deeply in love — or in such settings as Alcoholics Anonymous. When drinking, in a way, we were trying to live in the wrong story— a story that was not truly ours. At least that is one message I hear when I listen to the valid, fitting stories told at meetings of Alcoholics Anonymous.

But how do I come to know that story, the story that is real because it truly fits me — my story? It seems to me that its discovery is enabled by the Twelve Steps. A.A.'s First Step, terror-inducing as can be the concepts of "powerless" and "unmanageable," is also the breath of fresh air that allows us to see, first, that there is a story in which our drinking and our behavior are embedded, and second, just what point we have reached in the unfolding of that story.

A.A.'s Second and Third Step then present a possible development of our story — restoration to sanity — and indicate how that line of development might come about: trust in a power greater than ourselves. We are then invited more deeply to understand our story, the story of which we are part, by first taking and then sharing our inventory in Steps Four and Five.

I am not a businessman. Before A.A., my main exposure to "inventory" was as a stock-boy in a supermarket. Four times a year, we worked through the night, counting cans or whatever. I liked inventory: we were paid a bit more hourly, and there were no customers cluttering the aisles, looking for tomatoes in the fruit section and for pumpkin among the canned vegetables. I also liked the task of counting. For whatever reason, it engendered a sense of accomplishment. "Now we know," I remember thinking as I bicycled home in the dark. I had no idea what we knew, but I felt that knowing was important and that I had contributed to it.

A.A.'s inventory is different; yet, in a very deep way, it is the same. I marvel at the wisdom of our founders in choosing the precise term, *inventory*. A.A.'s inventory is different because we do not concentrate on counting. But the deeper meaning of this inventory is essential to our growth: we record both what is there and what is not there. To inventory is to examine both assets and liabilities, both credits and debits, both who and what we are and who and what we are not. "Examination of conscience" would not have served to name the process required: it tends to focus attention on the negatives. "Inventory" implies examining what one has in order to determine what one needs.

In the A.A. program, having taken and shared our inventory, we turn attention in the Sixth and Seventh Steps to our needs — to what we must re-order if we would become truly and fully human. This re-ordering, of course, involves not filling out forms and requisitions but the more literal re-ordering of seeing the necessity of certain kinds of order in our lives. "First things first"; but A.A. also teaches us less to engage in that re-ordering than to be open to it. As alcoholics, our track record at taking charge of any aspect of our lives leaves quite a bit to be desired. We must learn first to let go, even of the needs that our inventory has disclosed. And so it is suggested that we become willing and humbly ask: we count what is on and what is absent from the shelves, but we do not pretend ourselves to restock them.

The Eighth and Ninth Steps begin to teach us how we will be re-ordered and restocked. We take a broader yet also more specific inventory: more specific in that it focuses on our relationships with others; broader in that it extends over time, linking present with past (the Eighth Step) and with the immediate future (the Ninth Step). This is the point where inventory and telling stories link: we recount in order to re-count, even as we re-order in order to relate — another word with two interrelated meanings. Our stories relate our relationships.

All this comes to fruition, of course, in the Tenth Step, wherein the connection between continuing to take personal inventory and telling our ongoing story is explicitly set forth. Again, our recounting of our story is based on our re-counting of our stock, but we are able to re-count, to continue to take personal inventory, only because, now in touch with our stories because we recount them, we know what and how to re-count.

Taking inventory is not the same as keeping score. In fact, at times I am tempted to think that one of the most profound differences between a drinking alcoholic and a sober alcoholic — based on my experience with myself — is that the drinking alcoholic tends to keep score; the sober alcoholic takes inventory.

I learned the difference between keeping score and taking inventory by telling my story at meetings of Alcoholics Anonymous. Keeping score is counting; telling my story is recounting.

Let me be honest: at times, the old habit of keeping score tends to resurface. At times, locked into my own private world and contemplating the belly button of my supposed sobriety, I cannot even be sure whether I am taking inventory or keeping score. But at an A.A. meeting, as soon as I begin to tell the story that results from that self-examination, others can tell — they can tell the nature of what I am telling.

Tell and telling; re-counting and recounting; reordering and re-ordering; the relating of relationships: I seem, today, puckishly caught up in word-games, and word-games are the playthings of a child's mind. But in sobriety, I am a child. Each different glimpse that I get of A.A.'s Twelve-Step program delights me as much as the pleasure any infant finds in a new color, a new shape, a newly seen beam of light dancing from window to crib-rail. Let the psychologists make of it what they will: to be reborn in sobriety is to be reborn to life; and if I must then learn as does any infant, this time around I am going to enjoy it.

57

The sway of alcohol over mankind is unquestionably due to its power to stimulate the mystical faculties of human nature. . . . Sobriety diminishes, discriminates, and says no; drunkenness expands, unites, and says yes. It is in fact the great exciter of the Yes function in man. . . . The drunken consciousness is one bit of the mystic consciousness, and our total opinion of it must find its place in our opinion of that larger whole.

— William James

TAKEN OUT OF CONTEXT, THOSE WORDS might make one wonder at Bill W.'s tribute to William James as "one of the founders of Alcoholics Anonymous."

James is treating here of mysticism, seeking — as he always did — "to interpret to the philistine much that he would otherwise despise and reject utterly." What better way to open eyes and shake assumptions, for one with James's mischievous humor, than to point out the relationship between the mysticism that most of his hearers scorned while affecting to admire, and the drunkenness that most of those same listeners admired while affecting to scorn?

Yet James also had a positive point in the words quoted. Rational analysis divides and conquers; mysticism joins and unites. The more rational we become, the more some other part of our very selves yearns to escape the hobbles of pure rationalism. When drinking, some of us sought that escape in alcohol. Sobriety, because it is founded in honesty and especially in honest acceptance of our own reality, cannot afford to deny that quest. Important as it may be to diminish and discriminate, our very humanity requires also that we expand and unite. Essential as it is that we often say no, to live as human is also to find ways of saying yes. The question, of course, is how we express that necessary aspect of being human.

Two A.A. axioms guide us: "Identify, don't compare" and "Utilize, don't analyze." Each suggests to me that I find in

Alcoholics Anonymous an arena in which to exercise my affirmative rather than my reductive function. Identification involves the participation that signals self and other-than-self united in an act of a knowing that is more than mere knowledge. The admonition to utilize, of course, suggests applying a pragmatic test of truth: we come to know certain kinds of reality not by thinking about them but by testing them in our lives.

It also fascinates me that William James and Carl Jung intuited identically the same link between the use of alcohol and the quest for — for want of a better term — spirituality. Jung interpreted alcoholism as the struggle of *spiritus contra spiritum* — the conflict of spirits against Spirit. James saw in drunkenness "the great exciter of the Yes function in man," the enabler of affirmation. Many have written, recently, of our need to be affirmed. But we also, as human, need to affirm. One of our deepest needs is to say "Yes" to reality, to all reality.

Both James and Jung realized that reality involves more than the narrowly rational. Sigmund Freud, usually credited with the modern discovery of that ancient truth, refused to affirm it. The goal of his therapy is to make the unconscious conscious: the unconscious in itself can be only dark and threatening, and to embrace it is to risk self-destruction — destruction of the controlling ego — and that, for Freud, was not a desirable goal. James and Jung were at once more open-minded and more deeply accepting of the reality of "self." For them, healing — which means making whole — involves finding self's wholeness by accepting and affirming that which is larger and deeper than the self. Is it any wonder that Freudian thought has contributed little that is not laughable to our understanding of alcoholism, while Jamesian and Jungian insight find fruitful expression in the fellowship and program of Alcoholics Anonymous?

For a moment, let me think wildly and speak atrociously. Could it be that our task as human is self-destruction? — that we are born to self-destruct? Gregory Bateson has suggested that the very concept of "self" is a "false reification" — that systems theory and cybernetics finger its flaw by demonstrating that to be is to-be-part-of some larger whole.

The same insight, less modernly expressed, seems to me to underlie all the great religious traditions of mankind. Self must be transcended if we would truly find ourselves. And so we set out, both driven and pulled by an innate impetus that is life itself, to destroy self — to merge in some way with the other-than-self. The question is not whether but how we go about that task — the task that we call "love."

Drunkenness achieves it: who would deny its self-destructiveness? Mysticism approaches it, or so at least its practitioners and their students such as William James tell us. Is it too much to claim that I find in A.A. what I sought in alcohol? Bill W. did not think so. Hear his words, written to a student of Dr. Jung:

> More than most people, I think, alcoholics want to know who they are, what this life is about, and whether they have a Divine origin and an appointed destiny, and live in a system of cosmic justice and love. No doubt this quest, conscious or unconscious, is spurred by the neurotic pains which have preceded and which accompany their drinking. It is the experience of many of us in the early stages to feel that we have had a glimpse of the Absolute and a heightened feeling of identification with the Cosmos. I am satisfied that these feelings are generally more marked in the alcoholic than in average drinkers.
>
> . . . It is perfectly true, too, that alcoholics find in A.A. . . . a great deal more of what they glimpsed and felt while trying to grope their way toward God in alcohol. A.A. has of course seized this advantage. . . .

Have I grown up enough to accept that insight — to affirm it by finding its truth in myself, in my life, in the ongoing destruction of self that is involved in letting go of my self-centeredness? If I have come to accept it, is that affirmation truly growth? Does it meet the standard that can be my only claim as an A.A. member: "We claim spiritual progress rather than spiritual perfection?"

When drinking, I could have said in blasphemous mockery of the poet Paul: "I live, now not 'I,' but booze lives in me." Now sober, might I say with neither blasphemy nor mockery: "I live, now not 'I,' because I live in and through something greater than my 'self,' than my 'I' "? If I choose to interpret that reality as the fellowship and program of Alcoholics Anonymous, who can gainsay it? If I choose to understand it otherwise, can anyone who also knew me drinking dare to deny it?

If we transcend self-centeredness — the root of our troubles — only by dying to self, have I chosen — in finding Alcoholics Anonymous — not only a more fully human way of life but also a more more fully human way of dying?

58

Whenever we care what others think of us, we have given over to those others some degree of power to affect how we feel about ourselves. . . . Power-seeking individuals prefer to gain control in relation to others and also remain in control when in any interpersonal situation of human relationship.

— Gershen Kaufman

"PEOPLE-PLEASING" PROVIDES A PERENNIAL discussion topic. When drinking, whether because of the insecurity that led us to booze it up in the first place or because of the self-loathing engendered by our dim awareness that we were not in control of our drinking, many of us showed signs of becoming doormats. We thought we cared about what people thought of us, but actually we were terrified lest their disapproval destroy us.

When we first arrived at Alcoholic Anonymous, we were taught a fundamental, basic truth: self-respect comes not from without, but from within. We learned to esteem ourselves — not for heroic actions or grand designs, but because we were alcoholics who were able, with A.A.'s help, one day at a time, not to take the first drink. Some of us wondered how others, our former associates, would regard our not drinking. The guidance we received from older members was twofold. Acquaintances who mocked or objected, it was first pointed out, were probably not friends; any real friend would rejoice at our newfound health and would support the behavioral change that brought it about. My own experience with A.A.'s Ninth Step bore out the truth of that advice.

The second point inculcated was that it made little difference what others thought. If I did not drink alcohol, one day at a time, I would gain a self-respect far more precious than all the esteem others might offer. Back when I was drinking, a psychiatrist once suggested that I lived like a falling leaf — changing direction at the slightest breeze of anyone else's whim. When I found A.A., I discovered an anchor — or a compass; I became, if not self-directed, program-directed. The Twelve Steps charted my journey, and I learned to measure my progress against their firmly founded standard. What others thought of me became not unimportant but secondary — subordinate to those others' own adherence to the way of life with which I was striving to identify.

But sometimes, when this topic of "what others think of me affecting how I feel" comes up in discussion, I hear echoes — even in myself — of an earlier way of thinking, a way of thinking that does not jibe well with the understanding of sobriety suggested by A.A. The imp of self-direction emerges. We want to claim that we do not care what others think, so long as we are sober; and we warn each other about giving to others the power to affect how we feel about ourselves.

Usually, those warnings are well taken. The wisdom that inhabits most A.A. meetings seems almost instinctively to spot the signs of stinking thinking that underlie most fears expressed about what others think. Because, as we well know, "resentment is the number one offender" leading alcoholics to drink again, groups are lovingly vigilant to lay bare and to stamp out resentment's first buds. Because resentment is often rooted in projection, in attributing to others the devious thoughts and nefarious intentions with which we as alcoholics are ourselves overly familiar, that is a salutary exercise. It promotes the health of our sobriety and so also of ourselves.

But it seems to be also that we can go too far in our adulation of self-direction. If we are wholly self-directed, what are we doing at a meeting of Alcoholics Anonymous? If we do not care what others think about us, why do we listen so intently at those meetings to the thoughts of sober members about something brought up in our stories? If we claim self-direction as our goal, whatever happened to the decision we made — and, in my own case, remake daily — in A.A.'s Third Step? Alcoholics Anonymous teaches, it seems to me, not that we be blissfully uncaring of the thoughts of others, but that we choose a bit more carefully than we did when drinking which others' thoughts will make a difference to us, to how we feel about ourselves.

Because this has to do with alcohol, it concerns power. Kaufman, I believe, is right. A hallmark of the power-seeking individual is the refusal to grant to others any power to affect how he or she feels about himself or herself. That is not independence, which we should in any case be wary of claiming; it is arrogance. And pride, the *Twelve and Twelve* reminds us, "heads the procession" of "the Seven Deadly Sins."

Alcoholism has essentially to do with power and control — with the demand to be in charge, especially of our own lives. It seems to me that we surrender that demand, or at least acknowledge our utter failure at implementing it, when we first appear at an A.A. meeting and, however shyly, admit to being an alcoholic. In my understanding, we are not in control, especially of how we feel; and, because I am an alcoholic, the moment I think I just might be able to control my feelings, I will almost certainly again try to control them by controlling my drinking. Because I have been around A.A. long enough to see the results of such efforts by others, I would just as soon not start down that road myself. For me, at least, I suspect that any attempt to retain power and control over how reality outside me affects how I feel about myself is fraught with hazard. Any attempt to clutch to my bosom that power to control how I feel will likely lead to my favorite pre-A.A. posture: lying in a sweat-soaked bed clutching a bottle, wondering if it yet contains enough to sustain me until I feel well enough to get more so that I can feel good again. So much for my self-directed efforts to hoard power over my feelings.

In my Third Step, I surrender the claim to power and control over how I feel about myself. I give over that power to my Higher Power. My Higher Power, in this case, either is or chooses to work through, at first level, my A.A. group and especially my own sponsor, and more profoundly through those others in whom I see the A.A. way of life, whether they happen to be alcoholic or not. What such people think does make a difference to me and does affect how I feel about myself — and I am grateful for that guidance. It would, to me, be ultimate folly to resent it as intrusion, to fear the power it gives those others. How can my puny mind and blunted feelings ever plumb the depths of the wisdom of A.A.? Others know those depths and live that wisdom perhaps more deeply, certainly differently. Dare I deprive myself of their experience, strength, and hope out of some misguided fear of surrendering power or even of feeling bad? When that which those whom I respect think makes me feel bad, it is time for me to look to working my program. I need that reminder, then, even at the cost of "feeling bad," lest I feel much, much worse in the not-too-distant future.

"What others think of me" is a red herring: the phrase falsely objectifies the kind of human relationships that A.A. teaches me are possible in suggesting that I identify. Some others are not other to me. Those with whom I identify, on the basis of the A.A. way of life, are part of my sobriety. What they think of me is therefore what they think of and how they participate in my sobriety and its ongoing growth. If that is a surrender of power, it is also a victory of serenity.

I confess to being grandiose enough to apply to myself, on this topic, the words Dr. Silkworth spoke to Bill W.: "Hang onto it, boy: it is so much better than what you had!" What I had was booze, with all its empty promises of control; what I have now is the A.A. way of life, which comes to me in all its fullness through people. And for me, at least, it comes to me only if those people's thoughts make at least the difference to my feelings about myself that booze once did.

59

The only requirement for A.A. membership is a desire to stop drinking.

— The Third Tradition

AT THE TIME OF THE ORIGINAL WRITING AND publication of A.A.'s Twelve Traditions, the third of those guidelines began: "The only requirement for A.A. membership is an honest desire to stop drinking." I recall asking my first sponsor about it: "Why did A.A. drop the word *honest* in the statement of its membership requirement?" Phil's answer still echoes, reminding me of the mental and spiritual condition to which my alcoholism had reduced me. "I'm not sure, Ern, but it could have been because somebody foresaw you coming along."

Although I chuckle at that memory now, it stung deeply at the time. In fact, there is still sufficient bite in that recollection to make its recalling a salutary spur to "remember when." My drinking had messed up my life to the point where I doubt anyone thought me capable of an honest anything. Not that I was dishonest: alcohol is the great deceiver; the alcoholic is more deceived than dishonest.

A slipping newcomer at tonight's meeting led another memory to crowd in on that first one. The Third Tradition speaks of "a desire to stop drinking." My story includes eighteen months of hanging around Alcoholics Anonymous before finally joining the fellowship and embracing its program. I attended meetings, but I tended to come late and to leave early. I listened, but compared rather than identified. Because I did not know the difference, I thought myself more as one who goes to Alcoholics Anonymous than as a member of it. Looking back, it is not exactly surprising that someone who could not understand that difference did not stop drinking. What might be surprising to one who does not know A.A. is that I was welcomed at meetings, was still treated as a member by those who were members.

I probably did not learn much during those months, but I do

recall one conversaton. It took place at the coffee urn, during the meeting, for I was too edgy to sit still for a length of a speaker's entire story. Jimmy had followed me out — ostensibly to refresh his own coffee, more realistically, I suspect, to guard against my knocking over the refreshment table. Realizing that it was obvious that I had been drinking, I muttered something about A.A. "not seeming to be working for me."

I expected to hear the usual cliche so often tossed my way by others: "It works for you if you work for it." But Jimmy said nothing for a moment, apparently concentrating all his attention on stirring exactly the right amount of sugar into his styrofoam cup. Finally he looked up and spoke seriously, almost quizzically: "Well, you know, Ern, the only requirement is 'a desire to stop drinking.' It could be that the problem is that the only desire you have is to stop getting into trouble."

That hit home; for, in my case, at that moment, Jimmy was right. I was not yet ready to stop drinking. I was going to A.A. mainly because I hoped to find a way to cut back on the troubles that my drinking was increasingly causing me. It would be nice to report that that night marked a turning point, that Jimmy's comment helped me to become ready to stop drinking right then. The insight probably helped over time, but at that moment I had yet more troubles to go through.

A.A.'s Third Tradition, then, whenever I am fortunate enough to hear it discussed, awakens helpful memories — healthy memories of "what it was like." For some of us, A.A. did not come easily. Or would it be more accurate to say that for some of us, we did not come easily to A.A.? But did anyone, when you get right down to it?

Yet how difficult it was for me to discover and to learn that one need only desire to stop drinking. For too long, my desire was garbled. The Third Tradition does not read: "The only requirement for A.A. membership is the desire to drink without getting into trouble." Even after learning that, I almost slipped into a stupid attempt to examine my "desire to stop drinking" for "honesty." I, at least, did not come to A.A. honest; whatever honesty I have, I learned in Alcoholics Anonymous. Honesty was

A.A.'s first gift to me. How could I bring what I did not have?

There is also yet another bit of subtle wisdom in A.A.'s wording of its membership requirement. The desire to stop drinking is not the same as the demand to stop drinking. Active alcoholics, I think it fair to say based on my own experience with myself, have no desires. Cravings, yes; demands, certainly; aspirations and intentions, what else? But active alcoholics have as little desire as they have hope: how often the word *hopeless* appears in *The Big Book*'s description of our condition!

The term *desire*, then, in A.A.'s Third Tradition, contains a kind of catch. Truly "to desire" — as opposed to "craving" or "demanding" or "aspiring to" or "intending" — already implies the beginnings of letting go. We must learn to desire before we can hope; and we truly hope only if we have surrendered, only if we have really let go.

At large A.A. meetings, I learn much from watching oldtimers listen to newcomers. The conversations are usually brief, but they often have a pattern. The oldtimer, experienced in sobriety, listens to hear whether the newcomer is expressing desire and hope or demand and intention. If the former, the A.A. veteran nourishes the desire and holds out promise to the hope — perhaps by telling a bit of his or her own story that reveals A.A.'s promises coming true. If the latter, cautions are suggested about demands and projecting. Drawing again on his or her own story, the oldtimer illustrates the hopelessness of demand, the unmanageability of plans.

Each time I overhear such a conversation, and especially when I am privileged myself to participate in one, I recall again the subtle, profound wisdom of A.A.'s statement of its requirement for membership. And grateful for my own eventual fulfillment of it and for my own sobriety, I try, by my story, to pass it on.

60

Perhaps the will, at its deepest, does not connote self-assertion and dominance, but love and acquiescence; not the will to power but the will to prayer.

— William Barrett

OVER TIME, I AM BEGINNING TO NOTICE TWO things about non-A.A. literature, or at least about that portion of it dealing with alcoholism as it appears in human persons as opposed to technical treatises on such topics as alcohol metabolism or the biochemistry of ethanol absorption.

Let me introduce my two observations by noting that I do a first filing of what I read under two headings. First, those studies that approach alcoholism as if it existed primarily in test tubes and tissues form one classification. They may supply useful knowledge about alcohol, but rarely do they pretend to say much of practical value to the alcoholic. The second classification is comprised of those studies that at least implicitly build upon the humanistic observation that alcoholism occurs specifically in alcoholics — in human beings in all their complexities. They focus attention directly upon the alcoholic more than upon alcohol or alcoholism. It is the literature in this second classification that my observations concern.

The first point has to do with that literature's attention to and attitude toward the fellowship and program of Alcoholics Anonymous. Until about a decade ago, A.A. tended to be either ignored or mentioned only peripherally. With relatively few exceptions, those who adverted to A.A. presented its fellowship and program as either possibly a stopgap solution for the increasingly fewer people who still took religion seriously, or as a crutchlike pacifier for deviates who were so socially and psychologically deprived or depraved that recovery was sadly impossible.

Very few articles of that tenor still appear. Alcoholics

Anonymous has become, if you will pardon the expression, "scientifically respectable." Led by sensitive humanists such as Gregory Bateson, social scientists more and more approach A.A. with respect, open-mindedly exploring its demonstrated results. Many of their interpretations may evoke smiles, but even more suggest insight — and almost all reveal an intellectual honesty that will delight any serious student of the history of scholarly research on alcoholism.

Not all of these studies, by the way, enthusiastically approve of what they find in A.A. Yet even the gainsayers and critics, those whose interpretive frameworks lead them to find in A.A. "rigidity" and "dogmatism" and "ideology," reveal also respect. Their interpretations, in general, when criticized by other researchers in a scholarly way, can be seen as valid in the same way as was each blind man's description of the elephant. But the existence of serious scholarly discussion is itself of profound significance, at least in the narrow world of scholarly research. Perhaps A.A. and EAPs (Employee Assistance Programs) could work together more fruitfully. Perhaps more careful thought about the distinction between treatment and recovery, between acute crisis intervention and a chronic way of life, can help some who are still suffering to find sobriety. A.A.'s history reveals the fellowship itself as wondrously open-minded, so long as something worked. It seems to me, in other words, that the scholarly ideal of disinterested objectivity and the A.A. legacy of responsibility show signs of meeting on the same ground, and for that I rejoice.

The news is not so good on the second front, at least at first-level observation. From the very beginning of its history, A.A. has always confronted an alternative understanding of recovery — the insistence that "true recovery" for the alcoholic involves regaining the ability to drink safely, that the goal of treatment ought to be "controlled drinking." That impetus has not diminished, although its proponents now at least suggest more frequently and more explicitly that controlled drinking is an appropriate goal for only some alcoholics.

But I have noticed something else in that literature, as it has — you should pardon the expression — "matured." Those who urge controlled drinking, because of their own honesty (which, with one well-known exception, is impressive and should not be denied), are becoming more and more explicit about their understanding of control. And guess what? That literature's portrayal of the "successful controlled drinker" is coming more and more to resemble Dr. Silkworth's (and A.A.'s) description of the "active alcoholic" — one obsessed with thinking about his or her consumption of alcohol.

A light is beginning to dawn, in other words, and from a most unanticipated direction. To state its point perhaps too glibly but nevertheless validly, an active alcoholic is precisely someone who has to control his or her drinking. At least the first half of *The Big Book*'s definition of an alcoholic involves obsession, and the literature on controlled drinking ever more clearly reveals that the success of efforts at controlled drinking correlates directly with the amount of time and energy devoted to thinking about drinking. The question of success or failure of the effort to control one's drinking, I suspect most sober alcoholics would agree, is ultimately irrelevant. The difference between the alcoholic and the nonalcoholic is precisely this: the nonalcoholic does not have to control his or her drinking. We, as alcoholics, may find that as difficult to understand as most nonalcoholics find it difficult to understand our having to control, and failing at it . . . but that, I think, just happens to be the way it is.

Where nonalcoholics and members of A.A. would agree, I long suspected and now feel is verified by the literature on controlled drinking, is that, given a choice between having to control one's drinking and choosing not to drink, one day at a time, the latter is infinitely preferable. Who would choose obsession? Only one group, in my experience: those already obsessed with the idea and ideal of control — those who produce that literature.

The ultimate obsession, philosophers tell us, is precisely with control — the "Will to Power" so exquisitely delineated in the works of Friedrich Nietzsche and so penetratingly analyzed by such recent commentators as William Barrett and Dr. Leslie Farber. In reviewing the literature on controlled drinking, I find I am more reading shopworn philosophy than perusing the results of careful research.

I am rarely accused of being a compassionate person, but my heart bleeds for those addicted to the idea of controlled drinking. For the Will to Power is the ultimate addiction: it is addiction to addiction, in Farber's pungent phrase. We already have a "Controlled Drinker's Anonymous" — it is called A.A. But if anyone out there would like to begin a self-help mutual-aid group for those addicted to the idea of control, I have names to suggest: "Vicious-Circle Twelfth-Step calls" (who would be "in control"?) and (perhaps the ultimate name for the endeavor itself) "Gods, Incorporated."

61

It strikes me that those who don't have anything in their closet don't have much in their attic either.

— William Manchester (while being interviewed about John F. Kennedy)

TO BE A SOBER ALCOHOLIC IS TO HAVE BEEN a drunk. I have yet to meet an A.A. member who discovered his or her alcoholism the easy way. In A.A., as we know, "there are no dues or fees for membership." A common understanding of that clause from our "Preamble" suggests that we paid our dues before finding A.A. Many of us came, in fact, because we no longer could pay those dues, mentally and spiritually as well as physically and financially.

To be a sober alcoholic, then, is to have been a drunk; and, as drunks, we did things and acted in ways the very memory of which is painful. Fully half of the A.A. program, the middle six Steps from Four through Nine, seem designed to help us confront that reality. And not only to confront it, but also to transcend it. Transcending means to grow beyond; it does not simply imply overcoming, at least in the usual sense. Because we are powerless, we cannot conquer anything. Our way of life, we know, involves not managing but letting go. But how do we let go of that which remains a part of us because it is part of our story?

A.A.'s answer is clear and concise. We first take and then share our inventory; we become ready for change and then ask to be changed; we think in terms of, and then, as appropriate, act in ways that might repair the damage that we have caused. At best, we mend or repair: we cannot undo. Hurt, ours or others', may perhaps be transcended; it cannot be erased. Any reality that was, in some sense always is.

What, then, comes after the Ninth Step? The simplest and most obvious and truest answer is the Tenth Step. In a way, it recapitulates the preceding six. Practicing the Tenth Step keeps us mindful of the past and of the growth in which we are yet engaged.

I like the observation made by William Manchester, a good historian who does not blink at the truth.

His metaphor also reminds that any story — and all history is a story — is like a house. And because, as A.A. teaches us, our lives have meaning only as stories, that image may also teach us about ourselves. If so, what do we mean by our "closets" and our "attic"?

We have — and need — both closets and attics, I think, because of our propensity to put things away rather than throw them out. Some things we hide in closets less because they are ugly than because they have become unsuitable. We can find no fitting place for them. Even metaphorical closets, then, contain more than skeletons: they hold all those things that for one reason or another we cannot throw away. Those realities are there, and in general we remember that they are there, but that memory is not at the forefront of our consciousness. We remember them only when we need them . . . or when they start to spill over and out of the closets in which we tried to contain them.

In actual houses, many attics are like closets. In the image, however, attic implies upstairs. The metaphor shifts slightly, but its meaning is clear. Just as a well-appointed house has both closets and an attic, a fully human person has not only unsightly memories but something "upstairs." Can you imagine the A.A. program without the oft-called "housecleaning" Steps? That, in essence, is the point of Manchester's quip.

Many nonalcoholics labor under a severe disadvantage when they try to follow our Twelve-Step program. Deprived of the drama of drunkenness, even the spiritually inclined among them — perhaps especially the spiritually inclined among nonalcoholics — tend to slide from "making a decision" directly to "seeking through prayer and meditation. . . ." Those are both good practices, but their results seem to be a hollow shell of spirituality if not informed — even richly stuffed — by the insights and practices suggested by Steps Four through Ten.

Having empty closets, such spirituality seems devoid of both divinity and humanity.

As alcoholics, and especially as guided by Alcoholics Anonymous, we are unlikely to make that mistake. Each time we tell our story, we link our attic to our closet, reminding ourselves not only that we have both but also what their relationship should be. Especially when drinking, we were busily engaged in gathering unmentionables. At times, we paused and remorsefully tried to stuff those disasters out of sight, into our closets. Then we leaned against the door, surveyed the apparent success of our denial, and had another drink. When our closets became too full, when they could no longer hold the ever-increasing detritus of our alcoholic lives, some of us were fortunate enough to conceive the desire to stop collecting — the desire to stop drinking. The very fortunate among us then found, or were found by, Alcoholics Anonymous.

A.A. neither locked shut nor yanked open the door of our cluttered closet. In time, one day at a time, the fellowship and its program rather guided us in inventorying and then sorting out our closet's contents. A.A. helped us confront reality, guiding us to serenity in facing those things we could not change, offering us courage to change those things we could, and especially suggesting the wisdom that allowed us to tell the difference. Alcoholics Anonymous enabled us, in other words, to use our attic in a way that would put our closet in order.

Full closets, of course, do not necessarily imply a full attic — even within A.A. Here, Manchester's metaphor might present a problem. If attic signifies *upstairs*, what does upstairs imply? The image suggests that having and using an upstairs is important; but how am I to understand my attic, my upstairs?

Two possibilities suggest themselves, and they seem to me more complementary than contradictory. First, in Manchester's obvious meaning, attic signifies *mind*. Because the mental is one aspect of our recovery, A.A.'s program allows us to find and to use our attic. One aspect of hitting bottom is the dire fear that we are all closet. The house of my life that I brought to A.A. had precious little, if any, living space left. A.A., in a sense, helped me to find the home hidden beneath my "garbage"; and it did so by first freeing and then helping me to find and to use what I had been abusing and destroying by my drinking — my mind.

But mind was not all that I had misplaced, if not lost. Our malady, *The Big Book* tells us, is physical, mental, and spiritual. To me, then, the metaphor of upstairs means also that which is above me: a power greater than myself or, if you prefer, God as I understand Him.

Such an interpretation does not do violence to Manchester's metaphor, even if it lies beyond his intention. Psychological and philosophical as well as theological insight agree on this: "Religion is the lived admission of failure." If that is so, then closets and attics define each other. One cannot have one without the other. Usually, we approach that insight from only one direction: what is in our attic determines what is in our closet. But the reversal of that insight may be equally true — does the content of our closet define what is in our attic? Because my closet and my attic are interrelated as are the Steps of A.A., that merits thinking on.

62

A person manifests his own nature by the particular way he needs other human beings.

— Roberto Mangabeira Unger

A NOT EXACTLY NEW UNDERSTANDING SEEMS to be coming around again in the field of alcoholism studies — alcoholism as allergy. Those who find wisdom in the approach of A.A. will not be surprised by this turn of interpretation, but they may discover in its insight not so much confirmation of A.A.'s intuition as an invitation to think more deeply about the implications inherent in being an alcoholic.

First, let us be clear that the term *allergy* is used here in a broad sense. Alcohol is not pollen. Medical metaphors, as A.A. co-founder Bill W. well knew, can be dangerous. That is why Bill himself always preferred referring to our condition as a malady rather than a disease. Nevertheless the disease concept of alcoholism has flourished, paralleling the success of A.A., although pushed more strongly by Dr. E. M. Jellinek and the National Council on Alcoholism than by A.A. itself.

In A.A.'s *Big Book*, we recall, the idea of allergy more pervades Dr. Silkworth's contribution in "A Doctor's Opinion" than it informs the chapters labored over by the first "One Hundred Men." A.A., it seems always wise to remember, stands for Alcoholics Anonymous, not for About Alcoholism. A.A. is a fellowship of alcoholics that offers a program for alcoholics: it does not pretend scientifically to examine the nature of alcoholism. When reaching for a metaphor in Chapter Three, discussion selected "a passion for jaywalking" rather than for, say, strawberries as an illustration that the alcoholic's behavior is "absurd and incomprehensible." The early members of A.A., it seems, were as wary of the word *allergy* as they were of the term *addiction*.

And happily so, if the emerging recent understanding has any validity. For it now seems not that the alcoholic has some special allergy to alcohol, but that alcoholics lack an allergiclike protection common in others, in nonalcoholics. As are all the findings of modern science, this understanding is of course subject to refinement, revision, and even overthrow. Still, because provocative, it merits examination.

According to the theory, "normal people" — nonalcoholics — carry within their metabolism and tissues a built-in protection against overindulgence in alcohol, against drinking so much that it would destroy their bodies. The social drinker, when he or she exceeds a certain quantity in alcohol consumption, either passes out or becomes sick. In either case, the system has been triggered to protect itself by preventing further ingestion of alcohol. Even at A.A. meetings, I have never heard anyone tell stories of drinking while vomiting or passed out. This systemic reaction, then, although not a strict allergy, nevertheless functions to prevent further introduction of alcohol into the body. Nonalcoholics have a built-in physiological limit to the amount of alcohol they can consume.

Not so the alcoholic. The theory suggests that alcoholism has to do with the lack of that physiological, allergiclike protection. That is why, supposedly, alcoholics tolerate alcohol so well. Our system's metabolic and histological triggers barely function at all; over time, in fact, it seems that some of us can even defuse them altogether. It is not our tolerance that eventually breaks, in this understanding. Rather, what happens is that nature's protective mechanism having been totally destroyed, alcohol when ingested begins immediately to affect the centers that those mechanisms had been designed to protect. We are alcoholics, in other words, not because we have something, but because we lack something.

I happily leave to the physiologists the further testing and exploration of this theory. What interests me is its philosophical suggestiveness.

That we essentially lack — that we are who we are because we are lacking — strikes me as the core truth of the alcoholic condition, because it is the core reality of the human condition. The recovering alcoholic is always very conscious of what he or she is — an alcoholic — but an alcoholic is essentially one who cannot do something, who cannot drink alcohol safely. Recovery, then, involves knowing and accepting the reality of one's lack.

Only in such acceptance is the alcoholic freed from the tyranny of that reality.

Let me try to approach the implications of lacking from a different direction. Because we lack, we need. And we need not that which we lack so much as a different and, as it were, higher kind of wholeness. To know that one lacks is to be aware that one needs; to accept that one lacks is to acknowledge need without becoming needy. Our problem, as alcoholics, when we were drinking, was not that we needed but that we demanded. Consumed by our neediness, we consumed everything in sight that we thought might sate that aching neediness . . . alcohol and perhaps other drugs, money, and things — and certainly other people. And in that mad consumption, we destroyed not only what we consumed but ourselves — our very selves — for neediness is not need, and demanding destroys rather than fulfills our nature's needs.

In recovery, we know that we lack, and we accept that we need. And we find that when the demand of neediness is replaced by the acceptance of need, we become able to find a higher wholeness that can heal our hurt, a power greater than ourselves that can restore us to sanity.

I suspect that the study of alcoholism can offer, at best, only glimpses of the alcoholic. If we seek portraits rather than sketches, living pictures rather than detailed diagrams, we do better by studying *The Big Book*, best by going to A.A. meetings. But sketches and diagrams are also interesting, and glimpses always have a certain seductive quality. When we are in certain frames of mind, a glance can reveal more than a look. The very lack of information about the alcoholic in studies of alcoholism can thus at least invite sober thoughts — thoughts that shed new light on the depths of the riches of the wisdom of the program of the fellowship of Alcoholics Anonymous.

63

We become conscious of what we ourselves are by imitating others — the consciousness of what the others are precedes — the sense of self grows by the sense of pattern.

— William James

MUCH MODERN PSYCHOLOGY SEEMS FAR TOO subtle. The urge to surprise and the desire for novelty afford one reason, but a deeper cause lies in the nature of any profession. The professional establishes expertise most easily by claiming to have access to that not ordinarily seen. Professionals, in other words, thrive upon mystery.

That observation is not offered in condemnation. Few people would gainsay the benefits of x-ray technology, to choose a familiar and significant example. We need experts, and experts have rights both to make a living and to our respect if they aid us to live more humanly.

Virtually simultaneously with Roentgen's discovery of x-rays, however, came Freud's equally momentous postulation of the power of the unconscious. Each discovery marks a watershed: Roentgen's, in medical practice; Freud's, in psychological theory. However, there are some differences. Let us grant, for present purposes at least, that we have an "unconscious" just as we have a tibia. Physical medicine, it seems to me, has avoided the pitfall of studying everything only by x-rays. Many of the complaints that we bring to our physicians do not require consultation with a radiologist.

It is not clear that psychological thought has avoided the parallel pitfall, although that may be our fault as patients as much as that of the psychologists and psychiatrists who treat us. Even today, the more sophisticated we are or think ourselves to be, the more we seem inclined to judge the validity of proffered psychological understanding according to how deeply it seems to put us in touch with our unconscious processes.

This is not the place to review the history of psychological theory in America, but it does seem appropriate to observe that the evidence is clear and overwhelming that alcoholics have not been much helped by either Freudian depth-analysis or behavioral conditioning. How, then, have alcoholics been helped? Most obviously, by Alcoholics Anonymous. Is there, then, an implicit psychology in Alcoholics Anonymous?

It seems to me that there is an explicit psychology in Alcoholics Anonymous — the psychology of William James. James's thought is not popular today. One cause of his eclipse seems his utter abomination of all forms of mystification and his insistence on popularizing his psychology, his constant effort to present it in terms understandable by ordinary people. James deemed the ultimate test of both his philosophical and psychological thought to be the "Aha!" of recognition accorded by "the common man." In an age of political populism, James was an intellectual populist, firmly committed to the belief that ordinary people do think.

The psychological thought of William James reveals incredible riches. One generally overlooked idea, however, stands out to me. A while back, I rediscovered one of the psychologist's most forgotten insights — the role of imitation and emulation in the process of our learning to become human.

"To emulate" means to pattern oneself after so as to grow at least like: emulation is purposive imitation. We may learn best by doing, but seeing must ordinarily precede doing.

Let me propose a very simple hypothesis about A.A.'s classic suggestion to the alcoholic who still suffers: "Don't drink and go to meetings." By not drinking, the alcoholic learns by doing it "how to not drink." But it is by going to meetings, by attending gatherings of Alcoholics Anonymous, that the alcoholic sees "how to succeed" — how to succeed at not drinking without even really trying, and how to succeed at living by trying to follow the example, the pattern, held out by another sage bit of A.A. advice: "Identify, don't compare."

Imitation is the first and perhaps also the most potent form and motive of human learning, and the invitation to imitation and consequent emulation lies at the core of Alcoholics Anonymous. How, one might ask, can sharing experience, strength, and hope help others to recover from alcoholism? The simple answer is:

"Go to meetings and watch." Complex answers are also available. One might analyze the dynamics of "identification" or examine the theory of "cognitive change" implied in the practice of "telling stories." Or one could wax eloquent about all that is implied in such simple words as *share* and *hope*. But in the last analysis, it seems to me, all those peregrinations of the trained, sophisticated intellect come down to this:

> We become conscious of what we ourselves are by imitating others — the consciousness of what the others are precedes — the sense of self grows by the sense of pattern.

We are imitators in Alcoholics Anonymous: we imitate sober alcoholics because we wish to emulate their life of sobriety. In our commercially sophisticated culture, imitation has come to mean second rate. But there is a not-so-strange truth that ought to be remembered about noncommercial realities such as sobriety: imitating sobriety does not lead to imitation sobriety — it somehow rather begets the real thing.

64

Words are, of course, the most powerful drug used by mankind.

— Rudyard Kipling

WHEN DRINKING ALCOHOLICALLY, AND ESPECIALLY in the final stages of our denial that we were drinking alcoholics, we perpetrated atrocities on the English language. "Having fun" became a synonym for passing out. "A couple of drinks" never meant two.

In sobriety, as we clear up, many of those perversions of language do the same: our language and our thought both become more accurate. But some hangovers linger longer than others. Language has a spiritual quality, at least to this extent: it is one of those realities that degenerate first when we begin drinking alcoholically and that reanimate last as we begin developing sobriety. Certain words we so abused when drinking, that long into sobriety we remain wary of even their valid uses. The words I am thinking of are *unique* and *different*.

To scent denial in all thoughts that we are unique and different is, it seems to me, itself a species of denial. Even if we identify with every story we hear in Alcoholics Anonymous, does any one of us ever hear any story that is exactly like our own, in all its details? Because no other one can be this "I," no one else can make the unique claim on reality that is my existence.

Drinking alcoholically, the resort to chemicals, it further seems to me, signaled and served an attempt to deny uniqueness. We tried to fit in; or we turned to alcohol in order to enhance or to escape our own reality. At times, that reality was not pleasant; but it was our reality — part of that which was and who we uniquely were.

To identify is not the same as to fuse — to become one with in a way that destroys individual identity. We can identify only because we are distinct — an affirmation reflected in the A.A. greeting, "My name is ———, and I am an alcoholic." To deny our uniqueness, then, is to destroy our ability to identify in the A.A. sense.

The case with difference is not much different. We are wary of claiming difference, I believe, for two reasons. First, the claim of difference seems to echo the primordial alcoholic denial — the "But I'm different" muttered first within our fellowship by Bill D., who eventually became A.A. #3. The claim of difference recalls the pretext virtually all of us tried to foist at one time or another — the claim that although I drink like an alcoholic and live like an alcoholic, I am not an alcoholic.

Second, however, I believe that there is another reason for our wariness of difference in sobriety. When we drank, we were comparers: any difference we noted, we evaluated. "Different" never meant merely different — it always implied to our alcoholic minds "better" or "worse." The A.A. maxim, "Identify, don't compare," is directed, among other things, at that trait of our alcoholic personalities. A.A. practice makes clear that it is comparing that gets us into trouble, not the mere advertence to difference. How could we choose sponsors, or meetings, if we did not advert to difference? How could we follow the suggestion to "Stick with the winners"?

We learn in Alcoholics Anonymous, it seems to me, to think in terms not of "better *than* him or me or that," but of "better *for* me, just now." In a sense, we still compare; but what we engage in is not the comparison that involves mainly contrast so much as the attention to difference that invites growth. If we seek progress rather than perfection, we become able to attend to difference without comparing.

What we learn in A.A., it seems to me, is not that we are not different, nor that being different makes no difference, but that difference by itself does not make us better or worse.

A.A. teaches us also, I believe, how and when our differences do make a difference. The fact that as a White male I am different from Blacks in skin color and from women in ways too numerous to detail does not mean that I am different from them as an alcoholic. I can learn, and I have learned, from the experience, strength, and hope of Blacks and Hispanics and Swedes, from the physically handicapped and the emotionally deprived, from countless unique expressions of our shared alcoholic disability. Insofar as we are alcoholics, those differences make no difference — they are therefore not true differences insofar as we are alcoholics, and I am not different, as an alcoholic, from anyone I meet at a meeting of Alcoholics Anonymous.

But as an individual human being, I am different. As a White person, I suffer less cultural oppression than most Blacks I have met, inside or outside of Alcoholics Anonymous. As a college graduate, I have different employment opportunities — and disopportunities — than do many with less formal education, alcoholic or not. As an alcoholic male, the social settings in which I am expected to drink, and the ways those pressures are applied, differ from how they are met by alcoholic women. I also prefer classical music to rock, and small groups to large gatherings. I prefer watching football on television to going to the game, and I like smoked fish for breakfast and rich fudge for an after-dinner dessert. None of those preferences make me better or worse than anyone else, but they do make me me. And the freedom to be me is one of sobriety's, and A.A.'s, greatest gifts.

Alcoholics Anonymous has taught me how to use difference. Today, if you share my interest in classical music, I will at least explore your passion for Clint Eastwood movies. If, on the other hand, you revel with me in Dustin Hoffman and Woody Allen, I am willing to try to learn from your love of rock. Once I identify that we share something, I both want to share more with you, and I become open to your sharing more with me. I learned both to do that and how to do it in Alcoholics Anonymous.

A.A. opens us to our shared humanity by way of our shared alcoholism. In Alcoholics Anonymous, I learn the deep meaning of "First things first." If we are both alcoholics, you have something to give to me, and I have something to give to you, no matter what differences there may be. Your uniqueness, if you will share it, can add to my unique personality. Your differences, if I perceive them from the basis of our shared humanity, can enrich me, for such difference no longer threatens me.

65

Those who count don't matter; those who matter don't count.

— Attributed to Perle Mesta

TODAY, SOMETHING HAPPENED THAT ALlowed me to hear the hollowness potentially present in the phrase, "ninety meetings in ninety days." The work of art that is our sobriety is not painted by numbers. As a newcomer, I do not remember making ninety meetings in ninety days. But this evening I was reminded of the time when, as best I recall, I made perhaps a hundred meetings in about twenty days. I do not know for sure, because I did not count. But let me retell this day's story as a way of recalling that time.

Our group's current newcomer-slippee returned, again, tonight. He was met by A.A.'s usual combination, in such cases, of concern, exasperation, love, and suggestions.

It takes more than sheer guts to walk through the door into a meeting of Alcoholics Anonymous that one has attended with some regularity and to acknowledge that one has been drinking again. It demands a kind of courage, but even more, it requires desperation and humility. Every sober member present realizes that; and so, it seems, each contributor to the discussion seeks to tap each of those three qualities in the slippee.

With a facade of calmness, Robert assured the group that "this time would be different," for he had "decided to go to ninety meetings in ninety days." Under the prodding of our resident oldtimer, Robert went on to acknowledge that he wasn't sure he could learn much from "those who just came to A.A. and stopped drinking, bingo, right then." My thought ran to what did it mean: "just came to A.A."?

Many among us never drank alcohol again after their first A.A. meeting. I am not one of them. Sometimes, I wonder which was more difficult: going to A.A. meetings when I did not really accept that I was an alcoholic, or returning to those meetings after I had proven yet again that I was. In both situations, I recall being consumed with fear: in the former case, that I might really be an alcoholic; in the latter, that — being an alcoholic — I might have blown my only chance for sobriety by my earlier toying with A.A.

Perhaps not so strangely, given my boozed-up condition at the time, I remember no clear, definite line separating the two experiences. I do not really know when occurred the last meeting at which I "toyed," nor the first at which I "belonged." All I do know is that it happened sometime during one three-week stretch that, in memory, was somehow both the most desperate and the most hopeful period in my alcoholic life. The story of that twenty-some days is very simple, largely because, at the time, under the influence of both booze and A.A., I finally became very simple.

During what I hope, pray, and trust was my last withdrawal, I knew only three things: I did not want to and perhaps could not go through this again; the only way to avoid "again" was to stop boozing; and the fact that I was telling myself those first two things yet again seemed to prove that I did not know how to stop and perhaps even could not stop. There is no point in trying to label the feelings that encased those thoughts. I had heard, in A.A., the suggestion: "Don't drink and go to meetings." In my withdrawal, I of course wanted — needed — a drink. But somehow the idea came that what I needed even more was a meeting.

I do not recall fighting or arguing with that thought. I did not wonder how or why a meeting would "work." I do recall that somehow I craved to be sitting around a table, with other alcoholics, even more than I craved a drink of booze. The clock read 6:45 A.M., and I remembered that there was an "eye-opener" meeting available at 7:30. I had never attended it, but I recalled hearing of it, and it met nearby.

I made the meeting; and I sat and listened. The group was a well-formed one, and the members all hurried off to work directly after it. At the meeting's end, I still thirsted — for alcohol, but also for more A.A. There was, I knew, a 10:00 meeting in the vicinity. I supposed it mainly attended by housewives, but I knew I needed a meeting, and so I went. I was not the only male present, but again I was the only attendee who had been drinking in the past twenty-four hours. Again, I sat and listened, and someone mentioned a noon meeting. I went, I sat, and I listened. After that meeting, someone suggested coffee and a sandwich — on the way to a late afternoon meeting.

Throughout the day, I had — by trolley, subway, and bus — worked my way some distance from home. Now, then, I joined the rush-hour crowd returning to the neighborhood of my home and a more familiar meeting. That night, back in my apartment some fifteen hours and five meetings after leaving it, I still wanted a drink. But my trek had tired me enough, and perhaps I had heard enough, that I survived the day's waning hours without one. I even got a bit of sleep.

I awoke the next day still wanting a drink. In a way, I felt less need for A.A., but where else was I to go? My choice seemed simple as I walked down my front steps: the package store or an A.A. meeting.

On the day before, several A.A.s had informed me of other meetings in the area that met at the same time. I suspected that they had mixed feelings about hoping for my return, but I hoped that they were suggesting that I stick around A.A. even though I so obviously at that moment lacked comfort around them. So again I set off, marveling at the wisdom of my Higher Power in bringing me to a metropolitan center that had close to one hundred meetings daily, at virtually all hours of the day.

What was the second day like? Virtually a carbon-copy of the first: I went, I sat, I listened. It was only on the third day that my trembling abated enough that I dared risk approaching the coffee pot. Only some time during the second week of this routine did I venture to say anything beyond introducing myself as an alcoholic when called upon. A moment of humor occurred when, at a discussion meeting, I said "I pass" with a less broad "*a*" than the natives were accustomed to. They laughed, I suspect, because what they heard me say was perhaps already only too obvious. For some reason, at that time, going to meetings seemed more important than doing my laundry. I am not sure that I regret that particular perversion of "First things first."

I do not recall how many days my routine went on, nor how many meetings I attended. Sometimes, after a meeting, another alcoholic would take me in tow and talk with me for hours over a sandwich or a dish of ice cream. The main thing I remember learning, beyond "Don't take the first drink and keep coming to meetings," was not to order raspberry sherbet as a dessert for Roumanian pastrami. I simply do not remember hearing a single thing, although I have a vague recollection of echoes of "Easy does it" and "First things first" and "A day at a time." Maybe the significant thing that happened was that at some level I finally did hear them.

So I really do not know what happened, nor how long it took, nor even when precisely it happened; but at some point, after some days, I more or less suddenly realized that I no longer needed a drink. I had been there before, I recall thinking, so that realization mainly frightened me. Surely, I knew, now was not the time to stop my meeting routine. So I continued it, now doing more than just going, sitting, and listening. I began to read the A.A. literature, and I even began to try to work the Steps. In time, I believe, I began in one way or another to do most of the things that most of the A.A.s themselves did and do — to attain sobriety, to stay sober.

Those things, although important, are not, however, as I recall this story, all-important. I do not believe in magic, but somehow there is a magic in Alcoholics Anonymous. I may never be able to recapture it, but I know that I have experienced it. The closest I can come to putting that magic in words, is that if I go to meetings and sit and listen intensively enough, somehow I become changed. I know that because it happened.

Others have done it differently; still others will do it differently. But when the Roberts come around, the newcomer-slippees who still wrestle, on one level or another, with themselves as alcoholic, my memory comes back. I do not know how it worked, but somehow it did work. For whatever part the Roberts play in that, I am grateful.

66

I suspect that neither the nature nor the amount of our work is accountable for the frequency and severity of our breakdowns, but that their cause lies rather in those absurd feelings of hurry and having no time, in that breathlessness and tension, that anxiety of feature and that solicitude for results, that lack of inner harmony and ease, by which with us the work is so apt to be accompanied . . . .

— William James

SOMETIMES, PEOPLE COMPLAIN ABOUT THE occasional use of vulgar and even apparently obscene language by some individuals at A.A. meetings. I do not wish to enter that discussion here, beyond noting that I think Bill W.'s biographer, Robert Thomsen, in his description of A.A.'s early days, captured an understanding too often overlooked:

> But there was a sound reason for the raunchy reality of their talk. It was almost as though some men consciously used four-letter words in one sentence, knowing that in the next they could then use love, tenderness, humility, and even serenity, things they were beginning to understand as basically human, which their drinking had kept them from even thinking about.

When I first came around A.A., I sometimes attended a "for men only" meeting supposedly begun by a group of longshoremen but at that time populated mainly by academics. Many four-letter words flew at that meeting. But for me, and I suspect for many others in our early months and years of sobriety, the most obscene four-letter word that kept drumming in my ears at and especially after meetings was "time."

How can it be otherwise, when we are new to A.A.? One of our first perceptions is of the time we wasted in, and by, and through drinking. We had been squandering our lives. Is it surprising that we feel the need to make up for lost time?

As always for the alcoholic, of course, there is a pull force as well as that push impetus. We are attracted by the sobriety of the A.A.'s we meet. And, because we are alcoholics, we want it now. Delayed gratification was never any alcoholic's forte. Some of us may have deluded ourselves that we were verifying quality or being intelligent consumers when we carefully checked the proof-content of the booze we bought, but I, at least, was really making sure that I would get drunk with maximum efficiency.

In sobriety, serenity attracts us as did oblivion when we were drinking. Most of us come to A.A. with our lives at least somewhat in shambles. Suddenly, we find ourselves in the midst of smiling, happy, peaceful people. Having learned the difference between "mere dryness" and "true sobriety," we long for that sobriety. And so we begin to work for it — using the Steps not so much hopefully as demandingly, because we bring to our quest for sobriety a precise lack of serenity. Our first efforts at sobriety tend to be characterized, do they not, by "those absurd feelings of hurry and having no time," by "that breathlessness and tension, that anxiety of feature and that solicitude for results, that lack of inner harmony and ease"? Our very efforts, in other words, subvert our effort.

Wiser, older members caution us with what we hear as a curse: "time." Some even suggest that it takes as long to get sober in A.A. as it took to get us to A.A. We want to rebel against that understanding. It does not seem fair, and deep down we may even resent the suspicion that "that is the way it is."

The ancient Romans had a motto: *festina lente* — "make haste slowly." Although it is not an A.A. axiom, I have found it useful in my sobriety. My relationship to time, I discover in Alcoholics Anonymous, is in many ways the cornerstone of my sobriety. My story, each time I recall and retell it, reminds me that my life does have continuity — that nothing of value is built in a day.

Drinking alcoholically destroys our relationship with time. Perhaps that is the deepest reason why the abuse of mind-altering chemicals is so destructive of our humanity: our humanity is, in some way, our relationship with time. The alcoholic seems to be trying to live only in the past or the future, but the drinking alcoholic has no past or future. No future, not only because of alcohol's destructiveness of self, but because all drug use impairs the ability to make commitments, to relate constructively to what is to come. "Protecting one's supply" affords perhaps the world's most limited horizon. No past, because all efforts to recapture the past, to have something over again, are in vain and doomed to failure. Hear C.S. Lewis on the point:

> This itch to have things over again, as if life were a film that could be unrolled twice or even made to work backwards . . . was it possibly the root of all evil? No; of course the love of money is called that.
>
> But money itself — perhaps one values it chiefly as a defense against chance, a security for being able to have things over again, a means of arresting the unrolling of the film.

Or, to paraphrase Kierkegaard: Life must be lived forwards, even if it can only be understood backwards.

I recall once hearing a psychiatrist observe that the psychotic is disconnected from his or her past, the neurotic is overwhelmed by it, while the normal or sane person is able to build upon the reality of that past. Wallowing in is not building upon. As alcoholics, we begin to build on our past only when we arrive at A.A. and discover our story. A.A. gives us both our past and our future, and it does so by giving us our now — the present day, this twenty-four hours.

Time, then, is not a curse but a promise that can be fulfilled only if we make haste slowly — only if we accept that sobriety, precisely because it is the kind of reality we most want (and quickly), can come only slowly. The road to sobriety is best traversed by a purposeful walk, one Step at a time. If we try to run, we will almost surely stumble.

"Time," I try to realize today, reminds me of those truths about sobriety, about my sobriety. Today, fortunately, I speak that reminder more often than others have to remind me of it. Perhaps that is because, with A.A.'s help, I have to let go of "those absurd feelings of hurry and having no time, . . . that breathlessness and tension, that anxiety of feature and that solicitude for results."

67

There are many interests that can never be inhibited by the way of negation. . . . Spinoza long ago wrote in his **Ethics** *that anything that a man can avoid under the notion that it is bad he may also avoid under the notion that something else is good. He who habitually acts . . . under the negative notion, the notion of the bad, is called a slave by Spinoza. To him who acts habitually under the notion of good he gives the name of freeman.*

— William James

IT SOMETIMES TROUBLES ME THAT SO MANY people outside of A.A., including many who admire and respect our fellowship, think that the most significant reality about A.A. members is that we do not drink alcohol. In a way, of course, that is true. But it is not the whole truth.

How often do we hear someone use the word *sober* as a synonym for dry? Yet ours is not a way of negation. We are, in Spinoza's terms, freemen rather than slaves. We attain that status, it seems to me, through a sequential growth process — moving from drinking to dryness to sobriety to serenity. Spinoza's understanding of "freeman" and "slave" helps me to understand the nature of that process — "true sobriety" as that reality is understood by and within A.A.

Who would deny that we first come to A.A. as slaves to alcohol? We seek help to throw off the shackles in which booze has bound us, chains that we have proven unable to escape by ourselves.

But true freedom is never bestowed, never given. No one ever "frees" slaves. From the very nature of freedom as well as of humanity, freedom must be gained. Others may remove obstacles, but only we ourselves can attain our freedom. That attaining may require only acceptance; but it must be *our* acceptance if it is to be *our* freedom. We must lay hold of it for ourselves, even if only by our acceptance. All theologies acknowledge that even God treats humans in this way, and A.A. does not claim nor pretend to do otherwise.

For when we first come to A.A., we remain slaves. Dryness — putting the cork in the bottle — is the way of negation. One who stops drinking out of fear of drunkenness and its consequences, out of fear of alcohol, remains in a way still the slave of alcohol. Not to drink alcohol in order to avoid drunkenness is yet to act under "the negative notion, the notion of the bad." Few if any of us, I suspect, become freemen during our first months in A.A. What our participation in A.A. accomplishes, during that initial period, is the birth of understanding of the nature of our slavery to alcohol. We learn perhaps most importantly the truth glimpsed by Spinoza and James: ultimately, freedom is not from, but for.

We learn that truth, once dry, by seeing true sobriety. Slaves must understand the nature of their slavery before they can seek freedom. And slaves must somehow identify with freedom before they can become free. Once dry, we become able to seek sobriety. Drunks do not want to be sober: at best, they want to be not drunk. The drinking alcoholic cannot know the nature of true sobriety, any more than an illiterate person can read Shakespeare or a person addicted to sex can understand love. Those addicted to anything understand neither addiction nor freedom.

By participation in A.A., those liberated from the bonds of drinking alcoholically become enabled to outgrow the chains of thinking alcoholically. In sobriety, although we still avoid drinking alcohol, we do so less because drunkenness is "bad" for us than because sobriety is so "good" for us. We live not because life is the only alternative to death, but because life itself is good — not perfect, but good. Thus we become freemen.

68

Tried to practice these principles in all our affairs.
— from Step Twelve

THE FINAL WORDS OF THE TWELVE STEPS, Ed suggested in kicking off last night's discussion, are "the real clinker." "Maybe it means that I am getting 'weller,' because, as I recall, over the years I seem to have wrestled in a similar way with each phrase in the Steps; but just now, today, it is 'practicing these principles in all our affairs' that seems to be impossible and hopeless. The harder I try, it seems, the behinder I get. But I have come too far in A.A. to flunk out here. So let me ask for the group's help. How do you understand and live out that third part of the Twelfth Step?"

John and Tom, the group's reigning oldtimers, smiled. "What specifically is bugging you, Ed?" the latter asked.

Ed spouted forth his impatience and righteous rage at others' "stupidity" — all over a trivial incident in a supermarket checkout line. "So there I was," Ed concluded, "less than one hour ago: on my way to a meeting and thinking that I was sober, but also thinking and even acting like some rampaging drunk, or at least like the self-centered boozer that I was before I found A.A. Realizing that, I think I slinked through the door tonight with my tail further between my legs than it has been since I first came around, still drunk as a skunk. 'It gets better,' you tell me; and I know from my own experience that it does. But when and how does that kind of thinking get better? When do I learn how to practice these principles in all my affairs?"

"You have already begun, Ed," John suggested. "You said, I believe, 'one hour ago.' Back when you were drinking, where would you have been, and what would have been doing, and how would you have been thinking, an hour after such an incident? Practicing these principles in all our affairs means first of all, to me, noticing when they apply.

"It is probably trite to remind you — and myself — that 'we claim spiritual progress rather than spiritual perfection.' But let me suggest that although your nine words are the final ones of the Twelve Steps, they do not conclude 'How It Works' as we read that part of chapter 5 of *The Big Book*. And we read 'How It Works' rather than just the Twelve Steps, I think, for a reason — perhaps precisely for the reason that we need also to hear often that reminder about 'progress rather than perfection.' "

Others in the group offered similar reminders; and, by meeting's end, Ed seemed pacified. To remember that "we claim spiritual progress rather than spiritual perfection" is freeing. To realize that our way of life enables us to see things differently also verifies our liberation: sober, we perceive more of reality, even if, at times, belatedly. To recognize reality, especially the reality of ourselves, is no small gift.

But is that all there is to it? Do "progress rather than perfection" and a new "way of life" that enables us to see our own reality — great as these gifts are — capture all the richness implicit in A.A.'s challenge to practice these principles in all our affairs?

In a way, they do.

We come to know the good, it has been suggested, only by experiencing and participating in the bad. As one philosopher has put it: spirituality "is indeed able to teach us failure. And the latent assumption behind such teaching is that on earth everybody is a failure." Or, perhaps more profoundly:

> According both to the Bible [Genesis' story of the Garden] and to Freud, the capacity for guilt and shame constitute the human race as we know it. Guilt and shame are not merely intellectual performances, but rather involve a deeper questioning of one's own status in the cosmic order. That questioning springs not so much from a fear of revenge as from a feeling of awe that one is related to a world-harmony in a way that makes it possible for one to disturb it. The deeper anxiety results from the transgression not of a law, but of a taboo — which means that one has dared to act as if one were God . . . and found oneself able to do so.[1]

1. Based on Leszek Kolakowski, *Religion*, pp. 193-94.

I think we notice and discover who we are only by noticing and discovering who we are not. It is a precious "grace" to be able to see our "sins" as "sins." Precisely because we cannot perfectly "[try to] practice these principles in all our affairs," we are reminded who and what we are and are not: alcoholics who are progressing. In some matters, trying and progress are enough.

When we were drinking, we excluded that realization. In my drinking years, I was never at fault: other people, places, and things were always to blame whenever, rarely, I adverted to one of the manifestations of what I have since learned to call my defects of character and my own shortcomings. It was that tendency that troubled Ed this evening. Unhappy because frustrated, the alcoholic in him — like the alcoholic in each of us — laid the blame for his malaise on others' stupidity rather than looking to see whether perhaps that unhappiness was not more rooted in his own — our own — tendency to demand to be in control.

Someone once suggested that, ultimately, addiction — and in this sense, at least, alcoholism is an addiction — that "addiction is the twofold belief, the double certainty, that whenever 'there is something wrong with me,' something outside me caused it, and something outside me can 'fix' it." For me, the final words of A.A.'s Twelfth Step create a helpful mirror that leads me back to Steps Four through Seven. The A.A. program "ends," in other words, by not ending: it rather directs us back to reworking the Steps yet again, to building more solidly on the foundation we have laid down on our last journey through them.

69

Don't take yourself too damned seriously.

— A.A. rule #62.

WE ALL KNOW THE STORY FROM PAGES 103 and 104 of *Alcoholics Anonymous Comes of Age.*

I doubt that, today, many — if any — members of Alcoholics Anonymous would be inclined to undertake a similar promotional extravaganza. For one thing, there is that story — to remind us and to warn us. That is why Bill told it, in such exaggerated detail. But, as usual in Bill's stories there lurks another layer of meaning, a deeper yet simpler warning. "Don't take yourself too damned seriously" has to do with more than organizational hype.

I guess I am thinking most about those of us who work in that broad field called "alcoholism." In general, I think, we know and live the cliches: A.A.'s expertise concerns not alcoholism but the alcoholic; Alcoholics Anonymous is less a modality of treatment than a program of recovery. Remembering those truisms, because they help to keep us honest, adds to our personal program as well as to our professional effectiveness. But it also helps to remind us of the truth and honesty taught by A.A.'s famed Rule #62.

Because I regard my own ongoing recovery as a kind of wondrous miracle, I cannot but take it seriously. At times, however, I can get confused about what is recovery and what is just plain old me. My experience, strength, and hope, for example, are not the only experience, strength, and hope available at the meetings of Alcoholics Anonymous I attend. Still, when some favorite topic is discussed, or especially when a newcomer is present, too often arises the tendency to speak gravely and with a kind of emphasis that suggests: "This is the real poop." It probably is — although not in the sense that I intend.

It is good for me to examine both the intellectual and the spiritual dimensions of my tendency to seriousness. Precisely as "a scholar," I should be aware that my own experience of alcoholism and of recovery has but the slightest intellectual weight in my exploration of genetic or neurobiological theory — that, if anything, my sensitivity to my experience can be as much a hindrance as a help to cogent research design. At best, disciplined awareness of the significance of personal experience can help guard against the pitfalls of too-ready or too-sweeping generalization. At less than best, undisciplined self-consciousness can blind to the utility of new insights and new approaches. As *The Big Book* says in another context ". . . self-centeredness! That, we think, is the root of our troubles."

The case is similar in the field of treatment. The roads to recovery are varied, and the way of life suggested by A.A. is anything but a straitjacket. And, of course, treatment is not recovery. Treatment rather seeks to build a bridge, in each case, for an individual to embark upon recovery. Knowing that, what justification can there possibly be for, however implicitly, using one's own recovery as a model? There may, at times, be some validity in that approach, but each case — I supposedly know — must be evaluated individually, and in consultation with those skilled in the modalities of treatment. Perhaps I need to recall more often that skill in the modalities of treatment — the plural (modalities) carries the significance here — is more likely to be found in those not involved in a particular program of recovery.

But all that, of course — that which I know, the "intellectual" — misses the heart of the matter. As useful and as salutary as A.A.'s Rule #62 proves intellectually, its greatest benefit is spiritual. How does that passage go, the one that first helped the scales of denial to drop from my eyes?

> This is the how and why of it. First of all, we had to quit playing God. It didn't work.

"Playing God" signals less intellectual folly — although it surely is that — than spiritual suicide. This, I believe, is the ultimate importance of A.A.'s Rule #62. To take oneself too seriously is to pretend and to claim to be more than one is — a finite human being bounded and defined by the ambiguities inherent in being human. Seriousness tends not to tolerate ambiguity, the hallmark of our humanity.

Intolerance of ambiguity, then, marks the attempt to deny our humanity. And any attempt to deny our humanity involves also a denial of our alcoholism. If we, as alcoholics, have any advantage, it is this: we know that we are only human, and therefore we accept more readily the ambiguity and limitation inherent in all human beings. If, then, any quality should characterize our thought and work, especially in any area related to alcohol, that characteristic must be the one mandated by Rule #62 of Alcoholics Anonymous: "Don't take yourself too damned seriously."

I remind myself of that, of course, "seriously" — but I hope not as a way of taking myself "too damned seriously." Here again, we as alcoholics live in paradox and ambiguity. We must be serious rather than solemn, but we must also be serious rather than frivolous. As we have learned from our own experience, too much of anything can be dangerous. Our alcoholism serves as a symbol, a constant reminder of our humanity's common failure to comprehend the concept of "enough."

Here too, then, in the matter of seriousness, the appropriate goal is to be "serious enough." Serious enough to respect the phenomenon of alcoholism and the possibilities of treatment, but not so exclusively serious that I fail to remember that alcoholism comes not in test tubes but in alcoholics, that treatment is not recovery and that therefore treatment, unlike recovery, might involve modalities alien to my own experience. I need, in other words, to join the original formulator of A.A.'s Rule #62 in ready, healthy laughter — laughter directed at my own seriousness whenever that seriousness becomes too damned much.

70

Take my word for it, the saddest thing under the sky is a soul incapable of sadness.

— Countess de Gasparin

I FOUND IT DIFFICULT TO LISTEN AT TO-night's meeting. The speakers were good, but my mind had difficulty following them because my feelings were elsewhere.

Within A.A. we share many feelings. One, however, seems rarely mentioned: the feeling of sadness.

Sometimes, although not drinking and — I hope — sober, I am sad. In many ways, feeling sadness is a new experience for me. As an emotion, a feeling, sadness is slow. When I was drinking, there were no slow feelings. Emotions such as joy or anger either exploded or soon vanished with the help of alcohol. A drinking alcoholic does not have time for real feelings. Active alcoholics may think that they are feeling, but my own experience leads me to question whether — when I was drinking — I had feelings, or feelings had me.

It seems to me, that — just as there is a vast difference between passing out and falling asleep — before sobriety I experienced enthusiasms, but not joy; momentary pleasures, but never happiness; rage and anger, but not grief; morose self-pity, but never sadness.

Sadness is the emotion that flows from feeling the absence of something good. How can one feel an absence? Strict logic may balk, but the heart — the gut — knows whereof it feels. Did you ever walk down a familiar flight of stairs in the dark and, counting the steps, expect at last to place your foot solidly only to realize that there was no floor there yet? That is, in way, the feeling of absence, of nothingness.

One example more familiar to members of A.A. flows from when we first come around A.A. The first stage of clearing up, as I remember it, involves noticing the difference between our dryness and their sobriety. We are not sure what those others —

the "winners" — have, but we do feel its absence in ourselves. Although grateful for being dry, we experience sadness at not being sober.

But if sadness is the emotion felt at the absence of some good, how can one who is sober be sad? Because, although sobriety is a great good, it is not the only good. In fact, because sobriety allows us both to see and to feel things we never even noticed and surely never truly experienced under the influence of alcohol, I wonder if it would be too much to claim that sadness can be a hallmark of sobriety itself?

Although often confused with them, sadness differs from anger, from grief, from depression. Anger is directed at righting some wrong: it is dangerous to the alcoholic because it claims the right to control. Sadness has nothing to do with control. Grief, we experience over some loss; sadness need not imply that the absent good was ever possessed — indeed, it usually was not, for sadness tends to concern realities that cannot be possessed. Depression results from frustrated anger or signals inappropriately prolonged grief. Sadness verges into depression less when prolonged than when it is exclusive: when all that is noticed is the absence of good. True sadness, as opposed to angry depression, appreciates both present and possible good. One feels sad not because "the world is failing me," but because some potential or possible good is not among the goodness that one cherishes.

Nor, of course, is sadness the same as sentimentality. Sentimentality implies an inappropriateness of feeling response: one cultivates maudlin and mawkish and therefore weak and superficial feelings rather than allowing reality to impress one's humanity at depth. Sentimentality legendarily hallmarks the drinking alcoholic, for it flows from the fear of real feeling. One who feels only under the influence of alcohol does not truly feel. Perhaps that is why recovering alcoholics seem best able to appreciate the difference between sentimentality, which is essentially false feeling, and the sadness that is truly human.

In my occasional sadness, I find both a threat and a promise.

The threat is that, in feeling pain, I will turn to my familiar painkiller, alcohol. Once upon a time, that worked — although only at the expense of rendering me less human. Now, I know it no longer even works; and, even if it did, I have chosen a way of life that values full humanity above the false solace attainable by chemical use.

Many of us, when we were drinking, settled for less because we barely knew that there was more — or because we felt unworthy of and cut off from that more of human fullness and fulfillment. To feel sadness is to be reminded that I — like all reality — am capable of more. *Capable:* it is an invitation, not a driven demand. *More*: not more booze, which always only further distorted reality, but more reality, in all its undistorted ambiguity.

The promise of my moments of sadness, then, lies in the awareness that I can experience them only because I can also — now — experience moments of joy. Sadness is an experience rather than a way of life. Or at least it can be, if I remember that my chosen way of life — the way of life in A.A. — opens to sadness as it does to joy, neither imposing it nor excluding it.

Although provoked by the experience of the absence of good, sadness itself can be good, if it calls to attention the fullness of feeling that sobriety opens to those who cherish it.

71

We are tomorrow's past.

— Mary Webb

THE STORY TOLD BY TONIGHT'S LEAD SPEAKER, although brief and simple, raised a profound question: What is "the past"?

The ultimate philosophical conundrum, of course, is time. Everyone knows what it is, but no one has ever been able to explain it. Worried about or unwilling to live in the present, many people project into the future. That way of thinking characterized many of us when we were drinking. In A.A., we quickly learned at the beginning of our sobriety to take things "one day at a time."

But how does that axiom apply to our past? This day is, in a sense, the end-point of my story to now. Who and what I am today is largely the product of my past. "One day at a time," then, does not cut me off from nor close the door on my past.

My story is my past — or, at least, my story contains and connects me with as much of my past as is relevant to today. One experience we gain from any Twelve-Step program is learning that part of each day's task of growth involves learning more about our whole story, even as we add this day's stone to its structure. We never know our story perfectly. That is largely because, from our own point of view living it, we can never see our story as complete. If what I did yesterday influences the kind of person that I am today, it is also true that how I live today sheds light on the true nature of both what I did and the kind of person I was yesterday.

Tonight's speaker's simple story underlines the significance of such thoughts to my sobriety. A few months ago, Sally related, she had cut back her reading of A.A. literature and had stopped attending meetings. Those habits had begun to bore her, she commented wryly. Besides, "they took up too much of my valuable time." Sally continued her story:

Well, I have since learned a little bit about time, somewhat more about value, and, most of all, a lot about myself. Cut off from this program, I found myself not only doing less, but doing it less well.

I don't think I realized it at first, but the changes that my "added time" produced in my life turned me into a hurting — and a hurtful — shrew. I became difficult to live with as well as to work with. "More difficult," I guess, would be more honest. Anyway, I soon came to realize that I was hurting the ones I love, and that hurt me. And you know what you do when you hurt, if you are an alcoholic? I shouldn't speak for anyone else, but I start — started — thinking about taking a drink.

Oh, I wasn't going to get drunk! I never really was one of those drinkers — the ones who drank in order to get drunk. My drinking pattern was that I drank in order to feel good — only I always ended up passed out long before I ever got to feeling good.

Well, somehow I caught myself thinking of drinking. And so I called Pat, my sponsor. She had missed me at meetings, but she hadn't wanted to "pry," Pat told me. I had seemed so busy and even brusque recently, she noted, that she also had begun to wonder how I had time for A.A.

"So, Sal," Pat asked ever so sweetly, "how is it going? Are you finally finding out there what you couldn't find in here? I missed seeing you at meetings, as I said; but, of course, 'First things first!' "

Needless to say, Pat's pointed sarcasm touched a raw nerve. My pain and hurt became overwhelming, and so I told her that, and I also told her that I had earlier in the day caught myself thinking about drinking over my hurt. "What should I do, Pat?" I blurted out the simple question with more honesty than I had intended.

Maybe I should have mentioned earlier that I had that conversation with Pat just this morning. Her answer was to suggest that I get to a meeting, and she told me about this one and that our group needed another speaker to fulfill the commitment. So here I am and that's my story. It is good to be back, and now I am pretty sure that I will not drink for the rest of today, anyway. I have learned something, I think, about "First things first." Thank you for being here and for listening to me — for teaching me that lesson by your own happily sober example.

Sally's story of her recent past reveals something about all our pasts. Today, the story of her few months' "vacation" from A.A. fits into place within her larger story as a positive and useful learning experience, perhaps as the moment when she really learned the place of A.A. participation in her sober life. But let's imagine an alternative outcome. Suppose that this morning, Sally had picked up the bottle instead of the telephone — and that this evening, instead of telling her story at an A.A. meeting, she had suffered an accident while driving under the influence, an accident that left her maimed. How then would those few month's vacation, the interval between when she stopped attending meetings and this morning's experience of reaching for help, be interpreted?

In this hypothesis, that time would be seen — perhaps especially by Sally herself — as simply one long, tragic, downhill slide. There is nothing positive, for any alcoholic, about a period of time that culminates in a drink. The meaning, then, of Pat's vacation would change. This morning, in choosing to reach for the telephone instead of the bottle, Sal determined the nature of her recent past, turning it into an experience of learning rather than a prelude to tragedy. What one does today, that is to say, can and does shape both the nature and the meaning of one's past at least as much as that past shapes the nature and the meaning of who and what one is and does today.

Our power over our past is, of course, always limited. Nothing that I think or do today can undo the actual pain I caused those who loved me when I was drinking. But I can, within this twenty-four hours, live and act in ways that enable those loved ones to understand and therefore to interpret differently the pain that they suffered — and that does change something.

Shakespeare suggested that "What's past is prologue" — something that occurs before the main action of a dramatic story. In a sense, as an alcoholic, I find truth in that: sober, I am free to live this twenty-four hours of my own story soberly — building on my past but not overwhelmed by it. The drama of my sobriety begins only when I get sober. But also as an alcoholic who is trying to live soberly, I find a deeper reason to disagree with an understanding of the past as merely "prologue." Today's sobriety can change the meaning — and therefore the nature — of some past events. The occurrences themselves are immutable, but so long as I live, my past remains open to my present.

72

Simplicity of character is the natural result of profound thought.

— William Hazlitt

PERIODICALLY, JUST ABOUT EVERY A.A. GROUP lapses into discussion of one of the program's simplest slogans: "This is a simple program." Although the maxim elicits wide acceptance, its implications seem open to even wider interpretations.

Usually, I try to avoid thinking about A.A.'s adages. As adages, they are to be utilized rather than analyzed. But one suggestion, one distinction, put forth tonight, breached that defense. Jimmy asked, very simply: "What is the opposite of simple?"

Two answers appear possible, and the difference between them, I believe, sheds light not only on A.A.'s simplicity, but also on whatever simplicity I possess. For, similar as the words may seem, "complex" and "complicated" have very different meanings. "Simple," as it is usually understood within A.A., signifies less "uncomplex" than "uncomplicated." To understand "simplicity" in all its riches, then, it is helpful to understand that distinction between "complex" and "complicated."

"Complex" comes from two Latin words that give it the meaning of "woven or braided together." The complex is therefore that which is essentially composed of parts.

"Complicated" also derives from the Latin, but its origins signify "folded together; made intricate, difficult, or involved." To be complicated, then, implies artificially imposed combination.

That verbal distinction, remote from the concerns of daily sobriety as it may appear at first glance, contains an important and necessary reminder. "Simplicity" cannot be invoked as a denial of reality. Sobriety, like A.A., is not complicated, but it is complex. *We*, after all, are complex: beings who are neither more nor less than merely human, because we are both more and less than merely human. Our troubles may be seen, indeed, as mistaking complexity for complication.

Let me try to make that a bit more concrete. A.A., after all, suggests that there are *Twelve* Steps to sobriety, not one. If "simple" were the same as "not complex," A.A. would mandate but one Step: "Don't drink." Uncomplexity would exclude even the conjunctive phrase, ". . . and go to meetings." In fact, perhaps the most obvious witness that A.A. does not identify simplicity with lack of complexity, that A.A. understands sobriety as made up of more than one thing, is to be found in that simplest of injunctions suggested most often to those who seem most to crave complication: "Just don't drink and go to meetings . . . the rest will come in time."

Or take the stories that we tell at our meetings. They involve three essential elements: "what we were like, what happened, and what we are like now." However briefly treated, no one of those is ever omitted in any real A.A. story. Why? Because alcoholism — and recovery from it — is a complex phenomenon. To be an alcoholic, we also know, is to be afflicted "physically, mentally, and spiritually": a reminder that we are complex beings as well as that alcoholism is a complex reality.

But "complexity" is not "complication." Our problem, when drinking, lay not in our complexity, which we indeed attempted to deny, but in our tendency to complication, which served our denial.

We denied complexity, for example, by seeking — and even claiming to find — in alcohol a single solution to all our problems. If our team won, we drank. If our team lost, we drank. If it was too hot, we drank. If it got too cold, we drank. We drank to celebrate, and we drank for solace. We sought in alcohol not a simple solution, but a single solution. And "single" and "simple" are not the same, or we would never have had need of A.A.

Our pursuit of the "single" complicated our lives. Because we are complex beings, there are no single solutions for us. Learning to make distinctions supposedly marked our growth in maturity. Father was not mother; teachers were not family; the classroom was not the playground; wants are not needs. Looking back, I realize that I did not always acknowledge those complexities. More often, indeed, I complicated reality — and did so precisely by attempting to fold teachers into parents, friends into family, wants into needs. And when reality resisted, I complicated myself. Abandoning the integrity of my personhood, I assumed diverse and often fake roles — becoming mother's darling at home, the bully on the playground, teacher's pet in school, the gay blade on dates, the clown at parties, the drudge at work, . . . but why go on?

When I was in treatment for alcoholism, a perceptive counselor suggested: "Ernie, if you were ever on that television program and the emcee said, 'Will the real Ernie K. please stand up,' you really wouldn't know what to do, would you?" I smile at the memory now, but that all-too-true observation cut to the quick then. What was being touched was my complication — the refusal of my real complexity engendered by my single-purposed pursuit of others' approval.

"Keep it simple," I have learned in A.A., does not mean doing only one thing. It does, however, mean doing only one thing at a time. That too reflects the difference between complication and complexity. It is when I try to do more than one thing at a time, when I try to live more than one day at a time, that things get complicated and simplicity falls away and my program falls apart.

But keeping it simple — doing one thing at a time, one day at a time, — is complex. Just now, I am writing: that is a complex task, but I am enjoying it. Shortly, I shall attend an academic gathering to discuss a very different and very complex topic; and I shall probably enjoy that too. Back when I was drinking, my efforts to write would often be frustrated because I was planning what to say when I got to some meeting, and my participation and pleasure in meetings were blunted because I passed that time thinking about what I should be writing. Because I did not know how to keep it simple, I drowned in my self-created complications — or, more accurately, in the booze that I imbibed trying to render those complications bearable.

Today, keeping it simple does not mean that I only write, or only teach, or only cook, or only anything. My life is complex, but it is not complicated, for with A.A.'s help I am learning to "Keep it simple." Complexity means, for example, that I do many different things in my efforts to maintain and to grow in sobriety. I attend meetings and work the Steps. I read the literature and make Twelfth-Step calls. At meetings, I put out the ashtrays, sometimes, or set up the chairs or make the coffee as well as speak and listen. And, of course, with my Higher Power's help, I do not take the first drink, one day at a time.

Much A.A. humor concerns the distinction between complication and complexity. I am sure you have heard about the slipping member who strolled into a bar, ordered two drinks, and then carefuly drank only the second (a triple). That way, he did not "take the first drink." That is not really funny, of course: no alcoholic, drinking, is ever funny. But it does reveal where our tendency to complicate can lead us, if we ever forget the complexity of our devious disease.

I would also be inclined to drink, I think, if I ever again fell into the trap of confusing "simple" with "single." Doing only one thing, all the time, would soon drive me to doing the one thing, all the time, that got me here — drinking alcohol. Accepting life's complexity, indeed rejoicing in it, allows me to "Keep it simple."

Distinctions are only the most rudimentary beginnings of philosophy, and word origins are of little more help than word games in maintaining sobriety. But, for some reason, remembering that there is a difference between "single" and "simple" and recalling that "complexity" is indeed the very opposite of "complicated" — sometimes those thoughts seem to help whatever growth I am engaged in. For one thing, they help me truly to keep it simple, while remaining the person who I am.

73

I'm not okay, but you're not okay; but that's all right.

— Suggested book title

A COMMON NOTE IN A.A. STORIES, AND PERhaps an even more frequent theme of A.A. discussion, is "people pleasing." Most members can relate long experience in the practice — a history of self-abnegation in the attempt to purchase the approval of others. The sober mind clearly marks the irony of such efforts: the price is paid, but the merchandise never arrives. One who sets out to please others inevitably fails, and fails at the cost of the destruction of his or her very own being.

Most mentions of people-pleasing unite two common chords — "chords," because they resonate well with the experience of virtually all who are present and participating. The first concerns the self-hatred of the drinking alcoholic. When we were drinking, alcoholically drinking, at some level we feared and loathed ourselves. Devoid of self-approval, we craved the affirmation of others almost as much as we craved booze. Feeling certain, deep down, that there was something wrong with us, we labored all the harder to project an external image of being all right. Fearing that we were really no good, we desperately needed others' acceptance as "good people." It never worked, of course: even if we succeeded in winning some approval, the unboundedness of our need found that acceptance never to be enough.

The second theme concerns the hangover continuation of that quest, that need for others' approval, in sobriety. Within A.A., we attain at least the beginnings of self-respect — of an appropriate self-esteem. But we remain alcoholics. Mindful of our present disability as well as of our past more grievous failures, we catch ourselves at times slipping into our old pattern of people-pleasing, of trying to draw our self-esteem from others' affirmation of what we do.

The A.A. way of life helps, of course. It establishes us in a more healthy relationship with our defects of character and our shortcomings. It teaches us to seek — and to find satisfaction in — spiritual progress rather than spiritual perfection. By suggesting "First things first" and by locating us in a network that does approve us, A.A. blunts the tendency to self-destruction inherent in our people-pleasing efforts. The closing note of this second theme is almost invariably one of joyous freedom.

JUDGING. The religious tradition in which I was raised warned against it: "Judge not lest you be judged." No one ever told me, however, to the best of my recollection, that the maxim contained psychological as well as theological validity. I note this not to impugn my upbringing, but to suggest how early in my own life I can discern signs of alcoholic thinking.

It happened like this. As a member of an ethnic and a religious minority in my neighborhood, I was raised to be mindful of what other people would think of my behavior. As I grew older — I will not claim "matured" — and that ghetto mentality fell away, I nevertheless re-created its prison. After parties, for example, long before my drinking became a problem, I would take a very non-A.A. inventory — reviewing events in an effort to decide less how I had behaved than what others thought and might be saying about me. Had I spoken too much, or too little? Was my clothing perfectly appropriate, my demeanor absolutely impeccable? Needless to say, I rarely met those standards — and so I felt judged.

That was painful, but arrogance fueled by alcohol soon afforded a defense. If I could not absolutely avoid being judged, I decided, I could at least blunt the impact of such judgment by becoming myself one of the judges. I recall thinking of it as a way to direct attention: rather than wondering whether my shoes were sufficiently polished, for example, I could concentrate on deciding whether or not others' were. Instead of wondering, after a conversation, whether I had made a fool of myself by offering some silly suggestion, I began ranking the silliness of other's ideas.

I leave to the psychologists — or the theologians — whether crossing that line, the line between "judgee" and "judger," was connected with my crossing the line into uncontrolled, alcoholic drinking. Chronologically, the two crossings do seem related. Today, the connection between focusing on judgment and being an alcoholic is clear: both have to do with freedom.

PEOPLE-PLEASING. This, of course, also has to do with freedom — our freedom to be who we are. As all religious and spiritual traditions teach, passing judgment on human beings is a divine prerogative. Even in our secular system of government, only judges, courts, and ultimately our constitution itself are endowed with that aura: one is not judged by a human being, but by "the law" — by a power higher than any individual. To judge others, it seems, is in some way to claim to be God.

There is an ultimate irony, however, in such playing God — an irony both lived out and mocked in the phenomenon of alcoholism, as A.A.'s founders saw so clearly. Those who play God lose whatever God-like-ness is rightly and appropriately theirs as humans. That is why "First of all, we had to quit playing God." Only if we abandon that false claim can we regain our true being. The irony is that just as playing God makes us less than human, it is our passing judgment on others that saddles us with feeling judged and with being judged — and not by a merciful God or a just law.

That, it seems to me, is the treacherous trap implicit not only in our tendency to pass judgment on others but also in our sick need to please others. Seeking to please others implies the will also to be pleased.

We attain freedom from being judged, freedom from our tendency to people-pleasing, only by accepting and embracing the freedom that we are not compelled to judge, the freedom that we ourselves do not have to be pleased by others. Although we do need others in order to be who we are, our relationship with others within that need is based on neither judging nor pleasing.

The best and most concrete example is, of course, our relationship with other alcoholics within the fellowship of A.A. In my own case, I first became able to join A.A. and have found so much freedom flowing from my participation in A.A. precisely because Alcoholics Anonymous is so singularly free of the all-too-inhuman tendencies to judge and to please. Having learned, within A.A., that there are other ways of relating to people than judging them or being judged by them, than pleasing them or being pleased by them, I become — daily — more happily able to extend such relationships even outside of A.A. For an inveterate people-pleaser, for one whose life was once dominated by judging and being judged, that is a precious gift.

74

Cowardice, even more so than misery, loves company.

— John Douglas Mullen

THIS PROJECT OF ATTENDING NINETY MEETings in ninety days surprises some people who know me. Not that they think that I do not need it: it is rather that they know that I dislike and usually avoid large groups of any kind of people. Although not exactly a loner nor shy, I simply prefer smaller and more intimate encounters.

The idea of "loving company" was alien to my experience before I found A.A. and remains so now except for A.A. At times, I have wondered about that and about how it happened and what it means. An idea from John Douglas Mullen, then, sparks against that wonder to produce some light. It helps me to understand why I am so enjoying these ninety days.

There is, however, a problem with Mullen's observation: both courage and cowardice love company. The strength of his insight lies in the reason why. While courage and cowardice love company for very different reasons, cowardice and misery share a common motive — fear . . . fear of being who and what we truly are.

A.A. clearly teaches that one must confront self-as-feared if one is ever to find self-as-is. What the alcoholic fears most, just before hitting bottom, is that he or she may be an alcoholic. What happens within A.A. after that fear is faced? Alcoholics who accept that they are alcoholics begin to become the fully human beings they truly are. Freed of their fear, they gain the courage to *be*.

But what does it mean, to be "freed of fear"? We are freed from fear, in this case, not because we triumph over reality by defeating it, but because we confront reality and accept it. Reality must be confronted because, miserable as the active alcoholic is, he or she is more cowardly than anything else.

Miserable as I was in the latter stages of my drinking, I was more cowardly than I was miserable, or I would not have continued drinking. *Cowardice* is defined as "excessive fear," as "the lack of courage." And *courage* means "the attitude of facing and dealing with anything recognized as dangerous, difficult, or painful, instead of withdrawing from it."

One way of understanding my alcoholic career would be to see its active phase as characterized by ever-increasing cowardice, its recovery phase as involving the ever-wider application of courage. I first turned to using the chemical alcohol rather than merely "having a drink," out of excessive fear. Although I thought of that use as a way of dealing with my discomfort in certain social situations, the nature of the chemical rendered that "dealing with" more a withdrawal.

And so I progressed from a couple of belts with the boys through three-martini lunches in order to escape the tension that was trying to tell me something about my work; from a few drinks as a tool of seduction through steeling myself for both the joys and the failures of love by getting on a glow that made love itself unreal or inappropriate; from a glass of wine to relax at bedtime through sucking on the bottle until I passed out.

Somewhere, in each of those progresions, I recall dimly realizing what was going on — that alcohol had become a vehicle of escape. But the more I drank, the more I would have fought anyone who accused me of cowardice. Drinking was coping, I tried to convince even myself. In time, however, even I found that difficult to believe. And so I avoided challenges to that thin illusion by spending time not so much with others who drank *like* I did, but with others who drank for the same *why* I did.

The tensions of work and the paradoxes of love can be dangerous, difficult, or painful; they can also be fulfilling, joyous, and healing. But I refused that risk. Wanting all or nothing, I ended up with neither. One of the ultimate mysteries of human life seems to be that we always end up running toward and embracing precisely that which we tried to escape. And so my drinking brought me, in time, to alcoholism — a tension greater than any other job, a paradox as painful as any other love.

The moment one discovers the truth about alcoholism (about "my" drinking), the truth that drinking alcohol has become one's total work and one's total love: that moment is the moment of truth. Cowardice commands me to escape it, to deny it, to refuse its reality even to myself, usually by trying to drown it, too, in alcohol. For a time, many of us succeed at that cowardice.

But there is this flaw in cowardice: the more involved become one's efforts to escape, the deeper one must understand what one is trying to escape. Out of that understanding can arise at least the seed of courage.

For, unlike cowardice, courage loves company because it recognizes and accepts the ever-present danger of self deception. Courage thus seeks out company that will help it confront that danger rather than attempt to escape from it. Cowardice seeks company to support self-deception, and thus it seeks the company of cowards. Courage hopes to find self by avoiding self-deception, and thus it seeks out the company of honesty.

The Company of Honesty is a magnificent alternate name for the fellowship and program of A.A. We need — I need — both insight and courage. Only by combining insight and courage can I find and confront my self-as-feared. But self-as-feared, like insight and courage, is not a once-and-for-all reality embedded in concrete nor some permanent achievement chiseled in granite. The moment when I admitted I was "powerless over alcohol — that [my life] had become unmanageable" was only the model, indeed, only the First Step of my journey toward full humanity.

As I grow, other fears emerge — old fears, previously smothered in alcohol; new fears engendered by the confrontation of my limitations with what now seem limitless horizons. Regrowth, even more than rebirth, requires both insight and courage.

And the glory of the "company" of A.A. is that it affords me both. The Twelve Steps are an exercise in insight and courage. To practice them is to know myself, even as to practice them bestows the courage that that knowledge and practice require. Insight can embolden courage, and courage can open the way to new and deeper insights — but only if both are practiced.

As it draws to a close, my pilgrimage of ninety meetings in ninety days is offering me this: the insight to know my self-as-feared and the courage to confront that understanding so that I may be the self-that-I-am.

75

Psychological cure does not come through the patient's acquisition of psychological theory. The significant changes come deeper down, though our intellectual views may also change in consequence. The patient comes to feel differently about the world, about himself and other people, and as a consequence he will see things differently.

— William Barrett

After all, sobriety is but a start. The problem of finding out who we are, where we are, and where we are going next, is something that must eventually confront everyone.

— Bill W.

PERHAPS BECAUSE I AM KEEPING THIS journal, I wish to ruminate this morning on two A.A. axioms that might at first glance seem to advise against such an endeavor. Alcoholics Anonymous presents itself as a "simple program," and we are often advised: "Utilize, don't analyze."

Occasionally, I meet individuals in A.A. who seem to live at one of two extremes. Some few get so caught up in thinking about their thinking that they wince every time they are reminded that A.A. is a "simple program." Others seems to think that "Utilize, don't analyze" is one of the Twelve Steps — that "Don't drink and go to meetings" is the whole of Alcoholics Anonymous, and that even going to discussion meetings or reading the *Twelve and Twelve* is a falling away from some kind of pristinely pure sobriety.

Those I have met at either of these two extremes do not strike me as being winners. I neither can nor want to identify with their sobriety, because it seems to lack something I find attractive in the vast majority of A.A. members whose way of life runs between those two extremes. But sometimes I wonder about that broad middle space. How do we find the balance between keeping it so simple that we become mindless and analyzing ourselves into another drink?

Balance implies tension. Not all tension is bad. Balance and tension, in fact, insofar as they imply resistance to the tendency to rush to extremes, constitute both our humanity and our sobriety. The alcoholic, as Bill W. never tired of reminding us, tends to be an "all or nothing" person. We find sobriety, and ourselves, only by resisting that tendency. The A.A. way of life, indeed, seems well understood as a way of living in the middle — of fulfilling ourselves as humans, without falling into any of the extremes associated, in our drinking lives, with booze.

Let me try to come at that from a different direction. A.A. is a way of life for thinking human beings. The problem of the active alcoholic lies not in the fact that he or she thinks, but in the *way* he or she thinks. *The Big Book* does not say that the drinker's problem is his mind, but rather that "the main problem of the alcoholic centers in his mind, rather than in his body."

Therefore the A.A. way of life involves a way of thinking. There are different kinds of thinking. A.A., in a way, guides us to the kind of thinking that is healing rather than destructive. And it does that by suggesting that the first rule of that way of thinking is that a person "keep it simple" and "utilize rather than analyze."

A philosopher once observed that "Real thinking only begins at the point where we have come to understand that analytic reason is the most obstinate adversary of true thinking." There is a profound connection, that is to say, between thinking and simplicity. That is true because thinking looks to *wholes* more than it analyzes into *parts*. Any whole is in some sense simple, for as a whole, it is one.

Approaching the A.A. way of life as a whole leaves one free to accept or to reject it — but not to pick and choose among its aspects. That is the truest sense in which ours is a simple program: its nature is such that we can accept it only as a whole. Any attempt to deny that, to analyze it (and thus to break it) into parts, signals a rejection of the A.A. way of life. As a way of life, it has no parts. To see parts is to fail to know the way of life.

Speakers who remind me of A.A.'s simplicity simply recall me to thinking the A.A. way.

What is the A.A. way of thinking? First and foremost, it is the way of thinking that I learn by practicing A.A.'s Twelve-Step program. Reading A.A. literature and attending A.A. meetings of course help; but a *way* is learned only *on the way*. That is why I set off on the ninety/ninety especially mindful of the Sixth and Seventh, the Tenth and Eleventh Steps in my personal program.

What is the A.A. way of thinking? Telling and listening to stories is, ultimately, a way of thinking. That may seem too simple. But it reminds me of a favorite story, a classic story, that — although not an A.A. story — well captures and solves the apparent problems that we, failing to think the A.A. way, readily imagine are inherent in simplicity.

The tale, although it has many motifs in various traditions of wisdom, is most familiar in its biblical version, for it is one of the few Old Testament stories directly cited by Jesus of Nazareth. The story tells of a Syrian general, Naaman, who, coming to the prophet Elisha, sought to be healed of his leprosy. It helps my identification with Naaman to remember that, in ancient times, leprosy was as much a stigmatized illness as alcoholism is today. Elisha told the general to bathe in the Jordan River, but Naaman became angry at the simplicity of that suggestion and refused to do so. He started to leave in a huff, complaining that he had come too great a distance to get such simple advice when there were lots of bigger and cleaner rivers back where he came from.

As Naaman was marching off, full of resentment, his servants, who had made the same long journey for no apparent reason, prevailed upon the general to try out the advice. "After all," they pointed out, "if the prophet had told you to do something difficult that no other man could do, you would have done it. So why not at least try out this simple advice?" I am sure you know what happened: Naaman did, and he was cured.

To me, that story has to do with the kind of simplicity we talk about and experience in A.A. Although living sober can involve many complexities, although we are always invited to plumb the depths of wisdom embodied in the A.A. program, it is the simple things like not taking the first drink and attending meetings that get and keep us sober, the simple things that make it possible for us to handle the complex ones if and when we have to.

When I first came to A.A., I honestly believe that if they had told me that it was 2.46 ounces of alcohol that got me drunk, I would have been as happy as a clam. I would have run out and bought a chemistry set and a scale and a portable computer, and I would have probably carried the whole kit and caboodle into every bar I hit. That would have been worthy of my complicated intelligence.

But when they told me that it was the first drink that got the alcoholic drunk — well, even I can count to one on my fingers. There was no challenge in that, and so I almost resented it. Except, surprisingly, so long as I have remembered just that simple truth, A.A. has worked for me. It has taken time, of course. At first, I listened to the stories at A.A. meetings as if I were doing sociological research — fending off the boredom that was really my denial by counting and calculating: wrecked cars, time in jail, lost jobs, broken marriages, you name it. In my first six months hanging around A.A., I gathered more data than would fit on a whole shelf of scholarly journals. In fact, I probably could have published it, except that, because I was still drinking, I couldn't write a coherent sentence. I remember that the "scholars" in A.A., with whom I sometimes shared my findings, told me: "Identify, don't compare." That was such simple advice that, of course, I had to ask, "How?" "Keep coming," they told me, "and try." In time, I did.

And for that reason, I like to think that for me, "simple program" and "way of thinking," rather than being contradictory, fit together very well. Because I am human, it is inevitable and necessary that I think. The real question, the only question, is how I think. Remembering A.A.'s simplicity helps to keep me on the right track. Thus, I hear in the reminders of "Keep it simple" and "Utilize, don't analyze," not a prohibition of thought, but guidance to the kind of thinking that can aid my effort to make progress in the A.A. way of life.

76

The man who has come to imagine he is God may be unaware of it himself, but he very soon starts to behave in a way which makes it obvious enough to others. One minor symptom, for example, is a refusal to listen to or tolerate the presence of others unless they say what he wishes to hear.

— W.H. Auden

AS DR. BOB USED TO REMIND BILL W., "HONesty gets us sober, but tolerance keeps us sober."

When we first come around A.A., most of us are very fortunate. In hardly any time at all, we discover some groups in which we feel especially at home. Some meetings quickly become our favorites: the stories told at them seem to invite the identification that enables our growth in sobriety. A.A.'s own tolerance, thanks to Bill and Dr. Bob and many others, affords all of us the gift of diversity.

One lesson of ninety meetings in ninety days seems to be that if there are favorites, there must also be nonfavorites. On the one hand, that is okay. I can no more be equally at home at all A.A. meetings than I can be in many places at the same time or can read all the pages of a book in a single glance. But, on the other hand, it seems to me that one purpose of attending ninety meetings in ninety days is to grow beyond my usual meeting attendance pattern in quality as well as in quantity.

Necessarily, in choosing meetings to attend, I choose meetings not to attend. On some days, I quickly locate a particular, familiar meeting. For the rest of that day, I look forward with relish to attending it. On other days, however, no such meeting leaps out at me from the list's pages. Often, on such occasions, I fret within myself throughout the day, frequently rechecking the list in hopes of finding some overlooked "good meeting."

"A good meeting," I was told long ago, "is one at which you do not drink." Have I grown beyond that understanding, or am I forgetting an important truth?

It is only human, of course, I argue with myself, to want to find a setting in which I feel comfortable. The memory that I used to use the same argument to defend my drinking sounds a loud warning. So, alcoholic that I continue to be, I keep rationalizing. If growth in sobriety is based on identification, is it not wise to choose meetings where identification comes easily? That sounds pretty good — it even sounds quite intelligent. Another warning bell goes off: it was not my intelligence that got me sober.

Auden's words, penned in tribute to Dag Hammarskjold, pull me to a deeper understanding. Could it be that I am trying to find meetings where no one will say anything with which I disagree, anything challenging? My mind, even dry, seems riddled with pigeonholes, with categories that do not seem to be based in real sobriety. Who am I, after all, to judge some meeting as "too spiritual" or "too psychological," or to avoid other meetings because of "too much talk about drugs" or "too many (or "too few") newcomers or singles or oldtimers?

The need to identify remains real and constant in sobriety. But if my sobriety is to grow, so must my identifications. "Honesty gets us sober, but tolerance keeps us sober": tolerance implies difference. Agreement is not the same as identification. Identification, A.A. experience teaches, deepens when we hear very different others tell stories that at their most real level are all the same. Perhaps the most effective identification occurs in the shock of recognition — the blazing dawn of the discovery that at the most basic level, I am the same as every other alcoholic: an alcoholic.

If I ever forget that, if I ever lose sight of it, I am in trouble. Therefore I need to work to keep sight of it. And I suspect that maybe the best way to work on it just now is obvious: at least once or twice a week during the rest of this ninety/ninety, I should go back to meetings that on my first visit struck me as too intellectual or too whatever.

The Big Book does not often use screaming italics — but it does so in one place: "*Willingness, honesty, and open-mindedness are the essentials of recovery. But these are indispensable.*" They are "indispensable," they are "the essentials of recovery," because, without them, identification is impossible. Too readily, still, I seem to resist and refuse identification. Yet it is precisely identification that heals me — that heals my alcoholism because it makes whole my humanity.

I often talk and think about growth, about progress: sobriety and recovery, we all know, are neverending, ongoing processes of growth and progress. But those processes continue as they began — by identification. My identifications, then, must also expand and grow; and they will do so only if I allow them to do so — only if I invite and enable them to grow, to deepen. One way of doing that, the way to which I seem to be invited by this ninety/ninety, seems to be by attending different meetings.

The Big Book's italicized mandate haunts me: "*Willingness, honesty, and open-mindedness are the essentials of recovery. But these are indispensable.*" That is a healing reminder. Pondering it helps me to remember something that is very important to my recovery: I grow in sobriety by growing in — by broadening as well as by deepening — my identification with others, and especially with all other sober alcoholics. Perhaps that is why, as A.A.'s co-founders knew so well, "Honesty gets us sober, but tolerance keeps us sober."

77

If a man loves a girl for the sake of her money, who will call him a lover? . . . The Good is one thing; the reward is another. . . . When he, then, wills the Good for the sake of the reward, he does not will one thing but two. And this is double-mindedness.

— Soren Kierkegaard

THIS EVENING'S MEETING'S DISCUSSION CONcerned fringe benefits — the advantages that seem inevitably to flow from sobriety. Perhaps, Mel suggested, we would be better off if there weren't any.

That proved a provocative thought. In the first place, it is almost inconceivable that benefits not flow from sobriety. Sober, we become able to work and able to love; and we have all been taught that love and work both have and are their own rewards. Sobriety allows us to receive the goods around us that we closed off and rejected by our drinking: from a clear head and a calm stomach on awakening in the morning to the beauties of nature and art, the simple joys of calm reflection or active exercise. How could sobriety not bear with it inestimable fringe benefits?

The problem — and we see it often in newcomers and even, perhaps, too frequently in ourselves — is that it is possible to confuse the fringe benefits with the goal. Sobriety, Walter commented, if understood fully and correctly as its reality is presented by the fellowship and program of Alcoholics Anonymous, is an end in itself.

Norman observed that he was not so sure: it seemed to him useful on occasion to ask, "What did I get sober for?" But discussion soon agreed that the only ultimate answer to that question ran: "For sobriety, in all that it implies." The spiritual, which we most cherish, is after all not a fringe benefit. Someone else scented "blasphemy" in the affirmation of sobriety as an end in itself. Augustine insisted that " . . . Our hearts are restless until they rest in Thee" — and his Thee could only be a personal

Higher Power, "God, *as we understand Him.*" It is idolatrous, it seems at first glance, to make a god of sobriety. Yet more deeply, the group's resident spiritual philosopher reminded us, idolatry involves "absolutizing the relative," while blasphemy marks the attempt to "relativize the absolute." Accepting sobriety as an end in itself does neither.

After that brief flight, the group quickly returned to earth. The question, Helen suggested, was how to learn — and even more how to accept — that sobriety is its own reward. As always, when topics essentially philosophical are discussed at A.A. meetings (as they always are), no final solution was reached, but we all came away feeling enriched.

I have a piquant waking nightmare. Some evil force demands that I either take a drink or deny my God. If that strikes you — as it does me — as inconceivably ridiculous, then there is neither blasphemy nor idolatry in viewing sobriety as an end in itself. Life may present difficult and even impossible choices: sobriety does not. For although it is life, sobriety is also more: it is, by definitional concept, life-as-my-Higher-Power-would-have-me-live-it.

The problem, it seems to me, lies not in the self-deceiving direction of confusing sobriety with God, but in the too-common tendency of those who are not God to confuse sobriety with what one great religious teacher termed *mammon*, or everything that is not God. Because we are not God, we confuse sobriety with what is not God.

Mystics tell us that we are surrounded by God. Any fool can see that we are also engulfed by not-God: by wealth and physical beauty, by health and honor and career and comforts of every kind. They are good, but they are not God.

We have neither theologians nor mystics in our group, but Fred had an interesting suggestion on how to differentiate between the reality of sobriety and the realities that we term fringe benefits. The more I have of the former, the more others also have of it, from my very having. With more material things, it is different: the more one person has, the less other individuals at least feel that they have. Only that which is somehow infinite is enhanced rather than diminished by increased participation. Sobriety, Fred pointed out, meets that test.

Yet how many of us can say that we got sober in order to be sober? I would not pass that test. Most proximately, I wanted to get sober in order to stop hurting. And even that proved a false hope. I have learned in sobriety that not hurting is not one of the fringe benefits of sobriety. If anything, as far as hurting goes, sobriety allows me to feel the pain that, when drinking, I had tried to mask with booze.

Am I, then, disappointed in my sobriety? Hardly. In fact, I can identify with Floyd, who told the group that he was grateful sobriety had not brought him such fringe benefits as career, fame, even a regular job, a loving family, or flawless physical health. "Grateful?" several asked, thinking of the recent tracheotomy through which Floyd spoke. Everyone in our group listens carefully to Floyd — not because of his surgical disability, but because however little of worldly goods or good luck Floyd has, we are certain that we do want what he does have. I think every individual in the group measures his or her sobriety against Floyd's, and we always come away from that contact encouraged and inspired to grow.

"Yes, grateful," Floyd said. "If sobriety had brought me those things, I might have thought they *were* sobriety. And then, when I lost them, where would I have been? What would I have done? I'll tell you what I am pretty sure old Floyd, Floyd the alcoholic, would have done: he would have gone out and gotten drunk. My Higher Power has been very good to me by not letting me get confused about just what my sobriety is and is not. What you call fringe benefits would have just screwed up my thinking. I am happy for those of you who don't have that problem, and I appreciate how some of you use your fringe benefits to help Floyd. But Floyd himself is better off without them, because as sick as Floyd sometimes is, his greatest illness is his alcoholism. And so I am grateful that I never even had the chance to get confused about what my recovery — my sobriety — is all about."

Does it make me sound too sick if I admit that I almost fear Floyd's sobriety? His recovery beams a light that is almost blinding. But his ever-present example helps at least one group to be ever-mindful of the difference between fringe benefits and sobriety.

Perhaps that is why our group has such a constant flow of newcomers. Perhaps that is also why a number of them do not make it with us, at least the first time around. There is, in A.A., no "easier, softer way." We all know that. But perhaps not all who approach A.A. are ready for Floyd's message, even if they are ready to begin down the road to sobriety. It always interests me when some who do not "get" A.A. with us at first, later return to our group after beginning to taste sobriety elsewhere.

It is good, I think, for those of us who have been blessed with sobriety's fringe benefits to acknowledge them. But it seems to be also true that, if "our public relations policy is based on attraction rather than promotion," then it is also good for us to realize that only our sobriety itself can be the ultimate attraction. Any rational person seeking primarily wealth or health, love or career success, would hardly be advised to begin looking for them in A.A. Of course, when we first come around, few of us are very rational — fortunately!

78

A common characteristic of the inner world of the alcoholic is confusion. . . . Many times professionals too quickly jump to the conclusion that all the alcoholic is experiencing is simply the defense mechanism of denial.

Often the alcoholic is not able to establish a definite, solid, and irrefutable correlation between his/her life difficulties and the ingesting of alcohol. This causes confusion. After all, past history has taught the alcoholic that alcohol may still be a friend, a comforter, a support to lean on. The early positive experiences still have a "glow" and an attraction. The alcoholic many times sees others who can drink more often and in heavier quantities and they don't need any "treatment center." The active alcoholic has a hard time distinguishing the difference between abuse and disease.

— Dr. Joseph Emmanuel

THERE IS A DIFFERENCE BETWEEN CONFUSION and denial. Perhaps because of the enthusiasm of newfound sobriety, A.A. newcomers often ignore that distinction. More serious, however, seems the failure of many nonalcoholic professionals who are sympathetic to A.A. to understand that difference.

Because within A.A. "we are responsible" — because A.A.'s proven success has opened the minds of many professionals so that they are willing to learn from our experience, strength, and hope — it might be well for us to clarify that distinction for ourselves.

In addition to my recent reading of Dr. Emmanuel, this thought is occasioned by a newcomer's first storytelling at the meeting last night. Pat's story clearly described both confusion and denial, but she kept calling both "denial." I found that especially interesting because, earlier in the day, I had glanced through my copy of the unofficial, privately published "Index Concordance: Where Does It Say So" and learned that while "confused" and "confusion" are listed as appearing in both *The Big Book* and the *Twelve and Twelve*, there were no listings for "deny" or "denial." Also, offhand I would estimate that at the discussion meetings attended during these ninety days, I have heard "confusion" used at least three times for every usage of "denial," with both terms almost invariably being used in their correct meanings. Why, then, do especially newcomers and non-A.A.s seem to confuse confusion with denial?

Hearing Pat's story helped me to understand one possible reason: we rightly emphasize honesty so much that those not deeply familiar with and practiced in the A.A. way of life tend to see it as the whole story of our recovery. We know better, of course. Those who live the A.A. way of life soon discover that there are no "whole stories" except, in a sense, our own.

Most of us, when we first come to A.A. are mired in both confusion and denial. The denial involves self-deception: it is a species of dishonesty, and it signals our attempt to flee from ourselves — from the alcoholic selves we fear that we might be. Hitting bottom usually represents, if not the breakdown of denial, at least the opening of a sufficiently wide chink in it so that we can break out of denial and become able to identify with some A.A. members. That identification which derives from the heart and the gut proves to be the solvent that melts denial.

But there is also another aspect to identification — the identification that understands. The heart and the gut are connected to the head and the mind, but they are not the same. Denial, despite all the mind-games we play in practicing it, is ultimately a gut existential experience. That is why identification rather than education is required to break through it. The head may play mind-games in service to the heart's denial, and, cognitively, we are confused.

Confusion is not the same as self-deception. One reason why so many of us felt so out of place when we first attended an A.A. meeting was that we were confused about just what an alcoholic is.

But even at the beginning of our A.A. attendance, the cognitive aspect of identification works. We learn as well as feel as we listen to and identify with A.A. storytellers. Even the distinction between learning and feeling, of course, does not capture the richness of the identification that ushers us into sobriety: more accurately, we learn with both our heads and our hearts. Only one word adequately captures the process that in all its richness dissolves both confusion and denial: *identification.*

A Germanic distinction, implicit in Kierkegaard, I think, clarifies Dr. Emmanuel's insight: "heart-honesty" is not the same as "head-honesty." Denial signifies the absence of heart-honesty; confusion, of head-honesty. And it is as dangerous for those who work with alcoholics to mistake one honesty — or its lack — for the other as it would be for a surgeon to mistake one organ for another.

Most professionals who work in the field of alcoholism treatment, in dealing with their clients, encounter confusion at least as often as they confront denial. And while head-honesty cannot be ultimately separated from heart-honesty, perhaps some professionals can be especially skilled at working on the former, just as most A.A. speakers are especially adept at transmitting and eliciting the latter.

We do not, in A.A. ever tell anyone: "You are an alcoholic." We do share our experience, strength, and hope — and then suggest: "If you have decided you want what we have . . . then you are ready to take certain steps." *The Big Book* opens with a story, not a DSM–III diagnosis.

Whether themselves alcoholic or not, professionals acting in their professional capacity do not have what we in A.A. have — a context that is built on identification. Because of the very fact that they are professionals, their clients experience a gap that inhibits rather than invites identification. Professionals, then, can and need to say that we cannot and dare not say: "You are an alcoholic." And they have a duty as well as a right to use DSM–III criteria in establishing that diagnosis.

Professionals also, then, whether alcoholic or not, if they are wise — and very many are wise as well as knowledgeable — will look to members of A.A. for the knowledge that will help them not so much as to identify with alcoholics as to identify alcoholics. They and their clients can learn from our head-honesty even if they themselves cannot identify with our heart-honesty.

To be able to contribute, in that way, is to me both one of the glorious fringe benefits of sobriety and but one expression of gratitude, especially to all the professionals who kept me alive until I found A.A. It is also, I believe, an appropriate living out of A.A.'s service legacy: "We are responsible." For one fringe responsibility of A.A.'s success, it seems to me, is that we are responsible not only to be there when an alcoholic reaches out to us for help: we are also responsible for ensuring that at least the head-honesty that we can transmit be there for any person to whom a suffering alcoholic might reach out for help.

79

"Beliefs" are not intellectual entities which you receive, but decisions about yourself which you make.
— John Douglas Mullen

THE PARADOX OF THE SPIRITUAL, AS IT CONsistently arises at meetings of A.A. (it did again last night), seems to be this: on the one hand, how can one live the A.A. way of life without living spiritually? Yet, on the other hand, how can one who is an alcoholic embrace the spiritual as it is often presented without getting drunk? How can one grow in the acceptance of being a sober alcoholic without transmuting that acceptance into the claim to be special?

The answer, insofar as there can be an answer to any paradox, lies less in our A.A. literature than in our A.A. selves. Not that our literature, and especially *The Big Book* and the *Twelve and Twelve,* is a bad place to start. A modern philosopher has observed that the chief contribution of the religious thinker Kierkegaard was to make religious belief a difficult choice, and the chief contribution of the atheistic thinker Sartre was to make atheistic disbelief a difficult choice, and that is as both should be. Many will agree, I think, that their first reading of *The Big Book* or their first visit to an A.A. meeting had a similar impact: it rendered both continued drinking and the spirituality described as sobriety into very difficult if not impossible choices.

But somehow we made — and we make — the choice. Many postpone it for a time . . . some for as long as is possible. Many others spend years, even decades, trying to find some compromise . . . some way of evading the choice. Some die without making it: perhaps they are the lucky ones, if they die dry. Or at least so the evaders might think.

One of the paradoxes of being human is that although our being is both/and, our having can be only either/or. Rarely is that clearer than in the matter of our belief. Insofar as we have beliefs, we must choose. But insofar as we are our beliefs, we necessarily sustain paradox, without escape or compromise.

At least within A.A., the spiritual is a paradox. Our own argot signals that in our glib claim to live a spiritual rather than a religious program. If that claim be simply obvious truth, why have so many profoundly religious thinkers — among them Buddhists, Christians, and Jews — been able to find in our way of life a reflection of the best of their own faiths? Yet any truly religious person will also tell you that there is, in religion, no common denominator. How does A.A. do it? Exactly what does A.A. mean and do by its claim? I do not know: to me, at least, it is a reflection — or perhaps the nub — of the paradox.

Why is it that I come away from meetings like this evening's, meetings that wrestle directly with the spiritual, both refreshed and exhausted, both apparently more sober and surely more uneasy about my sobriety?

It is not easy to talk about the spiritual — it is perhaps impossible precisely insofar as one lives it. Is that the source of the unease . . . that we have attempted the impossible? Yet, A.A. insistently tells us that the spiritual is "the program." And so to touch on the spiritual directly is to tap most directly the core of our sobriety. Some realities, of course, are too precious — too sacred — to be touched directly. Talking about the spiritual can too easily mimic talking about love: those who can, do; those who cannot, talk. But our meetings are "talk."

Within A.A. we will tell our stories rather than attempt to explain our spirituality. Here, I think, is where something I recently read proves enlightening:

> "Beliefs" are not intellectual entities which you receive, but decisions about yourself which you make.

Spirituality is less the kind of reality that one talks about than it is the ultimate reality that one lives. And one lives it, in part, by telling the story of one's life — which is not the same as talking about it. To expand an aphorism is, of course, not to improve on it: but I hope that attempt today makes clearer my appreciation, today, of A.A.'s spirituality.

The answer to the paradox of A.A. and the spiritual lies less in our literature than in ourselves. That understanding suggests one way of comprehending A.A.'s claim that it is spiritual rather than religious. Most religions have a sacred book; indeed, some people — mostly outside our fellowship — seem to think that A.A. does, too. But we know that the reality is otherwise. For one thing, even though our book consists mainly of stories, they are *our* stories. More significantly, although we have literature, we are ourselves our stories.

Alcoholics Anonymous, that is to say, does not have and therefore cannot offer spirituality. Because we are Alcoholics Anonymous, A.A. is spiritual insofar as we — who are its essence more than its members — make decisions about ourselves. Now, decisions are not beliefs, for what we do flows less from what we think than from how we think. As our stories also testify, decisions — and their outcomes — are shaped by how we think rather than by what we think.

A.A. will exist — and exist as A.A. — so long as it welcomes very different people who have very different ideas about the spiritual. Our diversity of thought ensures that our unity derives from our way of thinking. That is important because we get sober and grow in sobriety not by doctrines but by practices; not according to what we think but according to how we think; not by intellectual entities that we receive, but by decisions about ourselves that we make.

Do we, then, "have" beliefs? The answer, it seems, must be no. As A.A.s, we do not "have" beliefs, because what beliefs hold us cannot be "had." Insofar as we do believe, our beliefs are our stories, for those stories tell the decisions about ourselves that we make. Those who would ask for more, those who would insist on defining exactly the nature of the spiritual in A.A.'s way of life, understand neither belief nor Alcoholics Anonymous.

80

Serene will be our days and bright,
And happy will our nature be,
When love is an unerring light,
And joy its own security.

— William Wordsworth

It isn't very intelligent to find answers to questions which are unanswerable.

— Bernard Le B. de Fontenelle

WAYNE ASKED A SIMPLE QUESTION AT THE meeting tonight, a simple question that provoked spirited and eventually profound discussion of the meaning of our sobriety: "Can the Serenity Prayer ever be a cop-out?"

He briefly detailed the situation at hand — how a change in his job's work rules threatened to disrupt his family life. His first reaction, Wayne admitted, had been anger. Although he did not think of taking a drink, the situation afforded a "remember when" of past sprees similarly triggered. "And so I said the Serenity Prayer — worked it to death, as a matter of fact. After all, who am I to decide on the rules: I do not know the whole picture. The setting in which I work seemed to me clearly to fall among 'the things I cannot change'; so, I decided, it is up to me to accept it, and to work rather on changing myself."

A few of the group's oldtimers, listening intently, exchanged glances as Wayne continued. "Well, Susie, my Al-Anon, did not see it exactly that way. She 'suggested,' if I may use that euphemism, that, if anything, my acceptance in this case did not console her as much as it frightened her, because it seemed to be the same kind of passivity and lack of self-esteem that I had exhibited back when I was drinking.

"Well, it seems to me that Susie has a point. The problem is that I need that 'wisdom to know the difference' that the third part of the Serenity Prayer asks. But until I get it — or maybe as a way of getting it — would the group tonight help by sharing how you learned to keep the Serenity Prayer from being a cop-out, if it can be one? I guess I am asking this: can any of you identify with the stage of struggling for sobriety where I seem to be stuck? And if you can, can you help me past it?"

The murmurs around the table as some members rose to refresh their coffee testified that identification would pose no problem this evening. Readily, a few of the newer members of the group told of similar experiences in their own lives, and how they had handled them and grown in sobriety, or at least stayed sober. Some of the veterans also eventually chimed in, less emphasizing similar situations than similar feelings of anger, frustration, and confusion over the meaning of "sobriety."

Reliable Ed, in his usual role of penultimate contributor, reminded the group that he has heard some of us say we had come to A.A. not in order to stop drinking, but in order to stop feeling bad. "It doesn't work that way," he pointed out: "we get what we need, not what we want." The others agreed that occasional moments of frustration and confusion seemed an essential part of any sobriety. Perhaps, several suggested, that is the ultimate acceptance we seek in the Serenity Prayer.

As the perhapses and the cliches began to outnumber the direct sharing of "experience, strength and hope," the group seemed to sense that it was slipping some mooring. The table grew silent and, as always in such situations, awaited the contribution of one of the oldtimer stalwarts sitting quietly and contentedly in the background. I have no idea how true this is of A.A. groups elsewhere, but I have become fascinated, in the course of my attendance at discussion meetings during these ninety days, how every group around here seems to have such monuments to serene sobriety — members quietly rejoicing in decades of sobriety who mainly just sit and listen, participating by their mere presence. Most often, they are content to say nothing unless specifically invited to do so. Because they come early and stay late, other members sometimes ask their advice privately, or the stalwart himself will offer some quiet suggestion in implicit response to some earlier comment.

Such status, I have observed, is neither seized nor bestowed: it somehow just happens over a long period of time. One manifestation of it happened now. Neither the chairman nor

Wayne called on anyone — this group does not do that. Somehow, everyone knew that it was time to hear from Floyd or from Tom — and that we would, if either deemed that he had anything to offer that we might not find elsewhere.

It was Tom, on this evening, who obliged, though he mimicked Floyd's deep rasp and terse style in doing so, perhaps as a way of informing us whence he had learned this profound truth: "There ain't no easy answers."

Instantly, the group was plunged into a deeper level of discussion, and perhaps of sobriety. The question, clearly, was not Serenity Prayer as cop-out, but our tendency as alcoholics to hope for, if not to expect, easy answers. Those sitting around the table re-embarked on the topic, enabled to share more profoundly the experience, strength, and hope that had brought us all together.

I must confess that I did not follow the ensuing discussion very carefully. My mind remained fastened on Tom's words: "There ain't no easy answers." The more I thought about it, the more that truism seemed to sum up an important lesson Alcoholics Anonymous has taught me.

When I first came around, there seemed to be an easy answer: "Don't drink and go to meetings." In my own case, of course, even that simple answer had not proven easy. Just about the time that it became easy, my sponsor threw an eternal monkey wrench into my dawning complacency: "You see those Twelve Steps? Well, you don't necessarily have to stop reading them, but you had better start working them."

"Working the Steps," although an answer, is not easy. Why do I always seem most in need of the Step that at that moment seems the hardest? The answer, of course, lies in the question: I need any Step because at that moment it seems the hardest. The same, I have found is true of the Serenity Prayer. There are three parts to that petition: we seek to become able "to accept," "to change," and "to know." We attain those abilities by asking for "serenity," "courage," and "wisdom." None of those, in my experience, is ever easy: and we must not only ask for them, we must practice them. We ask for them, indeed, in a sense, only by practicing them. And practicing such virtues as acceptance, courage, and the kind of intelligence that accompanies them is never easy. By why, I sometimes wonder, does the one I most obviously need at this moment seem least easy? The answer again of course lies in the question: because it seems least easy, that is why I need it!

Alcohol, I recall, was an easy answer. The only trouble was, it was the wrong answer, at least for me. In a way, putting the cork in the bottle signaled abandoning my quest for easy answers — only I sometimes too easily forget that. Tonight's discussion furnished a healthy reminder. If there were easy answers, I would not need Alcoholics Anonymous.

On balance, at this moment, I am grateful that the search for easy answers and the A.A. way of life exclude each other. If there were easy answers, I would not need the A.A. way of life. But that way of life has brought me — and continues to give me — so much that is true and good and beautiful that I do not think that today I would choose an easy answer even if such existed. Thank you, then, Higher Power, for teaching me, through A.A., that life itself, at bottom, is like the bottom of the bottle: one does not find easy answers in it.

81

[Freud] distinguishes between natural desires which are limited and those which spring from false opinions and are unlimited. Desire as such is not unlimited. In undistorted nature it is limited by objective needs and is therefore capable of satisfaction. But man's distorted imagination transcends the objective needs ("When astray — your wanderings are limitless") and with them any possible satisfaction.

— Paul Tillich

TILLICH HIMSELF DID NOT NECESSARILY agree with Freud, whose views he found prefigured by the Stoic philosopher, Seneca. For the Christian as for any theist, that which distinguishes the human from the animal is precisely a limitless desire that is not "distorted" nor "astray": the orientation of the human spirit toward infinite divinity.

But I am not interested here in theological distinctions. The point that seems valid, the insight that strikes me because it resonates with my own experience, concerns rather the nature of my craving for such mundane realities as wealth, fame, power . . . and alcohol.

Tonight, on the way home from the meeting, I began thinking about "craving" and "enough." One benefit of the A.A. way of life, one boon of these ninety days, is that the perspective afforded by my alcoholism on my craving for alcohol allows me to see that "desire" as a kind of model. Anyone who craves anything could learn much from the active alcoholic's craving for alcohol. And anyone who wishes to transcend the distortions visited upon any life by craving anything can learn even more from the A.A. member's experience, strength, and hope in recovery.

By "craving," I mean simply unlimited desire. More concretely, I use the term to signify how the active alcoholic desires alcohol to the point of needing it. Any alcoholic understands the meaning of the phenomenon of craving.

According to the point of view represented by Tillich's use of Freud, such unlimited desire springs from "false opinions." Freud wrote in German, but the word that he used — *die Meinung* — is well translated by "opinion" in this connotation: it implies a subjective attribution of value. The distortion of desire, that is to say, arises from false values.

But who is to say that any values are false, or that any values are true? One answer lies in this passage, and it seems a response that would prove acceptable both to Freud and to Tillich, both to the atheistic analyst and the Christian theologian. It is an answer that also has the perhaps even greater advantage of being borne out by the experience, strength, and hope of countless members of Alcoholics Anonymous. "False" values are those that drive one to seek the unlimited, even at the cost of destroying the best in oneself in the process.

"When astray — your wanderings are limitless." They are also self-destructive. The neophyte hiker lost in a forest tends to panic at the experience — to move wildly about in what are invariably circles. The more lost he feels, the more lost he gets. The experienced woodsman knows better: when astray, he does not wander but rather seeks and plots a point of orientation. Once oriented, one is no longer astray, even if yet unsure of the exact way out.

My alcoholic experience replicated that, on both the level of wanderings and the level of desire. The wanderings began when I realized that my drinking could just possibly occasionally be a problem — when I found myself "astray." I changed brands and physicians, jobs and life-style. Nothing, of course, worked — until I found the point of orientation afforded by Alcoholics Anonymous and its way of life.

That orientation concerned the nature of my desire, although A.A.'s vocabulary of "obsession-compulsion" and my own experience with other drugs as well as alcohol led me to think more concretely in terms of "craving." Clearly, I had proven my desire for alcohol, if not my capacity for intoxication, limitless. Only a fool would have failed to recognize that desire as distorted. The things I sacrificed on the altar of "my right to drink" revealed that that desire not only transcended objective needs but was totally incapable of satisfaction. Does a rational person sell his own blood in order to purchase the second half-gallon of booze so that he will be sure of having enough to survive a long holiday weekend?

I would like to claim that early in my A.A. experience I came to understand not only the obvious distortions in my alcoholic life but also the false opinions that permeated even my more socially acceptable habits. I would like to claim that, but I cannot. Only slowly did I come to see the aspect of metaphor in my alcoholism: how desires for wealth and fame and power and love tended also to be unlimited cravings. For some of us, at least, alcoholism, although not only a metaphor, is truly a metaphor — an image for just about everything that is wrong with our way of life. If I had died ten years ago, my epitaph would have most appropriately read: "He knew not the meaning of *Enough*."

Today, thanks to the way of life taught and enabled by my participation in A.A., that is different because I am different. I still have desires, of course, but they are desires, not cravings. And although I cherish many dissatisfactions, because they spur me to seek "progress rather than perfection," I have learned also to take satisfaction in progress: my objective needs are generally readily met.

For all that, I am grateful. Without passing judgment on the opinions or values of others, I have learned through Alcoholics Anonymous that in such matters as wealth and fame and power, there is such a thing as "enough." That I had to learn about enough by forfeiting my right to drink alcohol — by admitting that, for me, the first drink is too much — strikes me, in perspective, as the cheapest price anyone ever had to pay for such useful wisdom.

Most of all, then, I am grateful that, if I died today, my epitaph could appropriately read: "He knew the meaning of enough." Those who love me would know its significance: perhaps it would console them to realize that it applied also to my cherishing of their love. There is no greater gift than to know the meaning of "enough."

82

And, if God permit, I shall but better love thee after death.

— Elizabeth Barrett Browning

SAM AND I WERE NOT THE ONLY VISITORS from another group at the meeting last night — and thus began one of those after-the-meeting experiences that I suspect do as much for my sobriety as anything that happens between the Serenity Prayer that opens our meetings and the Lord's Prayer that closes them.

Ralph had arrived before us and obviously was anxious for the meeting to start. During the discussion, he participated with a peculiar intensity: I could almost hear him listening, as his watery grey eyes fixed on the face of whoever was speaking at the moment. Sharp featured and clean shaven, his skin was sallow except for the bright red patches where years of drinking had left their telltale pattern of ruptured blood vessels.

When he spoke, Ralph's voice came throatily, pushed forward by harsh, short breaths that hinted incipient emphysema. He offered ideas — or, more often, asked questions — choppily. Some around the table found it difficult to grasp his meaning, but the intensity with which this riveting visitor spoke hinted a plea that none could ignore. Here was someone, obviously not drinking and familiar with A.A., literally begging for sobriety.

As this journal entry already indicates, I had fallen into one of my usually not-so-sober habits: I was observing and studying rather than listening in order to identify. I realized that at the time, but I could not seem to stop — perhaps because, as it now seems clear, my Higher Power deemed that I needed that vivid picture for later memory. After last night, Ralph's memory will always live in my sobriety.

And so I noted how he was dressed: "shabby genteel," I believe the pop sociologists would term it. Clean and even neat, his clothing was worn. Ralph's plaid jacket and striped trousers would rarely have been seen together, except on skid row. His garish tie, held in place by an inept knot, partially concealed a row of disparate buttons carefully sewn but ill aligned on a shirt that had to have been ageless.

I confess to stealing a glance at this strange visitor's shoes — the ultimate revealers. As well worn as his jacket, they had been highly polished. Once, as he leaned forward to listen more carefully, I spied what appeared to be white string tied tightly around Ralph's ankle, futilely trying to keep a drooping sock from disappearing completely into its shoe.

As the meeting ended, the chairman announced that one of the visitors needed a ride home. Since Sam and I, the other visitors, had to drive clear across the city to get home, we seemed the obvious volunteers. Realizing us to be visitors, Ralph appeared to sadden in disappointment. He wanted, it was clear, to make some contact in this group, but no one else seemed to notice, and I deemed it unwise to unvolunteer Sam's trusty wheels. Besides, since Sam is my sponsor, I decided it might be well for me to "let go." Observers have no right to orchestrate.

Our ride proved warmer than I had anticipated. Ralph had clearly decided to make the best of it, so he began besieging us with questions — about how we understood A.A.'s slogans, about what we took for pain, about whether any loved ones were sick or had died, about how we "kept it simple," about what was "true sobriety."

The address Ralph gave Sam was unfamiliar, but I noticed we were headed toward a part of the city that I usually took care to avoid. Sam seemed to know the route, however, and I saw him steal a serious glance at his watch just before suggesting that if we were all going to tell our stories, we might as well do so over coffee and ice cream.

As we stopped at a familiar eatery, I became very aware of Ralph's discomfort. So did Sam, and he did not hesitate to pass it on to me. "This is going to be a real treat, Ralph. You see, Ern here owes me for about two dozen snacks from back when I was trying to Twelfth-Step him, so tonight, in honor of our being visitors together at that meeting, I am going to call in two of them. So this is Ern's treat, and if you want to thank me for driving you home, you can do it best by eating heartily." One reason that I had chosen Sam for a sponsor, I reminded myself, was that his sense of humor could be as sick as my own. There is irony in sobriety.

After some lingering hesitancy, our newfound friend ate like one famished. I could not help noticing that he ordered well: protein rather than sugars and starches seemed his obvious concern. As we ate, we talked. But again, as at the meeting, Ralph seemed far more interested in hearing our stories than in telling his own. Though still a bundle of questions, he proved a good listener. Again I felt that he was monitoring every incident, every word, as if trying to store them up so he could draw even on our vocal mannerisms for later use in staying sober.

I was puzzled: Ralph seemed in so many ways *so* sober. Sam, meanwhile, struck me as strangely oblivious to time. I sensed that he was less orchestrating our conversation than engaging in it with confidence that it would end naturally, when it should, as it did. Ralph suddenly remarked on the time, repeating his address. "It's time to go," he said simply but sadly, brightening when I suggested that he take with him an untouched dessert he had obviously not ordered for himself.

Back in Sam's car, I made a few feeble attempts to continue the conversation. But a strange silence had fallen on Ralph, and Sam seemed to acquiesce in it, so I shut up and looked out the window of the back seat where I now rode alone. As we turned a corner, I caught a glimpse of the street name Ralph had mentioned. Except for that faded green sign, I did not like what I saw.

Hell, like "bottom," I suspect, is more an inside than an outside experience. But if I had to devise an external setting for an alcoholic's hell, it would look and sound and smell like the street on which Ralph lived. Junkies and pushers, painted people and passed-out drunks, all littered a scene that was all litter. Some buildings seemed bombed-out shells: others, their drabness relieved only by occasional flashes of neon, signalled the businesses able to survive in such an environment — dingy bars and once-stately package stores crouched behind steel shutters. I closed my eyes, but it was too late: the nose and the ears are not so easily denied.

The mystery of Ralph suddenly cleared, only to be replaced by a deeper one. His clothing, his intense questions, his obvious hunger: all fell into place along with the shards of his story that I had only partially heard at the meeting. Ralph was married to — and loved beyond telling — a dying alcoholic/addict. Somehow, he had found A.A., but she could not. Our city affords little treatment for those dying willingly of addiction. It offers even less for those who love them.

Sam drove three long blocks slowly — partially lest an accident create a "recovered" alcoholic, partially because Ralph was blurting out enough of his story to "explain" what we saw. Now it all tumbled out: the loving marriage, the shared descent into alcoholism and then addiction, the lost jobs and the squandered opportunities, the moving ever downward — partially to be close to the drugs, mainly because of ever more pinching economic necessity as his own and Jeannie's health deteriorated. Ralph told of his own grave illness, of how he had chanced to find A.A. in the hospital; of how hopefully he had carried that message back to Jeannie. If I have ever heard love spoken, it was in the way Ralph said, "my Jeannie."

Ralph told more: how his Jeannie, in the pain of her own even more advanced illness, refused even to think of surrendering her habit. How he had sought help in a skid row A.A. group, but how his wife's continued adamant refusal even to want to change, now, so near the end, had led those A.A.s to tell him he had to leave her, for his own sobriety as well as for perhaps her only chance. How he could not do that.

As Ralph looked over to Sam, I noted that despite the strong intensity of his level voice, his watery eyes had teared. "But I don't think that means I am not really sober, does it Sam? I mean, I don't ever drink or take anything, even though I buy it for her and give it to her. It's the only thing for her pain, and I can't let her hurt like that — does that mean I'm not really sober? She's going to die very soon — we both know that. I wish she could get well, at least as well as me, but I don't want her going out thinking I have abandoned her. Does that make me not really sober, Sam?"

"You'll make it, Buddy," was all Sam said, his own voice choked, as Ralph clambered out of the car even as it barely stopped.

"Sorry to rush off like this, guys — but it's longer than I'm usually gone . . . she may need me. So, hey, thanks. I do have gratitude, too: mainly for each day that I'm sober, but today especially for that meeting and you guys. Thanks a lot. You've really helped, and I don't mean just the food. Thanks for talking. Gotta go." And he was off, down a dingy alleyway to a rickety flight of steps, calling as he reached them: "Jeannie, honey, I'm back. Guess what I brought you!"

It was almost midnight, and as Hell Street more or less cleared for the nightly police-pass, Sam and I drove home — slowly and silently. In parting, we said only "Good night . . . and thanks." We did not even rag each other about my "treat."

It is 6:00 A.M. now. I have been awake all night, trying to find the answer to one question . . . or perhaps to two. Is Ralph "victim" or "hero"? I do not know, and I have decided that it is a meaningless question. The second one may not be. I think that I am sober. But if I were Ralph, would I be as sober as Ralph? Again, I do not know: I do not even know that I am sure that Ralph will make it.

I have hurt, and I have begged. And I have wanted sobriety, and I have worked for it. But may God give me the grace, if I ever need it, to beg for sobriety as Ralph did tonight and probably does every moment of his life. Beyond that prayer, at this moment, I am speechless and idealess.

83

The reward of a thing well done is to have done it.
— Ralph Waldo Emerson

THE DISCUSION LAST NIGHT SUGGESTED AN interesting variation on the perennial question, "Why me?" The group sitting around the table contained several members well seasoned in sobriety. And thus when George, a relative newcomer, posed his problem, the veterans rose to the challenge.

"It seems to me that I have pretty well gotten past 'Why me?' " said George. "But sometimes, these days, I find myself asking my Higher Power, 'Why now?' Let me explain: I have learned, around these tables, that even sober life has its ups and downs. One of the main gifts of sobriety is smoothing those out: but insofar as sobriety allows us to live life as it is, those cycles will always remain.

"In fact, I even think that I would claim to like them: a life without ups and downs would be horrendously boring. And so I like my cycles, and I am grateful for them. When I am down — and realize it — I know that it will not always be that way, that the ups will come too. And when I am up, I remember to be grateful — grateful for the things that are going on that are helping me to feel so good.

"So I guess the answer I have evolved to 'Why me?' is, 'Because, in my Higher Power's wisdom, I *need* this.' Now I cannot claim that I ever make the act of faith and trust perfectly, but I have been trying — and in general it has worked out pretty well. Until lately. Lately, it seems to me, the 'cycle' is breaking down more than it is evening out. At times, I seem to be stuck.

"Not too long ago, for example, I hit a series of downs: the car, the job, the house, the kids . . . it just went on and on. In fact, it still seems to be doing that. Any one of those setbacks, or maybe even any couple, I think that I could handle — with my Higher Power's help and the help I get around these tables, of course. Well, I have been handling them — and without asking in so many words, 'Why me?' But I catch myself wondering about the pileup: I am beginning to say to my Higher Power, 'Give me a break — Why now?' each time something else goes wrong. My point is, I guess, that I think I am pretty willing to accept the ups and downs, but it is getting difficult for me to maintain that willingness in the face of a sequence of things that seem to be all downers.

"Now because 'Give me a break — why *now*?' is not exactly an Eleventh-Step prayer, I think I need some help. How do you handle the prolonged downs? What do you do when, even though you are sober and working the Steps, the cycle of ups and downs, instead of leveling off, seems to get worse — seems to get stuck in 'down'? What can I do?"

The group went off in many directions, offering a multitude of suggestions. Consensus agreed that "Why now?" essentially replicates "Why me?": it signals a lack of acceptance, the refusal of willingness to surrender the claim to control. I appreciated those insights, that reminder. But pondering the topic later last night, trying to converse about it with my Higher Power, another perspective on the question "Why now?" seemed to emerge.

As I repeated, "Why now?" I heard my voice whining. It struck me that, in my own case at least, the pleading, petulant query "Why now?" signals the return of the childish and the infantile in my way of thinking. Small children, like dumb animals, need and demand instantaneous rewards. Most of us are taught, when very young, that if we are good, someone will be good to us. And we quickly learn, or at least come to think, that a sort of contractual relationship is established by our being good. Just as the demand for instantaneous gratification characterizes infancy, the expectation of immediate reward hallmarks childhood.

I recall how, as a young boy, I disliked going shopping with my mother. And so I would behave brattishly — tugging at her and complaining or wandering away forcing her to look for me. My mother's response was to end each shopping trip during which I behaved decently with a special treat — an ice cream malted. My response, as I recall, was to shape up for about an hour or so, at which time I would begin whining for my "reward." "I've been good, where's my treat?" I would demand, and mother quickly learned to do her shopping in short spurts.

It strikes me that when I complain "Why now?" I am repeating that vignette of my childish story. "What I am like now" is coming perilously close to "what I was like" before my experience of "what happened" at the alcoholic bottom. Life does have its ups and downs. In sobriety, I have both learned that and learned to accept that. I no longer turn to alcohol in the attempt to force an "up" or to drown a "down." By my tendency to ask "Why now?" signals that my acceptance is flawed. I may accept that there are ups and downs, but I am still clinging to the myth of being in control of when and how they come.

As when I was a small boy shopping with my mother, it seems to me, I tug and tear at my Higher Power and perhaps even threaten to run away if my tolerance of the "down" that I do not like is not quickly enough rewarded by some "up." Then, I accepted that I had to wander among bargain basement counters, but I was willing to do so for only a short time before demanding my reward. Now, I accept that there will be days and events that will be "down," but I start complaining and become brattishly unwilling to accept as soon as I decide "Enough!"

But who am I to proclaim "Enough!" My track record with alcohol surely indicates that my sense of enough is stunted and hardly to be trusted. And I am dealing now not with my mother, who despite all her good qualities was not God, but with my Higher Power, who I would like to think is God. My mother may not have known the limits of my endurance: my Higher Power does. My "Why now?" is thus in a sense worse than childish. It signals a retraction of my Third-Step decision. One does not turn over one's will and one's life and keep an eye on the clock — or on the calendar.

A new insight for me seems to be emerging here. If the demand for instant gratification is the sign of immaturity, the reality that I am asked to sustain "downs" longer may hint that my Higher Power is treating me as if I were mature! That exclamation point is not rhetoric but wonderment, given my own knowledge of my own immaturity.

There is this profound relationship between "Why me?" and "Why now?": both kick against the goad of reality. When tempted to think the first, I have learned to find in it a reminder that neither I nor anything else under my control is the ultimate reality.

In a sense, to paraphrase many sick jokes with a healing insight: the bad news is that I am not God; the good news is that I do not have to be. I have a Higher Power who is leading me to maturity. What else could any alcoholic ask in progress toward recovery?

84

Goethe once remarked that the greatest difficulty about a problem lay in where one did not search for it.
— Helen Merrell Lynd

LAST NIGHT'S MEETING BEGAN WITH ONE OF my favorite questions. But it turned out to be, also, someone's unfavorite — and we had a rollicking discussion.

"What is your favorite A.A. slogan?" Before last night, I had always, in sobriety, liked that question for two related reasons. In the first place, it brings me back to basics. And second, it affords a good "Remember when."

When I first came around, I did not like A.A.'s simple slogans. I imagined that I was too sophisticated for them — that someone who hurt as badly as I did required more profound wisdom if I was to be healed. Needless to relate, I did not do very well in A.A. so long as I thought like that: my healing began only when I became simple enough for the program's simple slogans.

Fortunately, I like to think, that simplicity came less because further drinking addled my brain than because good sponsors and a benevolent Higher Power finally saw to it that I was given the humility that I so obviously and so badly needed. Still, I never will forget one oldtimer's response to my complaint that the slogans were too simple for me. "Keep drinking," he advised sagely, "and you will soon become simple enough for them."

Fred's problem with the question about A.A.'s slogans came from a different direction. He felt not that the slogans were too simple, but that too often they were prated too simplistically. "When I am hurting, and I ask for help," Fred observed, "it doesn't much help to be met with a vacuous grin and the mere reminder 'Easy does it.' Too often, I feel, some A.A.s use the slogans to avoid identification, to push off from engagement with another alcoholic's pain. The slogans have their place, but they are not cure-alls. And to treat them as such strikes me as dishonest. There is more to this program than 'Easy does it' and

'First things first,' just as there is more to recovery and to true sobriety than 'Don't drink and go to meetings.' "

Last night's was a tolerant group: Fred's outburst provoked sympathetic murmurs and a spate of comments agreeing that there are, in sobriety, no easy answers. But the general consensus suggested that that was precisely the message implicitly conveyed by the slogans. No one ever pretended that "First things first" and "Easy does it" and "Live and let live" are easy answers.

Several reached back to draw on the story of how their own experience had been able to become strength and hope only because of the apparent simplicity of the slogans. "When I first got here," Jerry explained, "I was twitching so bad I couldn't even hold, much less read, *The Big Book*. I know I couldn't focus my eyes well enough to read the Twelve Steps off that chart on the wall: hell, I doubt I even could have counted to twelve. Well, I clung to those slogans — to 'Easy does it' and 'First things first' for at least the first six months: they were my program. And so I sure as hell am not going to abandon them now that I am sober — they got me sober."

Others put it less dramatically but made the same point: if the slogans started us on the road to sobriety, they remain good guideposts. A favorite slogan emerges, from time to time, according to the requirements of our changing needs. The slogan that most irritates us might be just the one that we most need to hear. Those axioms are not substitutes for thought — they remind us how to act.

Perhaps because of Fred's comment, "Easy does it" won the "favorite" mantle, with "Live and let live" and "First things first" tying for a close second. No one in the group seemed to feel as put upon by some A.A.'s use of the slogans as did Fred. But later last night, I tried that shoe on the other foot. The question became not "Do I hear the slogans used thoughtlessly and perhaps even cruelly," but "Do I ever use them that way?" At times, I fear, I do.

It is not that there are people in A.A. with whom I find it difficult or unpleasant to talk — I doubt that I could ever feel that way about any other alcoholic who is willing to share his or her recovery with me. Shared recovery is the only recovery: I know that, and I do try to live it. But if there are not people whom I put off, there are times when I push off. Sometimes, I do not feel able to give.

Feeling unable to give may reflect a defect of character: insofar as it does, I am willing to ask for its removal. Meanwhile, I will not be too harsh with myself over it. Denying my limitations characterized my drinking; accepting them, even ungracefully, better serves my recovery. But the question here seems to be how that trait, character defect or not, manifests itself.

Belatedly, I think, I hear Fred's pain. The program of A.A. is precious to each of us. That which is precious to us, it troubles us to see abused. Abuse of the beautiful is a kind of blasphemy. And thus when, too tired or sick or unwilling for whatever reason to embrace another alcoholic at that moment, I carelessly mutter "First things first" or glibly grin "Easy does it" and move on, it almost seems that I am violating something sacred. A.A.'s slogans are not mindless cliches, unless we make them such by using them thus. And of that, I have been guilty.

For that insight alone I am grateful to Fred and to last night's meeting, but another intuition also emerges — a new way of seeing something I had previously only dimly understood. Often, the apparently cliched slogan suggests itself as the answer to a question. Someone asks, for example, how many meetings to attend, or when the craving for alcohol will cease, or whether a spouse is likely to return. Those questions, however honestly asked, have this in common: each is the wrong question. And to the wrong question, the best answer — A.A.'s wisdom seems to suggest — is one of the slogans.

Let me try to draw a parallel. In academic life many questions are asked. Some are even answered. But knowledge advances most rapidly when someone who understands suggests — usually not very gently — that the wrong question is being asked. To learn a new way of thinking seems to require learning a new way of questioning — a way of asking the right questions, or at least as close to them as present knowledge allows us to approach. The historically immature mind asks what caused the Civil War; the historian investigates how one nation endured so long half slave and half free.

Similarly, I think, to ask how many meetings one must attend each week in order to get sober signals a way of thinking alien to sobriety itself. We do not in A.A. say, as we perhaps too often do on campus: "That is the wrong question." We rather try to focus attention on the way of thinking that is sobriety; and our experience, strength, and hope have taught us that the slogans serve that purpose well.

Perhaps I am fortunate. When I was very new to dryness and yet lacking even a smidgin of sobriety, even though I disliked the slogans as simplistic, I knew that they were spoken to me by loving people who cared about my recovery. I thought many of those people ignorant then, I must confess; but I am grateful that I never judged them careless or cruel.

In time, as I look back on that experience from the perspective of last night's meeting, I came to suspect not only that the slogans and those who spoke them were not so dumb, but that perhaps I was. I came to abhor the slogans, in fact, only after beginning to suspect that they did contain the answer, and that I had somehow missed it. The answer they contained was that, in so many areas of my life even beyond the drinking of alcohol, I was asking the wrong question.

That was a painful revelation, and for a long time I resisted it and tried to deny its truth. Within A.A., however, we surrender to a new way of life; and if that surrender itself is honest, the new way of thinking that characterizes the new way of life slowly permeates our being. In my own case, I chart that progress according to my changing attitudes toward A.A.'s simple slogans. Each reminds me, always, of my tendency to ask the wrong question — of my alcoholic inclination to focus on quantity rather than quality or, for another example, to project results rather than carefully living each day.

I find it valuable, then, at times to ask myself not so much which is my favorite slogan as which do I seem most to need on this day. Usually, the answer is the slogan that I would most resent if spoken to me too casually or too glibly or by someone who did not really care about my progress in sobriety.

Fortunately for my sobriety, none of my A.A. friends are ever casual or glib about the topic of sobriety: they do care, because that is how and why they are sober. May I learn from their example, so that there will be less pain like Fred's within our fellowship.

85

We have met the enemy and he is us.

— Pogo

POOR BOY DESCENDED UPON THE MEETING I attended last night. No one present, so far as I know, could tell how Poor Boy obtained his nickname: it certainly has nothing to do with the quality of his sobriety.

The discussion topic was the Sixth Step: how do we become entirely ready for the removal of our defects of character? That is, the *Twelve and Twelve* tells us, "the step that separates the men from the boys." Perhaps because of the difficulty of the topic — of conceptualizing "entirely ready" and of talking about our "defects of character" — most participants focused on the point in their own lives when they sensed the transition from immature to mature pursuit of the goal of sobriety. I am glad they did, for Poor Boy's contribution proved priceless.

When I first came around (Poor Boy began), I thought I was pretty mature, and I sure as hell didn't have too many "defects of character." I was just a drunk, and I had proved to myself that I needed help if I was going to stop drinking. That's what A.A. was for, I had heard, so I came.

Now, I won't say that I exactly swaggered in, but I'll tell you honestly that at my first meeting, I noticed a lot of people who seemed to be less sober than I felt. I sort of filed that information: somebody suggested that I "stick with the winners," so I just determined to do so.

Well, over the first few weeks and months of my attendance, a funny thing started to happen. Several whom I had picked out as winners went out and got drunk again. In fact, two of them got killed in a car wreck while driving under the influence. And those who struck me as not sober, those who seemed stuck at the basics and who checked everything in *The Big Book*, those who seemed most intense about what they said and least cool about the A.A. part of their lives — why, you know, those s.o.b.s came back every week and seemed to be slowly growing. Although I was a bit confused, I had high hopes that some day maybe a few of them would get as sober as I had gotten so quickly — at least if I stayed around and helped them.

As you can imagine, I did not stay that sober very long thinking like that. But I was fortunate enough to survive my next binge, and so I came crawling back. It wasn't exactly a crawl, however: I was proud that I had enough courage to come back, and there was even a pride in my humility when I asked one of the group's oldtimers to help me understand the A.A. Steps, which some of the group's comments led me to decide I had not really discovered before.

"Can't do that," he surprised me by saying. "You've been around here before for a while — go ask your sponsor."

"Sponsor?" I said, hoping that I sounded less mystified than I was. "Yes, sponsor," he shot back. "You got one, ain't you?"

"Well, sort of," I replied, trying to think of at least one person I might have talked to once or twice after a meeting. "But he's not here tonight. In fact, I think he's the one I heard some of the others talking about a little while ago — the one who is out drinking and telling everybody he meets in the bars that he's in A.A."

Well, that oldtimer gave me a look I'll never forget. "Poor Boy," he said, "I sure hope your taste in booze was better than your taste for A.A. How the hell can you stand there and tell me that someone who is out drinking is your sponsor? Well, in any case, I guess you ain't got one, so I'll try. Sit down and let's talk."

I was happy about that, but it seemed again to be getting a little intense. So I asked, "Now?"

"Poor Boy," my new sponsor answered, "I got lots of things I was hoping to do tonight, but it seems to me you ain't never been in A.A. I've been watching you, however, and it seems to me this might be as close as you'll ever come. Besides, one drunk out there confusing people about us is enough. So yes, dag-nabbit: now."

Well, I sat down and old Luke gave me a pretty good going over. I forget all he tried to tell me that first night, because I had many other similar sessions with him — before meetings, after meetings, even in between meetings. And I began to discover that there was a lot to A.A. I also tried to plunge right in, to do everything that Luke told me. The one thing I did not do, as I later realized, was talk. Oh, Luke gave me the chance to, but I never took it. I wanted to learn, I told myself, and I used that as an excuse to keep from being honest about how I felt.

As time went on, however, I sensed that somehow there was still something missing. Now that I sort of knew what sobriety was, it seemed more and more clear to me that I did not have it. And that began to bother me. But I still never talked to Luke about it. In fact, because I was not sober, I sort of decided that that strange lack was probably my sponsor's fault. And so I slowly but surely moved away from Luke — attending meetings where he was unlikely to be; making sure, if he was at any that I attended, that he saw me talking with other oldtimers.

Luke did not chase me: I guess that real sponsors never do. But I sensed that he was still watching me when our paths crossed; and I felt that he recognized in me the same lack that I saw in myself — the lack that I had never talked about with him. For moving around meetings and choosing new sponsors did not help. As hard as I worked on my program, I could not seem to get sober. I could not, that is, seem to identify with those, like Luke, whom I now recognized as A.A.'s true winners.

Of course, I still wasn't telling anybody I talked to how I felt. In fact, one reason that I was jumping around talking to different people was that I was sort of afraid that somebody would spot it. I wanted to be thought sober. If you really want to know, I wanted to be thought sober more than I wanted to be sober. At least, looking back on it, that's the only way I can understand how I was acting, talking to all those people about "my program."

But one day, I finally couldn't stand it any more. I became afraid that I would go off on another binge; and I was deathly scared not so much that it might be my last binge as that if I went out on it, everybody in A.A. would know that I had never been sober. Now, I'm not going to pretend that that was a good motive for doing what I did, but I'll take it. Because instead of heading to the liquor store, where I honestly intended to go, I decided to try to find Luke. I really do not know why I did that: perhaps I wanted him to be the last person to see me not drinking; perhaps, in my grandiosity, I thought he could then help the others understand what had happened to me. Deep down, I suspect that I hoped he could help me understand what was happening to me, and thus save me from the drunk that at that moment I felt was inevitable.

"Luke," I said, when I finally found him, "I don't know what's the matter: my program just ain't working."

"Poor Boy," he replied, "you got it all wrong. Your program is working just fine. What I'm wondering is when you are going to try our program — the A.A. program. You got quite a program: it's the surest thing I've ever seen, the surest way to get drunk again. And it is working so well that I don't see what complaint you can have.

"Now, our program, the A.A. program that involves getting honest and working the Steps and lots of things you ain't got room for in your program, our program — although it has a pretty good track record with a lot of different drunks — it ain't nowhere near so quick and sure as yours. 'Course, A.A. is aiming at something else — at 'progress rather than perfection,' for example.

"So don't ask me to help you with 'your program,' 'cause, truth to tell, your program scares the bejeezus out of me. But if you want to trade your program in for our program, then I'm here to help you try to do just that.

"But let me begin by telling you just one thing I hope you'll never forget, Poor Boy: when you start thinking 'my program,' you in trouble. So don't you ever talk to me about 'my program' or 'your program' — 'cause the only way I know how to get sober is in our program, and you'd better never forget that for even one moment as long as you live."

Now, Luke, God bless him, so far as I can tell, is still working our program, even though now he's been dead about twenty-five years. He's still working it because every time I hear anybody say, "my program," as valid as that phrase may be in the particular context, Luke comes to life again inside me — I feel his love for "our program." And so I'm here tonight to pass on that message: if you're unhappy with your program, you just might try our program. Because that's what Alcoholics Anonymous and every one of its Steps means to me. And that's as close to "maturity"as I think I'll ever have to come.

I was one who had said, last night in discussing the Sixth Step, "my program." Although the words may slip out again, I doubt that I shall ever hear them in the same way. For I think I have learned an important truth: if there is something wrong with "my program," it is probably because it *is* "my program." To grow in sobriety, I need what I needed to get sober — the program of A.A., our program and the fellowship that makes that "our" real.

86

Success in psychotherapy — i.e., *the ability to change oneself in a direction in which one wants to change — requires courage rather than insight.*

— Thomas Szasz

DISCUSSION OF A.A.'S ELEVENTH STEP ALMOST always proves a richly rewarding experience. Its brief words compress at least seven topics, each of which I have heard discussed to the profit of my own progress in sobriety: *prayer, meditation,* two or perhaps three in *improve our conscious contact with God as we understood Him,* and another three or four in *praying only for knowledge of His will for us and the power to carry that out.*

Last night, as so often, attention focused on "knowledge of His will for us." Only toward the end of the discussion did anyone suggest that that knowledge, important as it may be, is only half the story — at least as the Step is worded. In our focus on the earlier parts of the Step, it seems that we too often forget or ignore its closing phrase: "and the power to carry that out."

That is not surprising. On the one hand, we live in a knowledge-oriented culture that tends to value insight disproportionately. And, on the other hand, specifically we in Alcoholics Anonymous tend rightly to mistrust the claims of "will" and "courage": we stopped drinking not by willing to do so, but by surrendering to our powerlessness over alcohol. We do not deny that courage has a place in our sobriety, but I suspect we tend to undervalue its role because of our wariness of the false claims of "liquid courage" that in the past fueled some of our drinking.

And yet there is a profound wisdom in the Eleventh Step's linking of "knowledge" and "power." For one thing, that explicit linking of the two discrete yet related concepts can preserve us from the trap of too glibly thinking that knowledge is power. Some knowledge is, in a way "power": such knowledge gives control over reality outside us. But the kind of wisdom that we find in A.A. is neither agent nor facet of "control": it signals and enables rather the willingness to accept — to accept as reality even that which we cannot control, that before which we are powerless.

That acceptance, that willingness to accept, requires and involves its own kind of courage. Too often, I suspect, we think in terms of courage as fighting and of cowardice as fleeing. But there are options other than fight or flight. In fact, for the alcoholic or addict, there are *only* options other than fight or flight. Neither fighting nor fleeing the bottle ever works, as most alcoholics can amply testify from their own experience. We can neither attack nor run away from our alcoholism successfully. Those who try those options — as we all did, for a time — learn the meaning of the reality encapsulated in "How it Works": "Remember that we deal with alcohol — cunning, baffling, powerful."

"Fight or flight" thus signals not courage or cowardice but futility. The alcoholic can neither fight nor flee: the alcoholic can only stand there. But there are two ways of standing there, and these are the alcoholic's options. Standing there, one can either confront reality or hide from — deny — its reality. The former, the confrontation that is acceptance, requires courage. Denial is the ultimate cowardice.

Thus I understand the linking of knowledge and power — of insight and courage — for which the Eleventh Step suggests we seek and pray. To confront reality, one must know it; to know reality, one must confront it. The knowledge and the power — the insight and the courage — sought in A.A.'s Eleventh Step are mutually related. It is impossible to have one without the other, for one attains each only by practicing the other.

How one does that is one of the conundrums of the centuries. Each age, as each individual person, tends to vacillate: first overvaluing insight at the expense of courage, then exaggerating the benefits of courage/power out of ignorance of the value of wisdom/knowledge. We do not exactly solve the perennial problem of philosophers in Alcoholics Anonymous; but, guided by the Steps and especially by the Eleventh, we come to terms with — we confront — its personal application in our daily lives.

For we learn and we practice two important realities: first, that "knowledge of His will for us" and "the power to carry that out" are mutually related; second, that both are to be sought, to be prayed for. Think first of wisdom, of "knowledge of His will for us." We accept that we need it, and we ask for it — we seek it. To know that one must seek wisdom is perhaps the ultimate wisdom. A.A.'s Eleventh Step thus guides us well.

But what about "the power to carry that out?" How can a program founded on the acceptance of being powerless enable and engender courage? Again, we seek it — we pray for it. But that is not the complete answer, for the Eleventh Step is not A.A.'s complete program. Indeed, here — it seems to me — the Eleventh Step turns our attention to A.A. as fellowship.

How does one who "stands there" learn to confront rather than to hide and to deny? The answer that I find to my seeking and my praying is identification with others who also seek and pray. My Higher Power does not tap me on the shoulder and answer my questions or my prayers directly. That is why I need Alcoholics Anonymous. In fact, that I need A.A. is perhaps the most direct knowledge my Higher Power has ever vouchsafed me.

I attain the courage to confront reality by identifying with others who do so. The sense that one is not alone cuts through hiding and denial. The knowledge that others confront begets the courage to confront.

We seek courage as we seek insight: "through prayer and meditation," but primarily in our identification with other alcoholics. Thus it is that each A.A. meeting, viewed from this perspective, may be seen as an intricate dialectical process whereby insight enables courage, and courage feeds further insight — whereby "knowledge of His will for us" and "the power to carry that out" reciprocally engender and fulfill each other in each member's sharing of experience, strength, and hope.

Most people accept the idea that insight — knowledge — can be learned, if sought. Too many forget or ignore that courage can also be transmitted and gained if sought by identification.

A.A. encourages us to seek serenity, courage, and wisdom. Of all three it is true that one cannot have one without the others.

Many people know that, or at least suspect it. Within Alcoholics Anonymous, we are privileged, when we reach the Eleventh Step, to learn not only that it is true but also how to attain its promise.

87

Now, hear the word of the Lord.

— Ezekiel

THESE SEEM TO BE MY "ELEVENTH-STEP days" — so be it. Last night, a different group sought to confront a different paradox implicit in that penultimate suggestion that is our program. This phrase was lighted on: "to improve our conscious contact with God."

Much inheres in that brief phrase. It seems to me that those words shed light both on A.A.'s claim to be "spiritual rather than religious" and on the vast difference between Alcoholics Anonymous and all other forms of therapy.

Religion, it seems to me, claims to put one into "conscious contact with God" as a particular expression of belief understands Him. I think it even fair to say that some manifestations of religion claim to be that conscious contact. Perhaps they are. Not only do many good people find this in their practice of religion, but the very concept of religion — which means "a binding back together" — seems to support such an understanding.

It is interesting, however, how Alcoholics Anonymous, in its Eleventh Step, takes care to *assume* what religion claims to *achieve* — that one has conscious contact with God. Perhaps the reason why that assumption is possible lies in the fact that A.A. does not try to explain or define God, but accepts its own members' understanding.

Having accepted that understanding, A.A. is left free to suggest neither that one attain nor perfect the contact that it represents, but simply that one improve it. To seek to improve implies that something is both present and imperfect. As always, then, A.A.'s claim and promise are of "progress rather than perfection." Progress implies that one needs to move forward, but the reason one can safely move forward is that one is on the right road.

Religious teachers traditionally claim to have "*the* way" and urge "striving for perfection." That is, I suspect, their proper function. But members of Alcoholics Anonymous content themselves with the "less" that, for them as alcoholics, is "more" — the progress of improvement. Those once addicted to playing God remain always vulnerable to that addiction: the muted understatement of the Eleventh Step's goal guards that vulnerability.

But "spiritual rather than religious" and even "progress rather than perfection" are old-hat topics. Valuable as are those reminders, they reflect but one-half of the story of A.A.'s place in the history of ideas, of A.A.'s significance in the story of twentieth-century modernity. For we live in an age not of religion but of science. And of all the human sciences, psychology is both paramount and paradigmatic. Despite all the reservations and qualifications of psychologists who also adhere to a religious commitment, in some sense psychology by its very nature seeks to achieve what premodern generations thought of as the task of religion — the healing of nonphysical disease.

"Therapy" is a widely used — and too generally abused — term for modern healing: let us simply accept it, in the sense of that which promotes healing by caring at least as much as by curing. To cure, in this understanding, is to restore to previously pristine, undiseased condition. To care implies enabling a sufferer to live with disease: the underlying condition remains. At least in this sense, Alcoholics Anonymous is therapy. We find healing in A.A., but we are not cured of our alcoholism: we remain alcoholics, but we learn how to care for ourselves and others as alcoholics. In fact, we care for our own alcoholism by caring for others' alcoholism, and we do this by sharing our experience, strength, and hope.

How, then, does Alcoholics Anonymous differ from other therapies and especially from psychological ones? One particularly significant difference seems hidden in an apparently innocuous word in A.A.'s Eleventh Step: *conscious*.

All other therapies, I think it fair to say despite their almost incredible apparent diversity, aim to make conscious that which is unconscious. The stated goal of Sigmund Freud, who is generally credited with discovering the unconscious as we conceive it, was "That where *id* is, *ego* may be" — perhaps the clearest statement of this thrust in modern terms. It seems, in other words, to be the goal of all therapy to accomplish what the ancients understood to be the nature of all knowledge — to manifest the hidden.

A.A.'s Eleventh Step, it seems to me, works otherwise. It focuses on a contact that is not only already present but also already conscious. Its aim is not to make conscious, but "to improve conscious contact." The Eleventh Step thus assumes not only contact but consciousness of one's contact with the ultimate reality that is God.

Whether the earlier steps also assume that conscious contact, or themselves establish it, seems open to interpretation. Because A.A. is — strictly — neither theology nor therapy, that question can be answered, in the case of each individual member of Alcoholics Anonymous, only by each individual member of Alcoholics Anonymous. But it seems to me that the Eleventh Step invites us to think on that question for ourselves, to examine its significance and meaning in the specific case of our own recovery.

What was the nature of my contact with God when I first came to Alcoholics Anonymous? And whatever that contact, how conscious was it? In A.A.'s Eleventh Step, we seek "to improve" neither our consciousness *of* contact nor our mere *contact* itself. We seek rather *to improve our conscious contact:* and that, it seems to me, is different — which is perhaps *why* it must be done "through prayer and meditation."

Sometimes, I wonder about "prayer and meditation" — about how to do them. Remembering their purpose, within the A.A. program, may help to solve that: prayer and meditation are to improve my conscious contact with God as I understand Him. The profundity of that simple answer becomes clearer the more I think about religion, and especially the more I think about modern therapy.

88

Man is a tool-using animal. Nowhere do you find him without tools; without tools he is nothing, with tools he is all.

— Thomas Carlyle

ONCE UPON A TIME, LONG BEFORE I BEGAN to drink alcoholically, a very wise and even holy man looked me directly in the eyes and said: "You simple tool." His eyes sparkled, and the words were spoken without rancor — in fact, they were offered as both compliment and challenge. And at that moment, I understood his message and its meaning: we are, at best, tools of a power greater than ourselves; and, if we can remember that, we might accept that the simplest tool can be the best tool.

In my years of alcoholic drinking, needless to tell, I forgot that message. Nor am I certain that I have yet relearned it — although the present pages may signal an effort to that end. But its memory lingers — always challenging me, occasionally shaming me. Perhaps because I am not adept at the use of what are ordinarily termed *tools*, I find the concept of *tool* fascinating.

A tool is that which is used to do something else. It has meaning only in the effect it produces. Long ago, my sponsor suggested, in what seems to be an unofficial A.A. axiom, that I "put away the toys and pick up the tools." And on page 25 of *The Big Book*, I read, under the heading "There is a solution": ". . . there was nothing left for us but to pick up the simple kit of spiritual tools laid at our feet."

Whenever I hear the term *tool* used in A.A., then, my ears perk up. As there were tools that first got me dry, then sober, there are tools, I suspect, that can further my progress in sobriety. If human beings are, as some thinkers have suggested, tool-making animals, then this animal wants to find or fashion the tools appropriate to sober growth. And last night, under Wayne's prodding, the group I attended chose to discuss "A.A.'s tools."

"Which tools of this program do you find especially helpful, and helpful for what?" Wayne asked. "They told me, when I first came around, that I had to use the tools. Well, I have tried to do that. But I have been around for a while now, and — as I look around this table and see the different kinds of growth that we have shared in — I wonder about the 'tools' that some of you may have used that I don't know about.

"The Steps, the slogans, the Serenity Prayer — meetings and phone calls and talking after meetings: that pretty well summarizes the tools I know about. Are there others? And even of those that I have named, how do you decide when to use which? Maybe those are stupid questions, but being a carpenter, I know how important it is to use the right tool for any job. So tonight I would like for us to discuss the tools of this program, because it seems to me that we mention them a lot, but we rarely discuss them in depth."

Perhaps because that particular group is attended by a variety of artisans, those around the table plunged into the topic with gusto. There are few art forms more impressive to me than a skilled craftsman wielding the tools of his trade, and I felt that — for all the diversity of the trades by which members of the group made their living — each person who spoke was first and foremost a master of the craft of sobriety.

The first point made was that sobriety is an entity fashioned by tools. And that means that any tool, and even the A.A. program itself, is then never an end in itself. Skilled mechanics learn to have faith in their tools, but the proof of any trade and any tool resides in the product produced. We know, in Alcoholics Anonymous, that we have the right tools, because we see all around us examples of sobriety produced by their use. There are other tools out there that other people suggest will produce the same results. In general, however, we have yet to see evidence that toolboxes other than A.A.'s simple kit of spiritual tools accomplish that, at least for us.

After locating the right tool kit, which we find in the program of A.A., it is of course necessary to choose the right tool. That is one reason why the Steps are numbered. For the first-meeting newcomer, going on a Twelfth-Step call is an inappropriate tool. Similarly, those who have mastered A.A.'s tools in their own sobriety often find it useful to suggest to mere apprentices how certain tools, such as the slogans, are to be used. "Easy does it —

but do it" and "First things first, but second things second and third things third" were among the suggestions offered.

Like most homeowners, I do have a toolbox, but often I am too lazy to get it out. And so I have been known to use good silverware to loosen a pesky screw, or the heel of my shoe to drive a nail. Even when I trouble to reach for my toolbox, I have also done such uncraftsmanlike things as poking a screwdriver into the garbage disposal: I do know enough not to use one in probing an electrical outlet.

It seems to me, in other words, that one must not only choose the right tool — one must use it rightly. And when I fail to do that, the reason is more often impatience than ignorance. The analogy seems to fit. I have been around A.A. long enough to know about its tools, even to appreciate their proper uses. But sometimes I am too lazy to reach for the tool I know I need; and at other times impatience can move me to ignore what I know to be the proper tool in a misguided search for "an easier, softer way." The result, invariably, is more destruction than construction of the edifice of sobriety that I supposedly want to build.

There is another level of analogy, one that better fits the tools that I do use in my profession. As pleasant and as satisfying as may be the proper use of tools, tools are not toys. Sometimes I suspect that the ultimate maturity may consist in knowing the difference between tools and toys. We never, of course, attain the ultimate. As I look around my desk, in fact, I am reminded of the truism known to all women: the main difference between men and boys is the cost of their toys.

In some areas of my life, that is a relatively harmless indulgence. But that is not true in what directly concerns my sobriety. Although we may at times be playful, there are no toys in Alcoholics Anonymous. Perhaps because I am yet — and always will be — a child in sobriety, I can forget that difference. Being reminded of the tools, however, helps me to remember it.

Despite the wisdom of my youthful mentor, my alcoholism led me to fail to be, myself, a simple tool. Insofar as I became, in my drinking years, "simple," it was only in the simplemindedness of my pursuit of booze. And insofar as I became a "tool," it was of alcohol — "cunning, baffling, powerful."

Today, in sobriety, occasionally I pray that I may regain my youthful vision, that squandered vocation to "simple tool-hood," in whatever way my Higher Power deems fit. But, meanwhile, more practically, I pursue that goal by using respectfully and appreciatively, the simple tools that A.A. offers me in my pursuit of progress in sobriety. To be reminded to do that is a great gift for which I am grateful.

89

No story is the same to us after the lapse of time: or rather we who read it are no longer the same interpreters.

— George Eliot

HOW MANY PHRASES DO WE USE EACH DAY, almost carelessly, that remind us of our stories — of the importance of knowing and remembering "what we were like, what happened, and what we are like now"?

"That reminds me"; "In context . . ."; "But remember what happened when . . ."; "In my own experience . . . ." Our stories are our selves.

"Self" is one of those terms of which we have learned to be wary. Used isolatingly, it signals the self-centeredness that we know is "the root of our troubles." But we must affirm ourselves: I can be connected, related, to others only if "I" exist. Our difficulty is that we too easily transmute that opportunity into a problem by losing sight of our relatedness.

Our stories relate our connectedness with all manner of reality. Note the term *relate.* It comes from a verb form that signifies "having been brought back." Telling — relating — our stories relates us to our relatedness, brings us back to our true nature.

Let me try to make all that a bit more concrete. Our stories tell of our relationships, not only with alcohol but with other realities. The most obvious realities in our stories, besides ourselves and alcohol, are our work and our loves — the two projects that humanize us, according to the ancient wisdom of all sacred writings as well as according to modern thinkers as diverse as Karl Marx and Sigmund Freud.

My own story involves three career changes and innumerable dabblings in search of love. It tells of being a student and becoming a writer, of moving from flirtations to marriage; and both journeys saw many intermediate stages. It is impossible to rehearse my story — to recite it aloud in detail — without coming to know myself better, without, by that very telling, relating myself more accurately to my present work and my present love. That is why living one day at a time is enabled by telling one's story.

Two concepts strike me in what has preceded: that of "process" or "journey" and the relationship between "myself" and "my self." Being human is not a "process": it is rather a journey and my story reminds me of that. Stories describe not processes but pilgrimages.

If we sometimes use the word *process* too glibly, we also too often speak the term *myself* too casually. My "self" is a true reality, but only as related to and in relationship with other, "larger" realities.

The necessary relationships, if my self is to be myself, seem three: that which we term *work*, which relates us to the realities that we have and do; that which we call *love*, which relates us to the reality that we are and can become; and that which we name *spirituality* or *religion*, which relates us to reality beyond speaking but not beyond be-ing.

Because telling my story reveals myself in a unique way, even to me, thus it is that my story is my self. Only by knowing my story can I find myself; only by understanding my story can I become the self who I truly am.

For one cut off from self, for the distorted perception that centers on self, there can be no more healing experience than discovering one's story. If to-be-human is to have a story, then to exist humanly requires understanding of one's story as a story.

Before finding A.A. I did not understand my self; with distorted perception, I thought my self was the center of the universe. Alcoholics Anonymous, by putting me in touch with my story cut through my double disability of self-destructive self-centeredness. A.A., that is to say, gave me my self. A.A. members did that, first, by making me a part of their story; then, over time, by becoming an ongoing part of my own.

Alcoholics Anonymous held out to me, in this way, the three relationships that enable myself to become my self. Its program less involves "work" than it teaches the meaning and value of "working the program"; but there are also tasks to be done, and so newcomers learn the value of work even in such simple chores as setting up the chairs and preparing coffee. "Love"? Who can describe the identification that allows the recovering alcoholic to see self in every other alcoholic, drinking or sober? I wonder at times which is the greater miracle: that a drunk see him- or herself in a sober alcoholic, or that a sober alcoholic see him- or herself in a drunk. As for spirituality, no doubt the less said the better, for all true spirituality is unspeakable.

Thanks to A.A., today I have my self because I can be myself. Realizing that, I will cherish every opportunity and invitation to do so. In return for that gift, all that Alcoholics Anonymous ever asks of me is that I tell my story — that I share my experience, strength, and hope with other alcoholics.

90

If well thou hast begun, go on; it is the end that crowns us . . . .

— Robert Herrick

Better is the end of a thing than the beginning thereof.

— Ecclesiastes

AS I CONCLUDE THIS EXERCISE OF NINETY meetings in ninety days, two things especially strike me about its course. First, although many topics, diversely inspired, have been considered, certain consistent themes keep reemerging. Second, among minor themes, although it is one I had consciously hoped to transcend, remains the mixed nature of human be-ing.

If that first point concerns content, the second involves vision. Not for nothing did I first taste the depths of true sobriety in an A.A. group that had chosen for its name, The Joy of Living.

Among the several unanticipated outcomes of this adventure, however, has been one that the attentive peruser of these pieces has probably already noticed. More frequently, in later meditations, the dark side of life — and of sobriety — has also emerged. No more than a beautiful symphony can sobriety always be upbeat. An aspect of pain also underlies much of our growth, and we ignore that reality at our peril. Indeed, if through this exercise my Higher Power has graced me with any single gift of which I am at this moment especially aware, it consists precisely in this: recognition and acceptance that sobriety, too, is a mixed experience.

Because, especially as alcoholics, we tend to be "all or nothing people," some reality within us wants to rebel against that realization. "It should not be that way," we tell ourselves. Sometimes we even seek out others who will tell us the same; or we may claim to hear that message whispered by some kind of voice that we can too readily confuse with our Higher Power.

The "we" in the preceding paragraph is, of course, more accurately "I": it represents the development of my own experience, strength, and hope over these ninety meetings in ninety days. The chief benefit of that exercise, in this light, is that it immersed me in A.A.'s company of honesty. Rather than seeking out specific others or particular meetings, and thus perhaps unconsciously choosing the message I wanted to hear, I sought to plunge into A.A. in all its diversity, to see and to hear and to touch and to feel and to identify with sobriety in all its wondrous forms. There is, in a sense, only one sobriety, but there are as many beautiful and thought-provoking and love-eliciting expressions of it as there are sober members of A.A. To dip into that ocean refreshes: it humbles even as it exalts.

Also, however, and this is perhaps purely personal, I tend to be wary of those whose relationship with their Higher Power seems too intimate, of those who seem so readily certain of exactly what their Higher Power thinks. Too many atrocities have been perpetrated in the names of "God" and "religion" and even "the spiritual." Danger lurks in all individuals possessed of such certainty. To hold such a view is not cynical. Bill W. himself shared it. Indeed, we owe the very existence of A.A. to the early members' wariness of the tendency of their nonalcoholic cohorts in the Oxford Group to claim such special guidance.

The words are strong, but they are Bill W.'s:

> Nobody can cause more grief than a power-driven guy who thinks he has got it straight from God. These people cause more trouble than the harlots and drunkards. . . . I have had spells of that very thing and so I ought to know.

And so there is a dark side as well as a bright side to sobriety. If sobriety is a rose garden, it also involves thorns; if life is a bowl of cherries, it contains also the pits. I am grateful to be able to embrace the whole of life, the entirety of sobriety of which I am this day capable. Tomorrow, I know, there will be more: another twenty-four hours in which to grow in knowledge and love of both my Higher Power and myself. Sobriety is one supply that I do not have to protect, and there is tremendous freedom in that realization.

I first came to A.A. not in order to stop drinking, but in order to stop hurting. Clearly, my sobriety has not worked out that way. I have stopped drinking; I have not stopped hurting. Today, in sobriety, I understand that hurting — and its meaning — differently. I would have said the same thing ninety days ago, but somehow that observation means something different this twenty-four hours, after those ninety meetings. Exactly what is different, I cannot put into precise words.